Charleston Community
High School Library
Charleston, Illinois

Presented by

Nell Wiseman
August, 1997

THE
LAST TIME
I SAW
MOTHER

THE
LAST TIME
I SAW
MOTHER

ARLENE J. CHAI

FAWCETT COLUMBINE • NEW YORK

A Fawcett Columbine Book
Published by Ballantine Books

Copyright © 1995 by Arlene Chai

http://www.randomhouse.com

Library of Congress Cataloging-in-Publication Data
Chai, Arlene J.
The last time I saw mother / Arlene J. Chai.
p.   cm.
ISBN 0-449-91068-7
1. Philippines—History—Fiction.   2. Women—Philippines—
Psychology—Fiction.   3. Identity (Psychology)—Fiction.
I. Title.
PR9619.3.C417L37   1996
823—dc20   96-5273

Manufactured in the United States of America
First American Edition: July 1996
10   9   8   7   6   5   4   3   2   1

To my parents.
And my grandparents,
wish you were here.

ACKNOWLEDGMENTS

My sincere thanks to my publisher Jane Palfreyman and my editor Julia Stiles for their enthusiasm and belief in my work.

My "readers" who patiently read through my drafts and gave me an endless supply of encouragement: Alan Barry, Cheryl Wong-Horne, Helena Lim, Yvonne Ellis and Suzanne Mercier.

Bryce Courtenay who, years ago, encouraged me to write.

My sisters Janiss and Adrianne for their assistance.

I AM WRITING THIS because it is the truth. And I fear it will be lost again or hidden, the way it has been in the last forty years. So I am giving it form. Words on paper become truth. They say, "It truly happened." They do not take wing like words merely uttered, which quickly disappear with the wind.

I am writing this so I can finally lay my mother to rest. For she continues to live inside me.

I write this, too, for my daughter, Marla, who often looks at me with questioning eyes. It is her story too.

I also write this for my husband, Jaime. Maybe he will read in these pages the message in my long years of silence.

But most of all, I am writing this to make peace with my past for there is much there I have not understood until now. In accepting it, I may move on at last. Before I knew of the things I now record in these pages, I lived a life filled with uncertainties. Perhaps you know of that feeling, when you are filled with little pinholes that show up in the light and you wait and wait for the answers that can make you whole.

This is the story of how I found those answers. I found them in the stories of three women. Do not judge them harshly for they are a part of me. And maybe you will see a part of you in them. After all, do we not all belong in each other's stories?

CARIDAD

"I have been summoned

by my mother."

My mother never writes. So when the mail arrived that day, I was not expecting to find a letter from her. There was no warning.

I had spent the morning running away from the lecture notes I had taken the night before at TAFE college. I was on my second term, doing a travel course which I hoped would get me back into the workforce.

By eleven I had run out of things to do. Outside, the Hills Hoist made squeaking sounds as it turned in the wind, like a giant weather vane stuck in a huge, flat, mossy roof. A gusty south wind blew and the clothes that hung from it flapped about madly, making snapping sounds. It wasn't so long ago that I had hung them out, carefully slipping hangers into shirts, pegging legs of pants onto the line, so they dangled there as if belonging to a row of people doing headstands, only their torsos, arms and heads had been chopped off by some unseen hand. They were almost dry.

The pot plants that lined the deck had all been

watered and fed. And the cobwebs that some industrious spider had intricately spun from one leaf to another like lace had been swept aside. Even the empty potato-chips packet that the fat kid next door had thrown over the fence had been picked up and deposited in the kitchen bin.

Three used cups stood in the kitchen sink and a small pool of coffee sat at the bottom of each. One last cup and I promised to settle down and study. My notes sat in a neat pile at the far end of the kitchen counter, looking at me reproachfully. I emptied the last few drops of milk from the carton. Not enough there. The liquid remained a dark brown. I took a sip. Then poured the rest down the sink.

TOURISM IN AUSTRALIA WAS written at the top of the first sheet in my neat handwriting. I looked at the page more closely, inspecting how I'd written out each letter. No open tails in my f's, p's and y's. My b's, l's and t's all had complete, closed loops.

"You're introverted and secretive. You're also the kind of person who finishes what she starts . . . that's what these loops say," so said an old college friend back home in Manila who dabbled in esoteric things like handwriting analysis. Now getting started had become a problem.

"Stop being so hard on yourself. What did you expect? A miracle? It takes some time to get used to studying again," Marla told me just the other night when I came home feeling frustrated, announcing to her I was quitting.

These days, my eighteen-year-old daughter preaches patience to me. Some of her words sound like the ones I used with her when she would sit in front of the piano, getting impatient with fingers that refused to play a Czerny passage with the fluidity required.

"I hate Kuhlau and Bartok is boring!" she used to complain.

"Be patient and you'll get it right," I would tell her.

Now Marla plays mother to me. Just last night when I got home from TAFE, she opened the door, an apron around her waist, gave me a kiss, and said, "I made some spaghetti bolognaise. Why don't you go take a shower and I'll heat some up in the microwave for you." I spent the rest of the evening sitting in the lounge room, hair still wet from the shower, a bowl of spaghetti on my lap, listening to her at the piano.

Marla is in her first year at the Conservatory of Music. I still find it hard seeing her in that classical institution. She is like a stranger in her new look: one morning she went to her hairdresser in Paddington and returned home with her beautiful long hair gone.

"Had it chopped off!" she announced as I stared at her razor-cut hair that barely made it to her ears. Soon after, the blues, reds, yellows and greens in her wardrobe made way for somber blacks.

"Black is dramatic," she explained.

"That's her growing up and making a statement," Jaime, my husband, said, shrugging in resignation.

As she sits in front of the piano, the picture she makes is of a punk playing classical music. The image is made even more jarring by her Chinese-Filipino-Spanish face. Her catlike, Oriental eyes, high cheekbones, and olive complexion.

I read somewhere that we may change our path, choose our future. But our beginnings stay with us forever. I had Marla while Jaime and I still lived in the Philippines. She was eight before we brought her to live in Sydney. And like every migrant, her country of birth has left its mark on her.

"To confuse the issue," she often says, "I'm not only Manila-born, convent-school-educated, speak English and Tagalog plus a bit of Chinese and curse fluently in Spanish, but now I reside in Australia as well."

Crazy mixed-up kid.

TOURISM IN AUSTRALIA. I read the title for the hundredth time. It was then that I heard the clink of the mailbox. I did not see the mailman come. The brick wall that enclosed the front garden obscured my view of the street. But every week day between twelve and two, he always came. I got up, glad for an excuse to escape my notes. Saved by the mailman.

As I stepped out onto the driveway, three teenagers with spiky hair thundered down the footpath on their skateboards. I caught a glimpse of them through the gaps between the timber palings of the gate. Across the street, Tripod, the three-legged dog that lived in number thirty-six, peed against a post as Big Tom, his owner, waited patiently for him to finish.

The mailbox scorched my fingers as I reached in to pull out the envelopes and rolls of junk mail that seemed to find their way there every day. The top envelope had a little window. A bill. The second had a tiny, almost illegible, spidery scrawl. From Jessie, I could tell.

Jessie—she hated her name—was an old childhood friend from my Manila school days who now lived in Michigan. She was a practising neurologist, a far cry from the girl whose hem Sister Bernadette once ripped out because her skirt rode too many inches above her ankles, showing more flesh than the nun thought decent for a young girl in a convent school.

Jessie wrote often then as her clinic was going through another slow month. "It's as if there's a season for being sick and a season for being well. The latter is very bad for business."

The last envelope had a Manila postmark but it was not from Mia. My cousin Mia did not write out her letters longhand. She worked off a keyboard. "I've become computer literate," she said over the phone. "Have to keep up with the kids." So I knew the angular handwriting, the long slanting letters that spelled out my name and address, did not belong to her.

Curious, I ripped the envelope open and pulled out a

folded sheet of blue stationery paper like the ones my father used to write on when he was alive. Only now the signature at the bottom read "Mama."

It was a strange sight that letter with the unfamiliar writing. Strange and funny for it occurred to me that if I were asked to put a face to those loops and dots, the way one puts a face to a name, I would not have been able to. After all the years of being her daughter, I had never seen my mother's writing until that moment. If it was the only way I could claim her, identify her, she would have been lost to me.

Not that the letter was a letter at all. It was a short note giving voice to a command. I could almost hear her say the words. For they were so like her. Curt. Brief. To the point.

"Come home, Caridad. I need to speak to you," was all it said. I have been summoned by my mother.

Was Mama sick? I rang Mia in Manila.

"No . . . no, nothing's the matter."

"So why does she want me to come?"

"She's old, Caridad, you know how old people are. They need to be humoured . . . So just do as she asks, okay?"

"I don't understand this . . ."

"You won't, until you come home."

Mia knew more but she wasn't telling. That much I was sure of because we had known each other forever. I was three, she, five, when we found in each other a sense of companionship that would last through the years. One crazy afternoon when she had come over to my house to play, we sneaked into the bathroom and opened the medicine cabinet where my father kept his shaving things. We took one of his razor blades. Then, after a few minutes spent summoning up enough courage, we cut each other's thumb and squeezed the cut to get the blood out before putting our thumbs together. With our blood finally flowing in each other's veins, we swore to be best friends forever.

Mia was my first cousin, Tia Emma's youngest daughter. Tia Emma was Mama's youngest sister. Mia was the youngest of six children and had no place in the games and chatter of her older siblings, while I, being an only child, longed for a friend. We were inseparable as children and remained close through the years.

When Jaime, Marla and I left Manila, Mia and I stayed in touch, writing each other long letters, exchanging hundreds of photographs and talking on the phone for longer than we could afford. It is she who has patiently passed Mama's messages on to me, for she has taken to calling on my mother to see how she goes. Not an easy task as Mama has always been difficult to deal with. So when Mia said, "Just do as she asks," I booked my flight, knowing she believed it was important I make this trip home.

That night as I lay in bed, a thought entered my mind. If Mama was well, was I being called home for another reason? Has she heard? Did she know?

———

JAIME DOESN'T LIVE HERE anymore. I have not told my mother, not even Mia. For I cannot begin to explain what I myself do not understand. Whenever I have tried to find the beginning to this knotted spool of things said and things done, I lose the thread, and find myself giving up.

I sometimes think of the scene in the film *Citizen Kane* where a young couple sit together at the dining table. They begin by sitting close to each other, happily chatting over a meal—breakfast, I think. Then as the years pass, they find less and less to say and sit further and further apart. Finally, they each sit at one end of this long table while he reads the papers and she eats in silence.

My friend Meg says, "So what's new?"

Meg tells me over thirty percent of marriages end in divorce these days. She quotes a lot of statistics to me. We are sitting on a bench on the grassy section overlooking Freshwater Beach where we often come for a stroll and talk about what she refers to as "our state." Meg, too, is alone again.

I explain to her that divorce is not accepted in Manila.

"It's this Catholic thing of yours that makes life so complex," she says to me, adding, "We have enough to cope with as is. Why add guilt as well?" Meg believes Catholics are fed a diet of guilt, that we're screwed up. "Loosen up, darling. Look at me, I'm a veteran of two divorces."

"How can you still laugh?" I asked her.

"Darling," Meg replied, drawling with her husky voice

as her hand flicked back strands of deep red hair, "she who laughs, lasts."

"That's a good line."

"Stole it from a book."

Meg devours self-help books, passing them on to me when she has read and highlighted them with a fluoro-yellow pen. I opened one the other night and this line leaped out at me: "Laughter is the shortest distance between two people."

It reminded me of the night Jamie took me out to celebrate our first month of marriage. He had booked a table at the Madrid, a restaurant in Manila we both loved.

We sat at a small candlelit table near the fountain where the trickling sound of water made a music of its own. On our table was a brandy balloon with a red rose floating in water. A singer walked around the tables, accompanied by a guitarist, as he serenaded the dining couples, singing the Spanish love song *Besame Mucho* in his deep voice.

Jaime held my hand and asked me, "So why did you marry me?"

Not knowing whether he was serious, I said, "The truth?"

"Nothing but the truth."

"Because you made me laugh."

"My jokes . . . you married me for my jokes!"

It has taken me twenty years to realise the truth in my reply. Now I ask myself a question I used to scoff at

when I heard it asked by others. Where has all the laughter gone? A cliché of a question asked by couples who
share that common experience called a rocky marriage.
Now that I find myself in one, I wonder how many
couples find themselves as distanced from each other as
Jaime and I now find ourselves. But there is no comfort
in numbers. Every unhappy person thinks her unhappi-
ness is unique.

"YOUR MOTHER AND I need some time to think about
things, Marla, time apart. We've decided it's best that I
move away for a while. I'm taking a flat in Neutral Bay.
It's not too far from the northern beaches and you can
come and stay whenever you like," explained Jaime to
Marla one Sunday.

"We're trying to sort this out, Marla, but sometimes
even parents don't have all the answers, not all at once,"
I said.

I remember wondering what she was thinking as she
sat across from us, listening but not saying a word. This
last year, Marla had changed. Her body had shed its fleshy
roundness, its awkwardness, to reveal bones that gave her
a new shape, interesting angles and a grace she never had
before. In her new found maturity, did she look on us
with disappointed eyes?

Later, in our room, I told Jaime, "Maybe we could
have found a better time."

"No, Caridad, there would never have been a better

time—there is never a good time to say these things."
The following weekend, Jaime left.

Marla and I ate out that first night. Since then, we have
been having our dinner in the TV room.

When the letter saying she had been accepted into the
Conservatory of Music came, I breathed a sigh of relief.
It gave her something to fill the empty spaces a missing
father leaves behind. It gave the three of us something
good to share again.

"You've lost the plot," is how Marla sums it up in
that tone of voice so like her father's. There is a lot of
Jaime in her. "Why don't you two talk it over?" she said
one night, a few weeks after Jaime had left. It was the
first time she had referred to our situation.

I shrugged.

"Say what you feel or think."

I shrugged again.

She got up and walked out of the room, her impa-
tience written all over her face.

They're here, inside me, the things I have refused to
say, won't say, can't say, am too scared to say because
they'll all just come out wrong. Unspoken words that
have fossilised.

"Talk to someone, go see a therapist," Meg advised
me. She had begun to see one recently.

"No. I don't want to talk to some stranger about my
personal life."

Meg said, "Watch it . . . people who keep things inside them develop all sorts of diseases . . . all that emotional gunk's got to find an outlet. Angry people develop cysts; stubborn people get arthritis; resentful people die of cancer."

"Which book is that from?" I snapped at her, instantly feeling guilty.

But Meg refused to give up on me. "Well at least stop hiding in the house. Go and learn something new, make a life for yourself."

Finally, after weeks of nagging from her, I enrolled at TAFE.

"I'm going back to school," I announced to Marla one evening.

She looked up and after a moment said, "Good," then went back to her book.

But now TAFE has to wait for I am going home. I have been summoned by my mother.

THE PLANE TOOK OFF from Sydney airport twenty minutes behind schedule. Typical, I thought. It was a Philippine Airlines plane. Back home we used to say PAL stood for Plane Always Late or Parcel Always Lost. Not much had changed.

Home. After ten years of living in Sydney, I still find myself saying, "I'm going home."

"Where's home?" people ask.

"Manila."

"Do you still think of it as home?"

I don't know when I stopped thinking of it as home but I still refer to it that way. I guess it's a habit migrants have, a habit we'll keep for the rest of our lives.

In my mind, I have two homes. Manila, where my past is. And Sydney, where Jaime and I came to live in search of better opportunities and a safer place to raise our child. So no matter which home I am going home to, I am always leaving another one behind. Some part of me is always absent. Missing the sights and smells of one as I go rushing to the other. Migrants, I think, are people who are never whole, never completely in one place. Ours is a fractured existence.

The last time I was home in Manila I buried my father. He had died unexpectedly straight after breakfast while he sat in his favourite chair reading the Sunday papers. He was old but I thought I would always have him to come home to.

Now all I have of him are pictures in my head and the sound of his voice that I hear in my mind. And one other thing. A painting. The going-away present he gave me. It hangs in the lounge room, over the mantelpiece, flanked on each side by a matching pair of terracotta vases. The painting is of a queen.

"I chose this, *hija*, because of its meaning. It is part of a series," he said. My father greatly admired the painter, having seen his first exhibition at a gallery in Makati in the mid-seventies. He had come away impressed by the artist's vision, and had followed his career through the years.

The painting my father gave me belonged to that first exhibition. He had asked an art dealer friend to trace this particular work. My father explained to me that its story began with a river up north. When the river's water flowed, the people who lived and farmed by its banks rejoiced for it kept their crops growing and brought them abundance. The artist, he said, created the queen as a symbol of prosperity, the bringer of good fortune. For as long as she reigned, life would be good.

"Hang this in your new home," my father told me, "and she will let blessing after blessing flow into your life."

The painting is in acrylic. Its hues are light, all pastel in shade, and yet it catches your eye, this graphic rendering of a queen's face with its rich imposing headgear, for the strokes are bold. It is of my father and my old home.

Let me tell you about the house I call home. It is a stately, two-storey house built on a huge block of land—close to two thousand square meters—in the old suburb of Malate in Manila, bought by my father in the late forties. In those times, the Malate and Ermita areas housed the more affluent families. The old rich. The houses were surrounded by a wide expanse of lawn, enclosed by high walls covered with creepers and a tall iron gate.

In the lower- and middle-class areas of Santa Cruz, Pandacan, Santa Ana, Paco, Tondo, San Miguel and the other old boroughs of Manila, life was different. The houses and *accessorias* stood close together. In these congested suburbs, children played on the footpaths, and women gossiped by doorways. Jeeps, buses, cars and even tricycles filled the streets, belched black smoke into the air, and honked noisily as they passed.

If you came home with me to the house in Malate, what you would first notice is the heavy black iron gate that creaks loudly every time it swings open. The gate leads to a concrete driveway that curves along the front of the main entrance to the house. The house itself is built deep into the block, a good distance away from the street, and the row of majestic acacias that stand like silent sentinels along the front wall hide it from view. It is impossible to see through the leaves of the tall trees. The entrance is an imposing one—solid double doors made from narra wood with symmetrical carvings done by hand. From here, there is a full view of the front garden, a rectangular block covered with Bermuda grass that grows densely, strangling every stalk of weed, for my mother hates things that grow wild and do not belong.

When I think of this house, I see my father reading in his study and I smell the old leather smell of his swivel chair, the back of which had long ago been impressed with his form so he fits into it perfectly. I see my mother in her bedroom sitting by the window overlooking the driveway, never missing anything that happens below. Home is this old house with its old smells and familiar corners where my parents continue to live in my mind, where they eagerly come out of rooms, flinging doors wide open, rushing to welcome me home. Except now the old house only has an old lady.

I try to make up for the distance between us. I write her long letters, once a month at least, as if words on paper, in great numbers, when added up, could transform themselves into my missing self.

I write to my mother about things big and small; I write to her about my housework, Jaime's business, about Marla, her music, her driving lessons, everything I can think of. In this way, she can still be a part of my life, for I am all she has left.

I used to call often but she disapproved of that. "Wasting money on long distance calls! Of course, I am fine." Mama had never lost her sense of frugality in spite of having married into a wealthy family. So I stopped calling, doing so only on birthdays and Christmas or when something special happened.

But the one-sided correspondence I kept up. Writing regularly, never expecting a reply, but writing just the same because I knew she read my letters. Mia told me so.

"Your Mama says Marla did well in her exams . . . She's been telling everyone how clever her granddaughter is. I'm beginning to feel she thinks my Susan isn't as smart!"

And it was Mia who wrote for Mama, often adding Mama's messages to her already long letters to me. PS: Your mama says you must do this. PS: Your mama says to tell you this.

The last eight months have been eight months of lies. I have kept the letters flowing, everything normal. As long as I didn't have to face my mother, I could keep up this pretence. But now my mother herself has written to me. And I sit in this plane with a head full of questions that only she can answer. My mother has always disliked my questions.

"ALWAYS FULL OF QUESTIONS . . . How many times must I tell you, better to listen than to talk. But you're always talking . . . asking useless things . . . whatever for?"

"Because I want to know," I would answer.

It wasn't that my mother was always like this. There were just things she never liked to talk about. Things about the past. I thought perhaps it was because she didn't like to remember the war. Maybe the war—the Japanese Occupation they call it—left painful memories she would rather forget. It must have been a brutal time for I remember my father telling me once, "Pray you never have to live through such a time."

So I stopped asking my mother about those years, thinking I understood her reluctance to remember. But it wasn't just the war I wanted to know about.

"Tell me about you and Papa before I was born. Tell me about me as a baby. Tell me . . ."

Part of it was curiosity, part of it was a need to understand bits of overheard conversation and make sense of strange incidents that peppered my childhood. But my mother refused to touch on these things. So I stopped asking after a while. Then I left for Sydney and resigned myself to never knowing. As Jaime often says to me, "What does it matter anyway?"

"EXCUSE ME, MA'AM, COULD you please straighten your seat and fasten your seat belt . . . The plane is about to land."

I looked at my watch to check the time.

"It's two hours behind Sydney," the flight attendant said, so I adjusted my watch to reflect the local time then leaned towards the window hoping to catch a glimpse of the city as we approached for landing. At first the view was partially hidden by a wispy curtain of cloud, but this slowly cleared and the rooftops of Manila at dusk became visible. Here and there, I caught the glint of GI sheets from the row of rooftops below, reflecting the last rays of a valiant sun that continued to hover over the horizon, refusing to call it a day.

In another few minutes, the plane landed and travelled across the tarmac, finally coming to a stop. I wondered if this was the same tarmac where the exiled Aquino, returning from the United States, had been welcomed home by an assassin's bullets as he stepped down from China Airlines Flight 8 1 1. The image of his body slumped on the ground, face down as blood gushed out of his neck, still burns in my mind. "Like a fountain" was how a witness described it.

I was safe in my Sydney home when it happened, but distance did not lessen the shock and anger and helplessness I felt.

"A gross political miscalculation," Jaime had said of the affair. He was right. It set off a chain of events that would finally lead to the overthrow of the government. Three and a half years later, it would culminate in a revolution. People's Power.

When it began, I remember watching the news on television, flicking from SBS to the ABC to Seven, Nine and Ten in the hope of hearing something new.

"It's not the same as being here," Mia said breathlessly over the phone. "I was out there, Caridad, when it happened." She spoke in a tone I'd never heard before. It was almost with envy, a sense of missing out, that I listened to my cousin talk of her march down Epifanio de los Santos Avenue—the long avenue that had filled with three million people who had come to show People's Power.

The poor and the rich, office workers and street vendors, old people and children, priests, nuns and prostitutes, sports heroes, movie stars and politicians—they would all band together in a fiesta-like revolution only Filipinos could have staged to finally overthrow the twenty-one-year-old Marcos regime. It was a revolution led by the Catholic Church. And it was filled with miracles, with tales of nuns taking the front line, stopping tanks with the power of their prayer.

But what I recall most is the strange tale told to me by Mia. "At one point we thought we were defeated. Nine helicopter gunships had circled Camp Crame where the rebels were holed up. But instead of attacking, the gunships landed and their pilots jumped out, waving white flags. They had defected and joined our side."

Later, a pilot of the fifteenth strike-wing of the Philippine Air Force would tell of his strange vision. As he looked down from his plane on the millions gathered below, for a brief moment, a giant white cross glowed over the crowd then disappeared. God was with the people. He could not fire at them.

"Oh, Caridad, how I wish you had been here when it happened. And now Malacañang Palace is open to the public. I will take you there next time you come home. Please come soon."

Now close to two months after the event, I was home. I wondered if there were visible changes. As I made my way out of the plane into the connecting passage leading to the airport, I experienced a mixture of contradicting emotions—excitement at being home mingled with a sinking feeling. I would soon have to face what I have come to think of as the "Manila Airport Shuffle."

During my last visit home, the airport—a project of the infamous First Lady, Imelda Marcos—already wore the first signs of decay. The harsh, fluorescent tubes that lit its interior failed to lighten its massive concrete greyness. Hailed as Asia's most sophisticated airport when it first opened, it now looked slightly sad, a low priority in a country that had more pressing problems than the comfort of travellers. I wished I was somewhere else.

By the time I reached immigration, I was hot, sweaty and sticky. So it was with great relief that I found myself at the front of the *Balikbayan* queue, the immigration counter reserved for visiting ex-residents. It literally means "homecomers." The service there was quicker.

With my passport stamped at last, I went to collect my baggage. One . . . two . . . three pieces. A suitcase and two boxes filled with fresh fruits.

"Is this all?" asked the customs inspector.

I nodded.

"Anything to declare?"

I shook my head.

"I'm allowed two boxes, right?" It was his turn to nod. He looked slightly disappointed. *Balikbayans* were given a tax-free allowance of two boxes of fruits, and I've always kept to that. No point getting taxed. He waved me through.

As I pushed my trolley through the glass door marked *Exit*, a wave of heat greeted me along with the din of hundreds of voices. The crowd outside the building pushed and shoved for a view of the arrival gates, hoping to spot the family members or friends they had come to welcome.

"Caridad . . . Caridad . . ." I heard my name called by a familiar voice. Turning, I saw Mia waving to me. She looked as she has always looked. A pixie with her bluntly cut hair, she stood out in her canary yellow shirt and electric blue slacks. Mia stood at five foot nothing and made up for her lack of height by wearing the loudest colours. Now standing behind a rail on the other side of the loading lane, she yelled, "Just wait there and we'll come in the car for you." I nodded, wondering just how long a wait it would be with all the cars parked bumper to bumper, waiting for people to get in, and behind them more cars waiting for the ones in front to move on so they could move forward. The loading area was jammed with trolleys full of baggage and boxes filled with *pasalubong*—fruits, blocks of cheese, chocolates, canned goods, all to be given away to friends and relatives.

As I waited for Mia, a fat matron, probably home from a trip to the States, walked past, sweating in her black, light wool coat, white skivvy, and red scarf twined around her neck. An Antarctic penguin lost in the tropics. She pushed an overloaded trolley. She pushed too hard. Like a film in slow motion, we watched the trolley slowly tilt on its side. Boxes toppled one after the other, and one box, crammed with goods, hit the concrete pavement and burst open. Out came apples and oranges, bars of Baby Ruth, Butterfinger and Hershey chocolates, cans of corned beef, a jar of Tang, tumbling . . . rolling . . . all over the pavement, then down to the loading lane and under the parked vehicles waiting for passengers.

A mad scramble began as onlookers dived for the escaping goods. Most were returned to the frantic and embarrassed owner, although I wouldn't have been surprised if a child or two had decided to pocket some of the goodies.

Twenty minutes later, Mia came in her car. She got out and gave me a big hug, kissed me on both cheeks, then quickly rubbed my face with her thumb to erase the bright red lipstick mark she'd left, speaking at the same time.

"Sorry about the long wait, but Manolo couldn't get the car out of his parking spot as some idiot parked right behind him. I should just have waited with you but I didn't think it would take this long."

"You're still here, Manolo," I said to Mia's driver who was busy loading my stuff into the boot.

He gave me a toothless grin, pleased that I had remembered him.

"He's been with us . . . oh, twenty-one years now . . . since Rey and I got married, isn't that right, Manolo?"

He nodded, giving us another one of his gummy smiles.

"God I feel old!"

"What are you talking about—you look great! All that housework must agree with you."

I laughed as I got in the car. I remembered all the times I had written to her during that first year in Sydney to complain about all the work I had to do. "It's the work of three maids—my hands look worn and wrinkled!"

In Manila, the maid did everything—the cooking, the laundry, the ironing, the cleaning, everything. The gardening was left to the houseboy. Public transport was something I was unfamiliar with for the family chauffeur drove me wherever I wanted to go.

Sydney was a totally new experience—"a humbling experience" I told Mia. The first time I cooked rice, I burnt it. Ironing collars and sleeves was a skill I took months to learn. Learning to drive was my biggest challenge—until we bought a decrepit old house that would take Jaime and I four years to renovate.

The first two years I ached for my old life. The comforts I knew, the taste of *sinigang* soup flavoured with tamarind seeds, green mangoes dipped in a sauce of tiny shrimps, dried fish and tomatoes served with salted eggs. But gradually these longings receded as I found more and more to like about my new home.

"You won't have to lift a finger while you're home. Tia Thelma will see to that." Mia's voice brought me back to the present. And, hearing my mother's name, I finally asked the question that had dwelled in my mind over the last couple of days.

"So why am I here?"

"She wanted to see you . . . No, don't look like that, I told you she's not sick!"

"Why then?"

"As I said, Caridad, old people get funny sometimes, so don't let her upset you . . . that's what I've been telling everybody."

So Mama has been at everyone. But Mia would say no more and I had to content myself with waiting. Mama will tell me in her own time and in her own fashion.

As the car inched its way forward, I looked around for signs of change.

"Too soon to tell, Caridad; you can't dismantle years of corrupt bureaucracy overnight. Even now there's already so much in-fighting and confusion. Same old politicians in new political guises. I'd hate to be Cory. Everyone's expecting her to perform miracles. The people have such high hopes, such unrealistic expectations, that I'm afraid they'll be disappointed," said Mia with a sigh.

"Well, she's given you one miracle already."

"True . . . and I guess even if she only achieves so much, at least it's a beginning. But I still wouldn't swap places with her."

The traffic had come to a standstill. Ahead of us, I imagined a series of clogged street arteries. A broken-down truck, a smash-up, a traffic light that had given up, drivers abusing each other, stubbornly refusing to budge, a Mexican stand-off in the middle of a Manila traffic jam. The hot climate, I believe, has something to do with the volatile temperament of Filipino drivers. As the traffic began to move once more, I watched children peddle leis of fragrant *sampaguitas*. Men in tattered cotton T-shirts followed close behind, walking around with their boxes of cigarettes, darting in and out of the traffic to sell a few sticks here, a few sticks there; and every now and then a woman carrying a child, or a blind person led by a street urchin, would come begging for coins. During a break in the traffic when suddenly everything surged forward, buses loaded with commuters raced each other down the lanes, overtaking, speeding, as I held my breath and wished for the safety of a traffic jam.

"Relax," Mia said, noticing how my hand gripped the edge of my seat, "you'll get used to all this in a day or two."

The traffic changed pace again.

"What's that?" I asked, pointing to a long, walled-in section, painted white, on the other side of the road. At an archlike entrance, children ran in and out. I caught a glimpse of what lay behind.

"A shanty town . . . a squatter area," Mia answered.

"Why the high wall enclosing it?"

"Well, from what I hear, the First Lady—"

"Former First Lady," I corrected her.

"Oh, that's right, it's hard to remember she's gone. Well, as the story goes, one day her limousine drove past here and she saw what an eyesore this place was. She didn't like so much squalor open to public view, so she sent in her battalion of workmen. The wall rose a few days later. Well, it is an improvement . . . if only a superficial one."

The place reminded me of the many walled-in exclusive residential subdivisions of Manila. Except inside these walls, there would be no plush homes, not even a functional, flushing toilet, and most certainly no security patrol at night to guard the residents and their worldly possessions while they slept.

Manila is a city of extremes. The poor are very poor and the rich very rich. They live side by side. The rich live in sprawling houses in residential subdivisions with fancy names like Green Meadows, White Plains, Corinthian Plaza, Bel Air, San Lorenzo, Magallanes and the very exclusive Forbes Park, a leafy enclave that was home to the famous Manila Polo Club. The poor are not far from sight. They live in little pockets on the periphery of these affluent subdivisions. A constant reminder to the rich that there is another side to life.

Near the harbour stands the historic Manila Hotel, a grand old hotel whose penthouse had been home to General Douglas MacArthur before the Second World War, and to the likes of Aldo Gucci, and where today the wealthy continue to dine and dance and where businessmen come to hold breakfast meetings involving million dollar deals. In the shadow of its modern tower, built in the mid-seventies, you will find Manila's biggest slum—Tondo. Tondo and its surrounding areas are home to the city's poor. The place is so congested that houses, if they can be called that, stand next to each other, most measuring no bigger than the size of a single bedroom. In this cramped area, families of five, six, even ten, sleep together.

In my convent school days, the nuns took us to Tondo on a field trip one day. It was intended as an eye-opener. To show us how the less fortunate lived so that we might learn to feel some compassion for them and in the process learn to be more appreciative of what we had. But compassion has done little to close the gap between our world and theirs. The structures that determine poverty and wealth have been in place for centuries.

Jaime explains it quite simply. He says, "Social and economic standing in this country is greatly determined by race. The Spaniards had a headstart of course. They ruled for three hundred and seventy years. Political power led to economic power. And don't forget the clever Spanish friars. They used religion to subjugate the masses.

"Then came the wily Chinese. They did not have political clout. The Spaniards saw to that. They treated them like pariahs, worse than the way they treated the Filipinos. The Chinese were made to live in a small area outside of Intramuros, no different from a ghetto. The Filipinos despised the Chinese as well. But nature balances things out always. The Chinese are a race of people born with great business acumen. Many of them wisely intermarried with the locals, and their offspring—Chinese-Filipino *mestizos*—gained acceptance into Filipino society. Soon they owned shops, houses, banks, haciendas. With their wealth, they eventually acquired power.

"Then the Americans came with their educational system which they cleverly used to influence Filipino thinking. Suddenly, Filipinos thought of themselves as American. We gave up the only thing we owned—our sense of self. How ridiculous we are as a people—why, we even lobbied to become the fifty-first state! In all this, it is the Filipino who is the most hard done by. The Spaniards and the Chinese have their wealth and political power but the Filipino who has never been a power in his own country continues to struggle. Have you ever seen a Spaniard or a Chinese living in a shanty?"

Looking about me at the faces of the beggars and vendors roaming the streets I realised how right Jaime was. Every one of them without exception was Filipino.

Although born a *mestizo* with Spanish, Chinese and Filipino blood in him, Jaime is Filipino at heart. And often sees with frustration the nature of the Filipino. "We have been owned so long we don't remember who we are. We think this is the way to be. We have become so accepting and indifferent to oppression."

When People's Power finally overthrew the Marcos regime, Jaime exclaimed out loud, "Are we not such a strange people, Caridad? We bow to four hundred years and more of colonial rule, suffering a thousand indignities, whereas all we needed to shake free of this state of servitude was a taste of homemade dictatorship. Still we put up with this regime for twenty-one years!"

I wondered what thoughts Jaime would have, had he been here with me right now. But then perhaps the traffic, so slow and so endless, would have been enough to keep him away. As is, it would take close to an hour to travel the few kilometres between the airport and the house in Malate. When finally Manolo pulled up in front of the gate and beeped, I let out a sigh of relief. I was home.

A MAID I DIDN'T recognise came and pulled open the heavy iron gate.

"She's new," I said.

"Well, your mama didn't like the last one or the one before, she says no one is as good as Rosa."

"Where's Rosa? She hasn't left, has she?"

"Oh, I thought I'd written you about that. Yes, early this year . . . said she wanted to go home to the farm in Pangasinan and live out her days there."

Rosa was Mama's trusted *majordoma*; she'd been in the family since I was a child and somehow I never imagined her not being here. Dear Rosa who never wilted under my mother's rule. She stayed on to see many others come and go, faces and names I no longer remember, and with time Mama had pretty much left her to run the house. She was strict with the other maids, often exuding a stern autocratic air not different from her mistress's. Now she was gone.

I entered the house where time had stood still long ago. The *sala* was as it had been. Like an image captured in a yellowing photograph. The same pieces of furniture in the very same places. My father's painting collection on the walls in the same position he had hung them oh so many years ago. The tall bamboo plant in the same big glazed pot with the dragon entwined around it still in the corner where it had first been placed over a decade ago. Some people like changing things, moving them around. Not Mama. She likes things to remain the same. Only now they look older. They have aged, grown old with my mother.

"Señora said for you to go up to her bedroom when you arrive," announced the young maid.

"Well, I'll leave you now. Call me later and we can make some plans," Mia said as she turned to leave.

"Aren't you coming upstairs with me?"

"No, I'm sure Tia Thelma would like some time alone with you . . ."

"That bad, huh?" I said to her, only half joking.

"Don't be silly," she replied.

I FOLLOWED THE MAID up the stairs to my room where she set my things down by the old Vigan chest at the foot of my bed. I ran my hand over it, feeling the wood, thinking how it needed a coat of Danish oil to condition it and restore its sheen. My father brought the chest back from one of his trips up north for I had always said I wanted one. I lifted the top to reveal the rows of little compartments with their promise of hidden treasure. I opened one of these and found two cowrie shells. I tried to remember when I had picked them. I took one and put it against my ear. My father told me long ago that if I put a shell close to my ear, I would hear the sea call. I would hear many secrets. I returned the shell to its compartment then I shut the chest and looked around the room. It looked the same but the curtains with their floral pattern had faded and from where I stood I could see a tear against the light streaming through the window. Someone had switched on the balcony light. Outside it had grown quite dark.

I opened the doors that led out to the balcony. The skies had suddenly opened as I stepped inside the house just minutes ago, releasing a burst of rain that washed the heat off the pavers, giving rise to that strong warm acidic stench that results from water coming in contact with a hot sun-soaked surface. I could still smell it. But the downpour stopped just as quickly as it had started. Now the only sign of it, aside from the stench, was the trickling sound of water droplets travelling from one leaf down to another on the old mango tree that grew by the side of the house where my room stood. Its long, thick branches now reached upward beyond the roofline, and the shadow of its branches that spread out like wide open arms reached into my room to embrace the walls.

I stepped back into my room where the air conditioner groaned. It was so old and probably had not been used since my last visit. The room was not much cooler for all the noise it made. But still, anything was better than being outside. Already the hot humid air had left my skin damp with perspiration. The brief downpour had not helped at all. It would take a few days to get used to this heat again.

With one last look, I walked to the door. No point delaying. She knew I was home. So I stepped out into the hallway and walked towards my mother's room. It overlooked the entrance to the house; from her window Mama would have heard the sound of the car going up the driveway and stopping at the front door, and our voices would have filtered up to her bedroom.

The old gilded oval mirror along the hallway caught my reflection as it had done so many, many times before. Only this time it was no longer the face of a child that stared back at me but that of a woman of forty, with stray strands of grey hair peeping out through the black; her face fuller than it used to be with fine lines at the outer corner of her eyes. And the sounds my feet made were no longer the patter of a child's feet but the footsteps of someone who had travelled the years and returned feeling lost and tired. The heels of my shoes announced my approach, ringing against the polished floorboards that ran from the top of the stairs to the end of the hall. Reaching my mother's door at last, I turned the knob and entered the room where she now confined her life.

Have you ever been inside a church when the lights are out and the only thing that shines is the row of glowing candles whose flame forms a curling trail of smoke that carries a prayer above where it will be heard by God? That same light and darkness is in my mother's room.

My eyes searched her out amongst the shadows. The only light came from the old lamp with the mother-of-pearl base that stood on a table beside her bed, casting dark looming shapes across the bedroom walls. At the same time it shed a soft glow on Mama, so I could make her out in spite of the dimness of the room. She sat by the window with its long, unmoving curtains. No breeze blew to shake their stillness. In her favourite chair, she rocked back and forth and back and forth, making creaking sounds that stood out in the silence of her room.

I hadn't seen her in three years. Not since we buried my father. Back then, at the funeral, she had stood rod straight, refusing to show any sign of grief. She had changed so much in so short a time. Her hair was all grey now . . . no, all white. She was older than I remembered.

Slowly I walked towards her, wishing my shoes didn't make such a harsh sound.

"Mama . . . Mama . . . I'm home."

She turned, slowly, the light on her hair creating a halo around her head, playing up the many, many lines on her face. Each line on our face, they say, is born of a worry.

"Ah Caridad, come here . . ."

"Mama," I said once more as I bent to kiss her wrinkled cheek. The skin felt cool and slack.

She raised her hand and put a finger over my lips and said, "No, Caridad, I am not your mama."

THELMA

"I am an old woman now . . .

I no longer fear the truth."

I RANG THEM BOTH. I said, "It is time to tell the truth."

"Why?" they both asked. Why now? Whatever for? It was so long ago. They argued, stalled, but I insisted.

Emma told me, "Leave the past alone."

My sister fears the past now that she is old, in the same way she feared the future when she was young. Is it because now that she looks back on it, she sees many other choices she did not see then? Emma sailed on turbulent seas in those early years. And water, stirred endlessly, looks dark and deep, its depth hard to judge. Emma, unable to see clearly, made her choices in fear. But storms blow away and seas become calm. Looking back to that time, does she think perhaps there was another way?

The other one was harder, angrier. "You made us keep our silence long ago and we have, why do you ask this now? Isn't it enough that we have kept our word . . . that we have kept to the terms you yourself set?"

Ligaya has not forgotten. Emma's eldest has a long

memory. And a tongue like a sharp knife, one that cuts with words. She thinks me hard and unbending but I look at her and see the set of her mouth and her face, all tight and harsh. I hear her described as beautiful. She is a terrible beauty. Dark and bitter. She has become all that she thinks me to be.

"You cannot keep what is not rightfully yours," she told me in anger so long ago. I remember her words clearly, the same way I recall many other things again.

Do not believe it when they tell you that you will remember less and less as you grow older. For I can tell you how little truth there is in that. Now that I come close to the end of my life, the beginning of it has come back to me. Little things that I have tucked away somewhere I am finding again. And I often ask myself with surprise, Why did you think of that? What made you remember?

Just now, on hearing the car come up the driveway and stop at the front door, I remembered many other times Raoul and I sat here and waited for her to come home.

She said then, "Why do I have to get picked up at ten? The dancing doesn't start till then. And the other girls get to stay till twelve!"

"Seventeen-year-old girls have no business staying out till midnight," was Raoul's reply. So long ago it happened but it has returned once more.

But what I remember most is this. "We must tell her the truth when she grows up."

Raoul said that to me when I first brought her home.

"What for?"

"Because it is about her. It belongs to her."

"Maybe when the time is right . . ."

I never found the right time because I never had the courage to tell the truth. I was afraid she would be hurt and we would lose her. But she left just the same and it was not even the truth that made her leave.

"CARIDAD AND I ARE thinking of migrating to Australia," Jaime announced over lunch.

Since she left home to be married, Caridad had dutifully come home every Sunday to be with us. First, just her and Jaime; then with Marla when she was born. Raoul and I waited for Sundays when the house would fill with conversation and laughter and mealtime was a busy affair. Raoul would discuss the news with Jaime.

"I could not have asked for a better son," Raoul would say of him. They both shared a love of reading and enjoyed their long discussions. "He has a good mind balanced by a sense of humour . . . He is right for Caridad, she is sometimes too serious," Raoul observed once.

So while the men talked, Marla would take an afternoon nap in her mother's old bedroom, and Caridad would sit in the kitchen and watch me prepare our *merienda*. I would make rice cakes which Marla never tired of eating, and serve them with a rich thick Spanish chocolate. They would sip this slowly, saying, "It's so tasty but so fattening." And I would reply, "Once a week it is all right to have Spanish chocolate." They would stay till late in the afternoon, often taking their leave around six or seven. Raoul and I would wave them off, and Marla, her head sticking out of the car window, would shout, "Bye Lola, bye Lolo . . .", knowing she would see us again the following week.

"What's wrong with here, what's wrong with Manila?" Raoul had asked.

"There's nothing wrong with Manila, Pa, it's just that there's a bigger demand for computer people in Sydney, and it will be good for Marla."

As they drove away that Sunday, Raoul, reading my thoughts, said, "It is just a whim . . . It will go away." But it did not. Eighteen months later, their papers came through and they departed for Sydney, Australia.

"Ayyy . . . Thelma," he said, "you must not feel so bad. She is all grown up now, a mother herself, and she and Jaime have their dreams. They must plan their life as they wish."

At the airport, they said to me, "It just sounds far, Mama, but really it takes only nine hours to get there; that's half the time it takes to go to the States . . . We can leave Sydney in the morning and be in Manila by six in the evening of the same day. It's not far for you and Papa to come for a holiday either."

"Now Marla," Raoul said as he held on to her hand, "you must not forget all you know, you must remember your Tagalog, and the Chinese words you've learned, and how to count in Spanish, and by no means must you speak English like an Australian or your poor *lolo* and *lola* will not be able to understand you."

Raoul and I never went to visit them. But Caridad came home with Jaime and Marla. Four times in the last ten years. The rest of the time, we contented ourselves with her letters, her phone calls, and the photographs she sent. Marla we saw grow up only in pictures. I would sit and listen as Raoul read the letters out to me. Sometimes there would be one from Marla, too.

"Write your *lola*," I can hear her tell the child.

From thousands of miles, we watched them move from a flat—"What we call a condominium apartment in Manila," she explained—to a town house—"Like an *accessoria*"—and finally to a real house—"Here it's called a free-standing house."

"Why did you buy that house? It is falling apart!" I said to her when she rang to ask if we had received her letter which came with many photographs. I was too ashamed to show them to anyone.

I remember how angry Raoul was when he saw the pictures. "It is a dump! It should be bulldozed! It does not look structurally sound. What could they have been thinking . . . Why, Jaime should know better!" he said.

The inside was worse. The photographs showed a house so old—older than the houses in Legarda, the ones that still stand with all their wood bare of paint. But this one had window frames that had rotted away, glass panes that were cracked. Its walls were stained and its ceilings were peeling.

"It is a short walk to the water, just ten minutes. Marla is so thrilled. She said she can pick from three beaches— Freshwater to the left, Queenscliff and North Steyne to the right. And the house itself has beautiful patterned ceilings. The original lead-light windows can be saved. The light streaming through the stained glass reminds me of a little chapel," she wrote. But we could not see anything beautiful in that house.

Raoul inquired as carefully as he could, "Is Jaime not doing well? Because if both of you need help, you only need to say . . ."

"No . . . no . . . Papa, everything is fine. It is not like Manila where people like to build a new house or buy a ready-built one. Most people here search for old places that still have original features and do them up. They renovate and restore. Jaime and I decided we wanted an old house. They have much more character. It'll look fantastic after we fix it up."

"Why not hire some carpenters to do the work for you? Why do you have to do it yourself?"

"We want to, Papa. We don't mind at all. Besides, unlike Manila where labour is cheap, it's smarter to do what we can ourselves and use the money saved for more important things."

"Here, you had three maids, a driver and a gardener. There, you do everything yourself. Is that what you call a better life?" But she insisted that everything was fine.

She said she was happy. The pictures kept coming. And slowly we watched her turn an ugly old house into a home. I showed those photographs to everyone.

After a while, I accepted she would not come back to live here any more. Raoul kept her letters in a box, according to when they arrived; the photographs he put together in albums—three of them—they sit on the coffee table in the *sala* downstairs. There are more pictures in the drawer of the table next to my bed. For Raoul is no longer here to slip them into albums. He, too, has left me.

IT HAPPENED WITHOUT WARNING. I held the bowl with my two hands. The blue and white Ming with the lotus painted in the centre. It was very old that bowl. It belonged to Mama's mama who brought it with her from China. I asked Mama for the bowl even before I was married, and I took it with me when I went to live with Raoul after we had wed.

I was standing in the kitchen with this bowl in my hands. One moment it was whole, the next it was half. It split before my eyes, as if a sharp knife had sliced through it. The cut was clean. I looked down and there was half a bowl in the palm of each hand. I knew then exactly what I had not formed with words in my mind, but I knew something bad had happened. What was whole was now half.

Raoul had gone into the *sala*. We had just finished

breakfast. It was his habit to take the papers into the *sala* to read.

"One must always know what is happening. It is important. Seeing only as far as the tip of one's nose is not enough." This he used to say to me and Caridad, and to Marla when he believed her old enough to understand.

So Raoul would sit and read the papers. He would begin with the front page and work his way to the back. He was like this with everything he read.

He was in his usual seat—the corner of the sofa next to the window where it was bright. His chin was tilted down towards his chest. Thinking he had fallen asleep, I touched his shoulder gently to wake him.

"Raoul . . . Raoul . . . why don't you go up to the bedroom?" He did not wake. That was when I knew for he had always been a light sleeper. I touched his hands and they were slack. I did not call the maids. I sat there for a while with his hand in mine. I spoke to him in my mind, sure he would hear me. I told him we had had a good life together, that I was thankful for all those years, that I would miss him. I said, "Don't you worry about me. I am strong and I will manage." I told him to be at peace. I lifted his hand and kissed it. Then I stood and took off his reading glasses—he still had them on. I folded them carefully. After that, I took the newspaper from his lap. He had not been there long when it happened for he had only turned the page once.

They told me he had a stroke.

"No pain . . . no suffering . . . he was fortunate," everyone kept saying to me at the wake.

Caridad flew home with Jaime and Marla. They came to bury him.

"Come and live with us, Mama," they begged me.

I refused. "This is my home and I would like to die here, not in some strange land with people I do not know. Besides, I am to be buried next to your papa; there is a space waiting for me."

He lies now in the Memory Garden at the Manila Memorial Park and with him we buried his story, the one I refused to let him tell.

I SPEND MY DAYS and my nights in this room, on this chair; sometimes I sit here until I fall asleep. Its rocking motion soothes me. The movement is like my mind, moving from today to yesterday and back. I live more and more in the past; I have little to do with people. The present serves no purpose. I am waiting for my time.

Vida, Raoul's sister, comes and visits me sometimes. I would rather she did not. Vida has not changed. But what was amusing in a young girl is irritating in an old woman. She talks without sense and does not know when to stop. So I nod and nod. I pretend to listen.

Mia, my youngest niece, comes by once a week. She comes because of Caridad. Her, I like. Mia draws me back into the world. She is lively and makes me smile. She reminds me I am still alive. Sometimes she brings Emma with her. My sister is no longer strong. Though she is younger than me, her feet have grown weak with the years.

Most days, though, I am by myself. I spend my time thinking. Since that day three years ago when we buried Raoul, I have spent many hours thinking about the truth and what Raoul said so long ago.

"It is about her. It belongs to her."

But what is the truth, I ask you. Is it not different for everyone? Do we not all look at the one thing, and each see it differently, so what is right to one may be wrong to another? Does it not mean that no one person holds the truth for it is arrived at when we all tell our part? Raoul, Emma, Ligaya and I, we all own a part of the truth.

Only, when Raoul died, one keeper of the truth—one of the four of us who lived through it all—could no longer tell it the way he saw it, felt it, in his own words.

There is something I have learned about the dead. They live on. They turn into dust and become part of the earth and the wind blows them up. They are in the very air we breathe. And their words live on in our minds, returning without being called. We hear them in our waking hours and hear them in our dreams, their words, more powerful and urgent than when they were first uttered.

Raoul whispers in my ear over and over. "Tell the truth," he says to me from the other side.

I am an old woman now and I must tell my part before I, too, leave this life. Besides, I no longer fear it. It is strange this life, for the things we are scared of, we find no longer scare us with time. It's like when you run and run and then after a long time, you look over your shoulder and find there is no one chasing you. You wonder what it was you have been running away from all this time. Many of our fears are but imagined ones bearing little resemblance to what is real. How much better our lives would have been had we known this while we were still young. How much more wisely we would have acted.

One day I decided not to run anymore. So I called the two of them. And with myself, we three will tell it so the picture can be as whole and as true as truth can be.

SHE IS HOME. FOR soon after I rang the others, I wrote to her, telling her to come home, knowing she would obey. She has always been a good daughter to me.

Now she sits before me confused and afraid. I see it in her eyes, this not knowing why she is here, why I have asked her to return. So I tell her. Maybe I could have said it in a different way, kinder, gentler, softer, but I say it in the only way I know.

"No, Caridad, I am not your mama."

Her eyes look back at me. A question in them. Unspoken yet not gone unheard by me. Why now?

Because I have stopped running. Then I tell her, "You know. Deep, deep down, deep inside you . . . here, where your heart is, you have always known. You have always asked. Or do you no longer remember?"

CARIDAD

"The past defines us as much

as the present.

Because mine was missing,

I never felt whole."

WHAT ARE YOUR EARLIEST memories? What do you remember? What were your questions? What did you want to know? What made you laugh and cry? What were your fears and joys? Where did you live and play? Whom did you love or hate? What were your dreams?

They say we remember everything we have ever seen, heard, tasted, touched and felt. That every experience is etched in some part of our brain. Nothing is ever lost or forgotten. Everything stays with us forever.

They say, too, time does not distance us from these memories. That some can remember things from their early childhood and some even further back, remembering sounds and sensations from when they slept in their mother's womb.

I remember many things. Shapes and shadows moving about me. Sounds of voices lilting, soothing and sometimes angry or sad and weeping. And warmth . . . the feel of a hand that caresses, loves and takes away pain. But most of all I remember things that I did not understand yet felt deep within me they held some truth. I asked about them as a child but was refused an answer. I asked as an adult but sensed that the answer would cause pain. I stopped asking. What does it matter anyway, it is only the past.

But it does matter. For the past defines us as much as the present. By never knowing my past, I was never sure of who I was. Because mine was missing, I never felt whole.

"Why?" is a word children learn early in life. It was a word I used often as a child. And it was a word I continued to use long after most children had moved on to other words.

The word itself creates an empty sensation. Try saying it now. "Why?" Notice how your tongue touches nothing when you form the word with your mouth. Feel the gap, the space inside your mouth, that it creates. The air. It is a place that needs filling. It is missing an answer.

I remember asking it as a four-year-old. We were still living in the old house in Santa Cruz. And every day, I would go out and play with the children who, like me, were not old enough to go to school. We played house by the front verandah, turning chairs into imaginary bedrooms and tables into sitting rooms. We played hide-and-seek under the house where many old discarded things had been tucked away and forgotten. And we played *piko*—hopscotch—along the driveway, marking its hard surface with pieces of white chalk. Throwing bits of chain or pebbles to mark our spot as we hopped and hopped, on one foot then on two. I can still feel my long braids whip against my back every time I hopped.

Sometimes we played dare. The biggest, scariest dare was to sit by the old acacia tree that grew near the wall in front of the kitchen door. A spirit lived there. An old woman in grey who sometimes showed herself to the servants at night. She had been seen walking—no, floating, her feet not touching the ground. She came out at night, a gossamer figure, thin as air, and see-through. Giggling with nervousness, one of us would go under the shade of that tree as the rest counted. The higher the number, the braver the person.

The tree loomed tall in my dreams and the old woman called to me one night. I wet my bed. Mama said my friends and I were never to go near it again, or she would make me spend a night out there on my own, and the servants were warned never to tell their tales.

One hour flowed into another as we spent the morning playing, laughing, screaming, fighting, then making up until we were called in. "Come in now and have your lunch!" The first cry would often go unheeded. Soon this would be followed by a second cry, "Hurry up before the food gets cold." This, too, we would ignore. But the third cry we always jumped to for it carried a threat. "Come inside this minute or you can forget about playing this afternoon."

For a while, silence would reign outside except for

the sound of passing vehicles. It would last another hour or two after our meal as we all took our afternoon nap. I never felt I needed that nap but there was no arguing with Mama or my *yaya* who was just as strict with me.

It was on a day like this that someone planted the first seed of doubt in my mind. That day, as we played outside, a *jeepney* stopped across the street and my Tia Emma got off. I remember feeling disappointed because she did not bring my cousin Mia along.

As she crossed the street that day, Teresa who lived next door said, "It's your mama, Caridad." The other kids giggled among themselves.

"No, it's not my mama. It's my Tia Emma," I said.

"It's your mama . . . It's Caridad's mama . . . Caridad's mama . . ." Teresa continued to chant, only stopping when Tia Emma came towards us. I looked closely at her but could see no resemblance between her and Mama. Her face was rounder and her eyes were dark like her hair and her skin was like milk.

Mama's face was longer and her eyes saw deep into you, her skin was a golden brown, and her hair sometimes had a touch of fire.

"Caridad, where is your mama?" she asked.

"Inside," I said, pointing to the house, "in the kitchen."

When she had gone, I turned to Teresa saying, "See, I told you it wasn't my mama." But she seemed to find that even funnier. I didn't like her much since that day, the day I started to ask "Why?"

I REMEMBER MY FIFTH birthday. My first one in the Malate house. Mama had invited all my cousins and the children next door to come to my party. She dressed me in a pretty pink dress the *modista* had made specially for me.

"Sit still, Caridad, I can't comb your hair if you keep moving. Stop scratching like you have ticks on you." I couldn't help it; the lace of my dress made me itch, so I scratched around my neck and around my arms where the puffed sleeves ended. Earlier, my *yaya* had dusted my whole body with baby powder to stop me from itching. But I continued to scratch and red marks were beginning to show where my nails had run over skin. Mama slapped my hand when I reached out to give my arm another go.

"Stop! And keep your head still."

I disliked having my hair combed out. It was thick and curly and long and every time Mama put the comb through it, its teeth would catch in my hair. She'd tug gently but it always hurt.

"Ouch!"

"It's almost done . . . Be still . . . How many times must I tell you a person has to be able to keep still because when one moves too much, one shakes off luck, but when you sit still, luck stays with you." Mama often told me things like this as she combed my hair in the mornings. I never dared tell her I did not understand her meaning. She pulled things out of some secret box in her head. She made things up depending on what it was she wanted me to do. Like this morning, to keep still.

Mama finally untangled my mass of hair. But instead of plaiting it, she gathered the front and tied this with a pink bow at the top of my head. The rest she left hanging down my back.

My *yaya* who was standing by watching Mama do my hair exclaimed then, *"Parang prinsesa!"* Like a princess. And, looking at myself in front of the mirror, I felt like one. The pink lace dress with its satin bow around the waist may have been uncomfortable but it made a pretty picture.

Mama had bought me a pair of new white patent shoes and white lace socks to go with the dress. And it was in these that I walked down the stairs to the *sala* to have my photograph taken.

"So this is the birthday girl," said the photographer who was waiting downstairs for me. He was a tall thin man with a slight stoop, which I thought must have come from always bending down to look into his camera.

He had set his camera up on a three-legged stand and put a black cloth over his head every time he took a shot of me. There were shots of the three of us—me sitting between my parents, me with Papa, me with Mama, and shots of me alone.

"One more shot to go and this time you choose where you want it," he said.

"Outside?"

"No problem!" He moved his camera to the garden, to my favourite spot, an arch formed by two bougainvillea vines. I loved playing under it as I imagined it to be the doorway to some magical place. I still have that photograph: a young girl with a smiling face standing under an arch of leaves and flowers that quivered in the wind.

The guests arrived soon after. Children my age that I could play with. But the one I waited for was Mia.

This is what I remember most about that day. This is what stands out in my mind, clear as the day it happened.

I heard Mama call out, "Emma, you're finally here." Tia Emma walked in. I was excited for that meant Mia was here as well, so I ran out to meet her.

I ran into the lounge room where the grown-ups were gathered. Tia Emma smiled at me and said, "Happy birthday, Caridad." She bent as I went on tiptoe to give her a kiss. Just then someone spoke out, I don't know who it was but I heard someone say in a surprised voice, "*Dios mio*, Emma, she looks like your Ligaya!"

"No, she does not!" Mama snapped back, sounding upset and angry. I looked at Tia Emma and she seemed upset too, only in a different way from Mama. Tia Emma looked embarrassed but there was something else . . . she looked sort of sad, like she was going to cry, while Mama looked angry. She didn't say angry words but her eyes told me she was angry. They always have a look to them, glassy and glinty; when she had that look, I knew she was angry. Her mouth looked angry, too, the lips were set in a straight, thin, hard line.

"Go out and play with Mia and the other children . . . Go on," Mama ordered, and I knew she didn't want me there. I went outside to look for Mia.

From that day on I would look out for my cousin Ligaya, Mia's eldest sister. Always hoping to see if I really looked like her. But Ligaya never came to see us. Often, I would look in the mirror and try to make out my features. Whose eyes were these, whose nose, whose lips, whose face. I had Mama's hair. The rest I thought was part Mama, part Papa so that I resembled neither one of them in a definite way. A mix.

I WAS AT MIA's house. Mama seldom took me there.

"Your Tia Emma's too busy to have visitors. Besides, there's no room to play there. Just wait till she comes next time . . . I'll ask her to bring Mia along."

But that day was different. She said we were going to my Tia Emma's.

"We must not be late or the other guests will have all arrived, so hurry up with your breakfast, Caridad."

I didn't need to be told again, and I didn't complain when she made me change into a party dress. I didn't mind the discomfort. I was going to Mia's.

"Whose birthday is it?"

"Not a birthday, but an engagement party."

"What's that?"

"Oh, you know . . . it's a party you have before you get married."

"Who is getting married?"

"Your cousin Ligaya."

"Who is she marrying?"

"Stop asking . . . finish dressing."

We arrived to find the *sala* already filled with people. It was not a big house, Mia's house, so it did not take many people to fill it. It was hot and warm inside and there was no seat or corner that had not already been taken.

"Where's Mia?" I asked. But no one answered me, everyone was busy talking.

I made my way to the dining room where Mama was already chatting to Tia Emma.

"Where's Mia?"

"Look outside, Caridad."

But Mia was nowhere to be found. I headed back inside. Maybe she was upstairs. Without another thought, I made my way up the stairs. I had only been up here a few times. This was where the bedrooms were. One for Tia Emma, one for Mia's brothers Miguel and Paolo, and one for Mia and her sisters.

Mia's bedroom was the middle one. There were two big beds there. She slept with Laura in one bed, and Ligaya shared the other with Celia. I never told Mia this—that I envied her this room. I would sometimes imagine myself sleeping in a big bed like hers with someone next to me to tell stories to, or just lie there not speaking but listening to secrets told by hushed voices, carried by a gentle breeze.

And under those beds lay a different world. We played under them once, amidst the boxes that were stored there. We pretended it was a cave in the mountains where we lived in fear, hiding from the *tulisans*, bandits that roamed the hills, preying on helpless damsels, just like in the soap operas the laundry woman listened to every afternoon, the radio loud and blaring as she ironed the clothes. So Mia and I rolled on the floor under the bed, inside a cave, not realising our lives were more in danger from our angry mothers who later found us dirty and sweaty with clothes that had picked up the dust the broom had missed.

But there was to be no playing that day. Mia's room was full of people, with Ligaya busy getting ready and Celia helping her dress. People were coming in and out of the room, many I did not even recognise. And still, Mia was nowhere in sight.

I turned to go and as I made my way to the stairs I noticed Tia Emma's bedroom door standing open. "Mia . . . Mia . . . are you there?" I walked towards it and looked inside. It was a simple room, small in size, with a bed at one end and a dressing table against a wall, opposite the window. But it was the picture on the cupboard that drew my attention.

The picture frame stood on top of a high cupboard and rested against a wall. It was a cream-coloured frame with touches of gold and the wood had curling patterns carved into it, like icing on a cake. It held the picture of a man. He was thin and pale, not old but not young. He looked serious except for his mouth, which seemed to be soft, as if he was about to smile just when the picture was taken, so it was too late to smile fully. Maybe it was from where I was standing, but it seemed like his eyes were focused on me, and I wondered what it was he was about to say.

"What are you doing here? Caridad . . . Caridad . . ."

Turning, I found Ligaya standing next to me. She was dressed and ready to go downstairs. I remember she looked so beautiful. I had always been in awe of her because of that and also because she always seemed so grown up and distant. I was a young child who very much wanted her approval. So I hesitated before speaking to her. I gazed back at the man in the picture first before finally asking her, "Who is that?"

Ligaya stood in silence and, like me, gazed at the picture. The two of us stood there for how long I do not know, until she replied, "That is Papa."

"Your papa?"

"That is Papa," she repeated. Then she looked from him to me, lingering on my face, before saying, "You have his eyes." Then gently she touched my cheek. A light feathery touch. I do not remember her ever touching me before. I looked at her without understanding.

"Come," she said, taking my hand, "it is time for me to go down . . . People are waiting for me and Mia must be looking for you."

She gently turned me around and guided me out of the room. She took my hand and led me down the stairs.

I wanted to ask her one other question but in the excitement that followed, I forgot what it was. Only later as I lay in bed did I remember. I had wanted to ask her this, "Is it true that I look like you? Is it true?"

"A HUNDRED TABLES! SHE will have a hundred tables!"

My father promised a hundred tables at my wedding *lauriat*. A banquet for a thousand guests, ten to each table. When a couple was invited, the children, sometimes even grandchildren, came along, easily taking up a whole table.

My parents took a while coming to terms with my marriage. I was eighteen when I met Jaime through a friend who said she had a cousin who was brilliant with numbers, and who could help me with my statistics class. Jaime was already working then, being four years older than me, but he handled tutorials to make extra money. At first he came once a week for two hours, explaining things like the T-Test and the F-Test, and the difference between mean, median and mode, and how to work out standard deviations. But these discussions quickly gave way to long talks about books and films and travel and many other things that led to friendship and beyond. The day Jaime refused his fee was the day my father realised my tutor had become my suitor.

Jaime was only half Chinese, his father being Spanish-Filipino, and his family was not well-off like mine. But my parents' main objection was my age. I was twenty and had just graduated from college when Jaime proposed. But Jaime refused to be deterred by anything.

"I am not a wealthy man but I am hard working and I promise you I will take good care of your daughter," he told Papa when he asked for my hand in marriage. "And while it is true Caridad is young, wouldn't you rather see her securely settled and happily married while you are both still around, than wonder and worry if she will be all right on her own when you are gone?"

My parents were in their early sixties and Jaime had touched on their unspoken fear. Papa gave in. And a date was set. So I was married at twenty and was given a hundred tables to celebrate the event.

During the wedding banquet, we moved from one table to another, all one hundred of them, accompanied by a friend of my father who served as toastmaster. The guests drank to our happiness. While we made the rounds, I sipped tea, avoiding anything alcoholic. So it was with a sober mind that I remembered someone saying as we walked past one of the tables, "This one . . . this one came after . . . but she is the lucky one . . . the others, you know, had a hard time for many years."

All these memories I pushed to some recess of my mind. And there they remained until I discovered I was pregnant.

"MAMA," I SAID, "MAMA, Dr. Santos said I tested positive. The baby's due in July."

"Good . . . Oh, that's good," she exclaimed, sounding really pleased. "Your papa and I have been wondering if we were ever going to have grandchildren to play with. I'll put him on the phone so you can tell him yourself."

Jaime and I had been married almost fifteen months before I got pregnant. I was beginning to think maybe there was something the matter with me, for Jaime came from a large family and I was an only child, a late in life child.

"Maybe I'm like you . . . You had a hard time conceiving . . ."

"Nonsense!" Mama said, cutting me off before I could finish what I was saying. "There's nothing wrong with you."

As my pregnancy advanced, I began to remember the many little unexplained bits and pieces of my past. They trickled back into my consciousness. I mentioned them to Jaime one night.

"You're just imagining things," he said, giving me a hug.

Jaime would always say I liked imagining mysteries where none existed. But there is something about expecting a baby that makes you think of your childhood. I think it has to do with all the little scenarios I would imagine—of my child growing up and asking about my life, of the wonderful stories I would then tell—all these imaginings brought back my sense of incompleteness. I couldn't script the stories because I didn't know all the facts. So I began to ask questions again and the more I asked, the more upset Mama became.

"Tessa said I am going to have a boy," I told Mama one day over lunch.

"What would Tessa know. It's a daughter you're carrying," Mama said, sounding so sure of herself I could sense Jaime smile.

"Your mama is infallible, like the Pope," he said jokingly to me once.

"What would Tessa know," Mama continued. "Round . . . your stomach is round, that means it's a girl. If it is pointed, it would be a boy."

"You should have told us sooner, Ma, then we could have painted the room pink," Jaime said as I glared at him across the table. He liked teasing Mama and I always feared she would take offence.

"We painted it off-white—a very pale cream—so it would suit a boy or a girl," I explained.

"*Basta!* It's a girl," she said once more, as if daring anyone to contradict her. Papa glanced up from his plate once, a twinkle in his eyes, and Jaime winked at me but I pretended not to see.

"Besides," Mama added, "you're looking good . . . blooming . . . baby girls do that . . . baby boys make your skin go dark, your neck and the skin under your arms start to take on a deeper colour."

Jaime looked at Papa and said, "I don't think I want a son after all."

"So you mean, you looked really pretty when you carried me," I said, teasing her. She took it wrongly.

"Always full of questions . . . always asking . . . whatever for!"

MONDAY'S CHILD IS FAIR of face they say. But no one warned me how difficult it would be to bring one into the world.

If Marla had had her way she would have come into the world feet first. She was a big baby. Unusual they say for a first child. She clung in there, refusing to come out. No amount of regulated breathing and no amount of pushing could coax her out. Finally, after twelve hours in labour, my doctor took pity on me. I was too tired to weep by then. So she operated. At 8:58 in the evening, Marla was finally delivered by Caesarean section. She weighed eight pounds six ounces. She was a beautiful baby. She was not fair-skinned but she had a beautiful face. But what caught everyone's attention were her fingers. They were the longest tapered fingers I have ever seen on a newborn.

My parents, who had kept Jaime company in the waiting room, felt their anxiety transform into relief, then joy. Mama was beaming when she came in to see me and my father had tears in his eyes. At last they had a grandchild to give them pleasure in their old age. We named her Maria Larissa. Marla for short.

My hospital room was filled with fresh flowers. The

first bunch came from Jaime. Bright yellow roses because I have always loved yellow. To Marla's nursery, which had been painted an off-white, I would now add a yellow touch.

Mia came the next day accompanied by Tia Emma. They had missed Mama by a mere ten minutes. They brought with them a basket of strawberries from Baguio and a small container of condensed milk.

"I thought you'd like to have them now and you'd be wanting some condensed milk to dunk the strawberries in, so I brought some with me." Mia knows my every weakness. As she went looking for a plate, Tia Emma sat by the bed next to me.

"No one is with you today . . . Where is Thelma?"

"Mama has gone out to buy some things for the baby," I reassured her, adding, "Jaime had to go to work but will be taking the afternoon off. Papa is in the office but will come tonight."

"We've seen the baby, Caridad," Mia informed me on her return. She had managed to get a plate and a fork from a nurse. "Mama and I went by the baby ward before coming here. She's beautiful."

"She will grow up to be a beauty, Caridad. You and Jaime must be very pleased," Tia Emma said to me as she took the plate from Mia and put some strawberries on it for me.

"Here, you eat now. They are very fresh."

I smiled and took the plate from her. In between mouthfuls of strawberries I told them, "You should hear

Jaime, the way he speaks about the baby you would think he was the only one responsible for making her!"

"That sounds familiar. Maybe all men are the same!" Mia quipped.

"Did you see her hands, Tia Emma, her fingers are so long!"

"Long fingers . . ." she repeated after me, her voice trailing off. After a while I heard her say, "My Alfonso . . . you never knew him . . . he said long fingers . . . talented people have long fingers."

"Oh, does this mean I am terribly untalented?" Mia said, holding both hands up with her short fingers spread out.

We all laughed. Mia had always referred to herself as the midget in the family. Everything about her was small. She was barely five feet tall. Had size five feet. A twenty-three and a half inch waist. And small hands too.

We chatted for another half an hour, then Mia stood to leave. "We have to go. I have to bring Mama home and then do some shopping, but I'll come see you again. You're here another two days, aren't you?"

It was then that Tia Emma took out a small parcel from her bag which she hastily put in my hand. "It is nothing . . . only a small present . . . I want you to have it, Caridad. It is important, this time . . . the birth of a first child."

I held the parcel in my hand, quickly looking at her then at Mia who stood behind her mother. Mia nodded to me indicating I should go ahead and open it. Inside was a heart-shaped pendant. I could see it was not new. I understood it belonged to my aunt.

"But Tia Emma, I cannot take this. It's very pretty but I can see it is yours. I mean . . . don't you want to give it to one of your children or grandchildren?"

"No . . . no . . . this I want you to have."

I caught the look Mia gave me. Take it, her eyes said.

So I thanked my Tia Emma for it, accepting with reluctance and embarrassment her gift to me. "I will keep it, I promise to take care of it. Thank you . . ."

She clasped my hand then, the one that held the pendant. She said, "It is not much, you understand, no need to tell your mama, yes? Only a little something."

I have never worn it. But I have kept it. That old heart-shaped pendant is wrapped in tissue paper and lies in a red silken pouch inside my bank vault at Westpac in George Street where I keep most of my jewellery. Expensive pieces, even trinkets of sentimental value, are safely kept there. To tell you the truth, I had forgotten all about the pendant. Once when I had to go to the bank to take out a piece of jewellery to wear to a function, I saw the small pouch and couldn't recall what I had kept inside. I opened it out of curiosity and only then remembered the existence of that heart-shaped gold pendant. I should have asked Mia about it then. It hadn't occurred to me that it might have meant something. Something more than just a present from an aunt who was fond of me.

"So what are you going to be when you grow up?" Tia Vida asked Marla.

"A pianist."

Marla was eight and had just won her third award in her school's piano recital. She was the youngest performer in Division Two. The other kids her age competed in Division One.

"I don't know where she got her talent," said Jaime, "no one in my family has an ear for music."

"And I've never played well. Mama had me take lessons but I wasn't interested at all."

Tia Vida laughed. She was Papa's younger sister and came to visit my parents every now and then. "Yes, I remember you playing the piano as a child . . . *walang pag-asa!* You were hopeless."

"It's a stray gene then, a throwback to some ancestor," Jaime said.

"Oh no, it is from your mama's side, Caridad."

"But Mama doesn't play."

"Your cousin does, your Tia Emma's eldest . . . What's her name?"

"Ligaya. I didn't know Ligaya played the piano."

"They say she was very good. Marla took after Ligaya . . . *mana kay* Ligaya."

"That explains it then," Jaime concluded, "nothing strange in that."

"No . . . not at all . . . same family," Tia Vida replied, "not strange at all."

"What's not strange?" Mama asked, entering the

sala, a tray in her hand, the *leche* flan she had made still warm from the oven. Marla loved her cream caramel.

"*Lola*, Vida says I took after Tia Ligaya. Was she really good at the piano, *Lola*?" asked Marla.

Mama stiffened. She continued walking towards us, then stopped by the table to put the tray down, the maid close behind her, carrying the plates and forks. I caught the swift glance Mama gave Tia Vida.

"Was she, *Lola*?"

"Was she what, Marla?"

"Tia Ligaya . . . was she very good at the piano?"

Mama nodded, "Yes, she was, but that was long ago. Now, how big a piece would you like, Marla?"

With that Mama ended all discussion about the piano and Ligaya. Tia Vida and I exchanged looks but kept our silence. I never asked her about it for it would have been a betrayal of my mother. And Tia Vida looked sorry enough for having said the little she had. Mama always said, "Vida's tongue runs away from her, she has no control over it."

"YOUR PAPA WANTED YOU to know . . . I didn't."

Mama's voice brings me back from all those years . . . back to the present where I now sit and listen.

Why now then? I asked with my eyes. As if hearing my question, she replied, "I am old now and one day I will take the truth with me, and you will never know my part in it . . . never hear my side. And hearing it from the others . . . you may think I was wrong."

"So tell me from the beginning."

She shook her head, "The beginning," she said, "the beginning is not mine to tell. It belongs to my sister . . . to your Tia Emma."

EMMA

"I think now there may have been

other choices had I been brave

enough to see them, choose them."

LAST NIGHT I DID something I have not done in many, many years. I unlocked the drawer in the cupboard upstairs, the one that stands in the corner of the spare bedroom, the one I seldom open but have taken with me each time I have moved in the last forty years.

At first I could not remember which key it was that opened it. There were many keys dangling from the heavy, tarnished silver chain. Alfonso's old chain. Some for pieces of luggage that have long been thrown away, too old to be of use, others—I do not recall which ones—for those I have stored things in; they lie hidden, under the spare bed. I cannot even recall what is in them.

So I took out the chain that held these keys together, trying them, one after the other. Inserting them into the blackened keyhole of the old *aparador* until I found the right one. It slid in easily, and as I turned it, the lock clicked open. I pulled the drawer out, releasing the air of many years, an old musty smell.

The box lay at the bottom where I kept it many years ago. I lifted the lid and took out the album with the photographs. It is strange how the years can seep into everything, even things kept hidden under lock and key. The pages had always been black but now they felt grainy and brittle as well. The photographs all looked older, browner, darker, stained by the passing of the years. But as I looked closely at them, eyes glittered and smiled once more, and I began to hear voices again as conversations returned. No, I have not forgotten. Who can?

Now I am ready to tell it again.

I DID NOT WANT to but my sister insists. Thelma, how she has grown strange and more difficult with the years. I pray I do not become like her. She has never learned to bend. I remember my grandmother comparing the two of us when we were children.

"Thelma is like a strong narra tree, hard and unbending. You are like a bamboo, you sway easily. Half of you and half of Thelma would make a better tree, one that will survive storms, floods and strong winds."

"She drives everyone away . . . Why, even her maids don't last," said Ligaya. But Ligaya can be unkind where Thelma is concerned.

To Mia, she often says, "Why you even go and see her is beyond me."

"Because she's lonely. Tio Raoul's gone and Caridad is

so far away. She has no one really, no one who comes home to her. Besides, I promised Caridad I'd look in on her every now and then."

It is true. Thelma is lonely. But she is too proud to admit it. All alone in that big house with no one to talk to. I cannot live like that. She seldom comes to see me, expecting me to be the one to go to her. I make the trip even if it means taking three *jeepney* rides to reach her house. One to Avenida Rizal, one to Malate, and another one to her street. I used to not take the last ride, preferring to walk the distance to her house, but these old bones no longer move well, they no longer carry me with ease. But I go as often as I can. Mia scolds me when I go without her. So now I take the maid along. But she does not like that either. "Why didn't you tell me you wanted to see her? I would have taken you in the car." Mia does not like me to ride jeeps and buses.

I do not mind the inconvenience. I must see Thelma. She has done much for me. *Utang ng loob.* My debt of honour. I must show her I am grateful, even if at times I have felt resentful. It is what those who have needed help must suffer: to receive with gratitude and resent having to receive at all.

But life is strange in how it balances out all things in the end. Thelma is strong and life has left her to stand on her own. I, who never had her strength, have been given many children to be with. It is not such a bad thing, I think now, to be the way I am. The children, who were a burden to me when Alfonso died, have become a blessing in my old age.

My children come home on Sundays. Not all of them together. But at least one of them. They ring during the week to tell me who is coming. So I am never alone. They come, sometimes bringing the young ones, sometimes on their own. But always, I have someone.

So Sunday is the day I do the cooking myself. I know what each of them likes to eat and just how they like it done. Sundays I cook for them.

This Sunday is different. Caridad is coming home for the first time.

I asked the maid to clean the apartment well.

"But I just waxed the floor the other day and yesterday, I husked it. See, it is shiny."

Ah yes, I remember seeing her do it, polishing the floor with a coconut husk gripped by her bare foot. Yes, the tiles had a nice sheen to them but I tell her to make sure they are really clean.

"Sweep them once more."

"Susmariosep!" I hear her mutter under her breath.

I check the tabletops for dust. Old places seem to gather dust quickly. This has been home to me for the last twenty-one years. I moved here the year Mia got married, the last of my children to leave home. It has only two bedrooms so it is easy to keep clean.

The food is almost ready. This morning, I got up early to go to church then I passed the market on my way home. I like to buy everything the day I do my cooking, that way all the ingredients are fresh. I bought two plump ripe eggplants. For Caridad, says Mia, likes to eat *rellenong talong*. It is simple enough to make. First I throw in the chopped garlic when the oil is hot then the meat follows. I add some soy sauce and a pinch of salt. When this is done I set it aside. Then I boil the eggplant until it is soft. I slice it in half then dip this in egg. I spread some minced pork on top and fry this until each side is brown.

I bought two cans of corn kernels to make her dessert, for Mia also told me, "Make her some *ginataang mais* . . . I know she likes that." And I made sure I added a bit more sugar than usual. "She has a sweet tooth," Mia said.

"Mia, are you sure there is nothing else she likes?"

"Oh, Mama, stop worrying. It'll be fine."

So I cook Caridad's favourite dishes with care, tasting the eggplants to make sure they have the right amount of salt, enough garlic, not too much soy sauce. Making sure the corn is soft and sweet enough. As I cook and stir, I think to myself how I am so blessed after all. That what I believed I had lost, what I had given away, is returned to me once more.

But a thought comes to my mind. When it all happened it seemed the right thing to do. I think now there may have been other choices had I been brave enough to see them, choose them. For it is about choices in the end. Will she think I chose wrongly or will she understand? Will she be kinder than Ligaya who said I was weak?

———

SHE ARRIVED TWENTY MINUTES ago, kissing me on the cheek as she came into the *sala*. "Tia Emma, *kumusta ka?*" she said, greeting me and asking how I was before handing me a bag of fresh fruits.

I tell her I am well and that she should not have gone to so much trouble. She has brought me big red apples and a dozen oranges. Fruit is so expensive in Manila. "No, it was no trouble at all. I just checked the boxes in. I did not have to carry them at all," she reassures me. Then I hold up this strange fruit. I have never seen anything like it. It is brown like a *chico* but it is not round and it has short fine hairs on it.

"Oh that, that's a kiwifruit. I brought some for you to try. It's very tasty and nutritious." She tells me fruits are cheap in Sydney, they have apples and oranges all year round. Some people, she says, just pick them from their backyards.

"These are from your backyard?" I ask her.

"No, no, we didn't grow these. I bought these from the fruit market near the house. But we do have a lemon tree in the garden and a small vegetable patch."

I smile at the picture of her growing vegetables and herbs and I say to her, "It is the last thing I would imagine you doing. Why, when you lived at home, you never even got up to get yourself a glass of water. Thelma, your mama, had a little bell in every room which was rung when you needed something. And now you dirty your hands growing vegetables." I find the thought pleasing.

We sit and talk some more. I get up and turn the electric fan on. I can see she is uncomfortable in this heat. I ask after Jaime and his work. She says little about Jaime but is eager to talk about Marla and her music.

"She is very talented and she wants to be a concert pianist." She pauses, then says, "It is funny that it should show up in her . . . this talent . . . and not in Ligaya's children."

Ahhh, this is her way of saying she knows the truth, and now wants to hear it from me. Oh, Thelma, you may have raised her as a child, but she has none of your bluntness. I see there is some of me in her. She is a little shy and unsure.

"Tell me," she says softly.

I wonder how much I may tell her.

"Tell her your story," Thelma said. But it is not easy, for where my story runs, also runs Thelma's story—they meet and cross. I see it like the stitches on a piece of clothing. I see it as a stitch that has come loose. When you take the cloth in your hand and pull at this loose thread, there is the danger that more stitches will come loose. One leading to another, one stitch after another coming loose. Telling the truth is like that, it is much like telling a lie—one leads to another. And soon all the stitches unravel, and the hem falls free because you pulled at just one loose thread. How much can I tell her? When do I stop?

"*Mula sa umpisa.*" She asks me to tell her from the beginning. So I do.

WE COULDN'T FIND A coffin for his body. It was just after the war, you know—the Japanese Occupation. Ten months after it ended, ten months after Liberation, Olongapo, where we lived, was still in chaos. Things were hard to come by. Clothes, food . . . everything. So when he died, there wasn't a coffin to be found in the whole town.

My poor Alfonso. He lay in our bed while we tried to find a coffin. Finally Kumpadre Lucio thought of getting a carpenter to make one up. There were some old *palo china* crates in the warehouse where he worked. So he himself dismantled these crates and took the pieces of old pine wood to the local carpenter. The man then worked all afternoon to make a long box we could use as a coffin.

We laid Alfonso out in this box. Inside, the wood was bare and rough. I draped a piece of old curtain on it. So young . . . he was only thirty-nine. He had not been well, you see. A few months before, he started to have chest pains. "Go back to Manila, go see a doctor there," I kept begging him, but he would not listen. He did not want to be taken away from his work so he went to the local doctor. The doctor told him he had a weak heart, he should take care.

There was no sign he would die so soon. He would be

fine most days and go out into the fields, laying electrical lines through the rice fields. He was an electrician. He and Kumpadre Lucio had come to Olongapo to start an ice plant.

The work took him out early in the mornings into the fields, and often he walked across stretches of swamp lands. "Be careful," I told him over and over, "it is not good getting your feet wet all day, and you don't know what is out there." But he was like a bull sometimes, stubborn, when he had an idea in his head. He did not watch his health. So the week he died, he was home most days. He woke up tired every day. Still, I did not expect to lose him. Maybe he knew. Because he asked that we send for Ligaya. She had gone back to Manila a few weeks before and Alfonso hadn't seen her for a while. I thought nothing of it. Just him missing her. She was his favourite.

I remember the morning it happened. He said he wanted to go back to the bedroom to rest. I got up to help him but he waved me aside.

"No . . . I can manage," he insisted. He did not like being helped, especially in front of the children. So I let him go up on his own. It must have been half an hour later, maybe longer, but not much, when I went up with a glass of fresh *calamansi* juice for him. He liked a cold citrus drink on a hot day. He was sleeping when I entered the room. His head was turned away from me. I was about to walk out of the room when I decided to leave the glass of juice on the bedside table. I walked over to his side and put the glass down. Then I decided to lift his head, put it back on the pillow, and I noticed his face, the greyness of it and his bloodless lips, his mouth in a line of pain.

I called to Paolo who I knew had gone back to his room. He must have known from my voice—I do not recall if I was shouting—but he came rushing. He knew something was wrong. Paolo came in just as I was lifting his father's head. He was still breathing. I told Paolo to run for the doctor. To hurry. I could not wake Alfonso. The doctor arrived and listened to his heart, felt his pulse. He shook his head, no, he could do nothing for him. His condition did not change. His breathing remained shallow, his mind gone. He clung on, long enough for Padre Luis to come and bless him. He never woke again . . . just slipped away.

Sometimes I wonder if there was something he wanted to say as he lay there. I wonder, too, if as he lay there he could hear us, hear me weeping. Maybe I should have said something, then maybe he would have come back.

He laid there until early in the evening when Lucio came with the coffin. It was too late to take it to the church so we waited till morning. Two days later, we buried him. It was the day before Christmas.

It was not a good time to die. Not only did we not have a decent coffin for him, we did not even have a funeral car. We asked around; not me, you must understand, I did not quite know where my mind was then;

even now, there are many things I cannot recall about that time, so it was the others, they looked for something to take the coffin to the cemetery but there was nothing.

Then someone suggested we hire the local garbage truck. This is my shame, my regret, that we could not give him a proper funeral. A garbage truck. My Alfonso was buried, *parang pobre*, like a poor man.

We followed on foot. A procession of mourners. Our neighbours came and just about every Chinese in Olongapo. They collected money for the family. It helped see us through the early days. It was a very warm day and we had to walk in the heat wearing black. I had no black dress and had to get one made in a rush. Black is for mourning and I had not expected to bury a husband at this age. I can still feel the sun burn through my black dress and my black veil. I thought I would faint. Even my feet could feel the heat for the ground was so hot I could feel it scorch through my shoes. As we walked, the music blared from the loud speaker they had put on top of the roof where the driver sat. The cemetery was not that far from town but the trip was slow and painful.

Padre Luis was there. Alfonso would have approved. Every Sunday, Padre Luis said mass at the church we attended so it was right that he was there to bless and bury Alfonso in the end.

He let us follow the Chinese ritual. Maybe he did not approve, being Catholic, but he let us do it anyway. The funeral was part Chinese and part Catholic. We prayed

Catholic prayers, but before we left, we burnt temple money for the dead. Thelma brought a bundle from Manila. The night before, she showed Ligaya, Celia and Laura how to fold the money and they sat in the *sala* carefully arranging these on a tray. We burnt them during the burial so Alfonso would not go without on the other side. We also lit sticks of incense and offered fruit. After the burial, we distributed the fruit. Everyone who came to the funeral took some home. It is for good luck because this fruit is blessed. It is offered first to the dead then given to the living. The luck is shared. Padre Luis said nothing while we did all this. He was a kind man.

After the funeral, we all walked back. All of us on foot. It was hard. By then it was afternoon and the sun was high, missing nothing. Mia cried all the way home and Ligaya had to carry her. I remember my feet ached so much, every step made me wince. The two boys had to help me all the way home. Blisters had formed on my swollen feet by then. When we finally got home, Thelma boiled some water and when it had cooled a little, she put some salt in it and made me sit down and soak my tired feet. You know how it is when you are heavy with child—your feet swell up.

Yes . . . yes, I was pregnant then . . . I was carrying you.

ALFONSO AND I ALWAYS wanted a big family. I grew up with three sisters and a brother and could not imagine a child growing up alone as Alfonso had. He often said it was so lonely not having a brother or a sister in the house. He was born in China; his mother died when he was eight and his father took him to Olongapo soon after to live. A new land, a strange language, no mother to comfort him, no friends to play with; he never forgot the loneliness.

I met him on a Sunday afternoon. Remember your Tia Cora, my second cousin? Yes, the one who lives in Caloocan. Well, she played matchmaker. Cora was dating your Tio Ramon then and it was really his idea. Alfonso and Ramon went to school together. They were best friends. And he kept wanting Alfonso to meet me so he and Cora planned it. Later, Alfonso told me he did not want to come along that Sunday. Your papa, he was a very shy man. But Ramon was very insistent.

It was in May. You know how warm it gets in May. Well, Cora said she would come over on Sunday to visit. She came just before lunch after we had returned from church. After lunch, Mama and Papa retired to their room and everyone else followed. It was siesta time. Cora and I sat in the *sala*. Gossiping about this and that but mostly about her suitor Ramon. I had met him before at Cora's. After a while, Cora stood up and said, "It is so warm in here, let's go and sit out on the verandah."

I remember she even took Mama's *abaniko* with her and fanned herself while we sat on the chairs out front. We were there, oh, maybe fifteen, twenty minutes, when Ramon walked past with a friend. He waved to us and Cora, sounding surprised, exclaimed, "Look, it's

Ramon!" She waved back to him saying, "What are you doing here? Come in . . . come in for a while. . . ." Well, it is not hard to imagine what happened. They introduced your papa to me.

That Cora, she should have been an actress! Anyway, the afternoon passed pleasantly. Ramon talked a lot while Alfonso—I could see he was shy—spoke softly, asking politely about me and my family, and telling me about himself and his studies and the small business he had started. I liked him a lot. They stayed a while, and when they were leaving, Cora said, "Oh, we should do this again." That was the first of many Sunday afternoons the four of us spent together.

Ramon and Cora married soon after. Alfonso and I followed ten months later. I cannot remember being happier in my life than I was then. So happy that I forgot what had been foretold of my life when I was a young girl.

I WAS EIGHT YEARS old when I accompanied my mother to a shop run by an old Chinese couple. I think it was somewhere in Binondo, but I cannot be too sure. It was a small dark shop with lots of jars and trays inside a long glass counter with sliding doors. The jars contained dried leaves and stalks, seeds and grains, dried flowers and twigs, even black things that looked like the bark of trees. The inside of the shop was warm like an oven and the smell of the strange things hung over it like a cloud that refused to move.

"What are they?" I asked my mother.

"Medicine," she said, "Chinese medicine . . . they are made from plants and come all the way from China."

I made a face. My mother had made me drink them in the past, a cup of black liquid that tasted as bad as it smelled. Now I knew why. Every cup was made from these strange dried things.

I moved closer to the counter to peer at the things that were laid out on the trays. I tried to identify them. I saw pieces of ginger, some dry flowers with white petals and then, on another tray, something that made me feel sick. I had only seen them once before, moving about slowly in a fish tank in the house of my father's friend. Papa had said they were seahorses. But the ones here were all dried up. I shuddered at the thought of drinking anything that contained a seahorse.

An old man stood behind the counter. When we entered the shop he was busy attending to another customer. So it was his wife, an old lady with her hair in a bun covered by a fine black mesh, who asked my mother what she needed. They spoke in Chinese, which I did not understand well, for at home we spoke Tagalog more than Chinese.

But I sensed her eyes on me. As she spoke to my mother she kept looking at my face. She slid the glass door of the counter open and spooned up some dried things. I watched what she chose because I was afraid she would include some seahorses, but she didn't. After scooping up an ingredient she would put it on a scale to weigh. Finally, when she had about eight different kinds all measured up, she wrapped them in a big sheet of paper and handed the parcel to my mother. There were three packets in all.

Then I watched her fingers flick the beads of an abacus, up one row, down on another. She did this several times, moving quickly. Finally, she looked up and told Mama how much it all cost. As Mama searched in her purse for money, the old lady asked a question and Mama glanced at me then nodded in reply.

"Your daughter?" was what she asked my mother. I understood the Chinese word for daughter.

The old lady came around to the front of the counter where I stood. She raised one wrinkled hand to my face and held my chin, bringing her face close to mine. I smelled her stale breath as she spoke to my mother. She had long crooked teeth with big gaps so you could see their sides. They had dark stains on them like rust. And some bits were black. Then suddenly she opened her mouth and I stared at this deep dark hole.

"Aiiiyah!" the old lady exclaimed and I jumped back in surprise. She pointed to my right eye as she continued to speak to my mother. Here, this was what she pointed at. Do you see it? The mole in the corner . . . No, not outside but inside. The mole at the inside corner of my eye.

I did not understand what it was that had been said, but I knew it was not good. Children have a way of knowing when they are being talked about and they can sense whether what is being said about them is good or bad. I sensed she had said something bad about that mole.

Mama nodded without smiling, and soon after, we took our leave. Once we were out of the shop, back in the sunlight, I turned to her and asked, "What did she say?"

"It's nothing . . . nothing important."

"So what . . . what did she say about my mole?"

I would not stop asking. Tired of my questions, Mama finally gave in. She said, "It's just some superstition."

"What?"

"She said when you cry, your tears will touch it, and that it is not good to get it wet."

"It's *malas* . . . bad luck."

"It will bring you grief," she said. "But don't pay attention to this . . . old people believe in many superstitions."

I WAS TWENTY AND Alfonso, twenty-three when we married. My marriage was not as good as your mama's. When Thelma married your Papa Raoul, he was already helping manage his family's successful construction business. Alfonso, on the other hand, did not come from a wealthy family. He and his father had very little money when they arrived from China. They settled in Olongapo for a while, that is why it was there that Alfonso chose to live after the war. When we married, I knew we would never have much. But that didn't matter to me because Alfonso and I were happy.

Alfonso was an electrician and ran a little repair shop where he fixed radios, lamps and irons and sold electrical parts. It was a short *calesa* ride from where we lived in Sampaloc. He'd come home for lunch sometimes, but most days I'd pack his lunch in a *pimbrera* and he'd carry this to work.

Ligaya was born in the first year. All this family planning business did not exist then. Everyone started a family as soon as they married. Why, it was the reason people married in those days. Children were important not just for your old age but for a family's business. Whether it was a store or a farm you had, it was better to have your own children help you than to depend on an outsider. People didn't wait a year or two before having babies. The ones who didn't have a child soon after getting married would worry. I know couples who have had to go all the way to Obando to dance in the streets in the hope of having a child. So I was lucky. I had no trouble at all conceiving. I was a lot of trouble to Alfonso though.

I remember I had this craving for *buco* when I was carrying Ligaya. But I wanted the coconut to be young because the meat was still soft and the juice much sweeter. Alfonso would often have to go by the market on his way home from work. Even the small coconuts were heavy and bulky, but he didn't mind. He would pour the juice out into a jug then scrape the soft white meat off. This he would spoon into the jug as well, adding sugar to make it even sweeter. On a warm day, I'd have the juice with cubes of ice. My mama—your *lola*—said that's the reason why Ligaya is so fair. It's because of all the soft white *buco* I ate while I carried her.

Ligaya was born at home. It was a Saturday afternoon and the people next door had come for a chat the way they always do on a Saturday. We had just finished our *merienda* when I felt the first pain. I did not say anything, thinking it would go away.

It was my neighbour . . . Maring, I think, was her name . . . it was she who noticed me wince. A woman understands these things. She had Alfonso fetch the *komadrona*, the midwife, who lived a few streets away. She helped me to my room then went to boil some water.

The pain was unbearable. I tried hard not to scream and cry. I bit my lips until they bled. It was not till night time that Ligaya was born. We kept the afterbirth in a box which we buried under the house to make sure she would grow up to love her home and not wander off to strange places.

Alfonso came into the room and knelt by my bed. "I am sorry it was so painful. I promise you, we won't have any more children," he said. Thinking about that now makes me laugh. We had, as you know, another half a dozen after Ligaya.

When I realised I had a daughter I wept. Alfonso had looked forward to the birth of his first child and I had disappointed him. I wanted to give him a son. But I could not have been more wrong about how he felt.

He named her, did you know that? I wanted to call her Maya, after the pretty little birds that chirped in the trees outside, but Alfonso named her Ligaya, for happiness. And she was that to him. How I could ever have thought he would love her less because she was not a boy I do not know.

She was a small baby. They say the first-born is usually smaller than the babies who come after. And she was very red. The *komadrona* reassured me saying it was a sure sign she would grow up to be fair. The red ones, she said, always turn out fair.

When he first saw her, Alfonso said, "She is beautiful. She is very fair and look at her fingers . . . so long . . . She will be a pianist when she grows up." He would tell this to everyone. So it was no surprise when he had a piano delivered on her fifth birthday.

In the mornings, I would have to push him out of the door. "Go to work. Go and make us some money!" I would say or he'd stay there playing with the baby and not leave at all. He was good with her. At night, he would get up to help change her wet *lampin* and he enjoyed helping me bathe her.

When he came home in the afternoons, he would come straight up to the room to have a look at her. But he would not carry her; not until he had washed and was clean would he carry her.

Then, of course, the other children followed and maybe I am wrong, but I don't think even the birth of Paolo, our first son, meant as much to him as Ligaya's birth. It was not that he didn't love the others, he just loved her best.

The old lady whose husband owned the *sari-sari* store at the corner of our street used to call out in a loud voice, "Ahhh, here comes the daughter worth ten thousand pieces of gold." She would tease him saying, "Not to bother, only a girl." But he would take her out every chance he got and show her off to everyone he knew. Why, before she could even walk, he'd take her to the shop. So while he worked, I'd talk to the customers who always spent some time admiring Ligaya. Alfonso liked that.

It was a good year that first year we were together. I can say it was one of the happiest years of my life.

When Ligaya was three, we moved to a bigger house in Sampaloc, a few streets away from where we used to live. By then I had Celia and was pregnant with Laura. She was the first to be born there. We liked the house because it came with a backyard . . . a small one, but with enough space for the children to play in. Upstairs, there were three bedrooms. The big one we eventually gave to the girls. The boys shared the small room. And Alfonso and I had the one facing the stairs.

It was a friendly neighbourhood. Down the street from us, about five houses away, lived a childless widow in her forties—Lagring was her name. Behind her back, the children in the streets called her Santa Lagring for all the *santos* she kept in her house. Lagring lost her husband in her twenties and never married again. Few men, after all, would choose a widow for a wife because widows are considered *malas* . . . unlucky. With no children and no husband to share her life, she spent her day praying.

Lagring was a very devout woman who woke early every morning and walked to the church to say her *novena*. She owned two dresses—a black one and a brown one.

In Lagring's spare bedroom was an altar with a statue of Our Lady and on either side of it stood several *santos*. In front of these were three fat candles that burned all day and all night. Her landlady Mrs. Sotto was also our landlady. She was a loud, heavy woman who owned most of the houses on our street, having been left them by a gouty husband who was found dead next to his young mistress. The girl went mad, or so they say.

Mrs. Sotto had threatened many times to evict Lagring from her house, not because she sometimes failed to pay the rent, but because the landlady feared the house would burn down one day. Santa Lagring lit candles all day but kept the windows in the altar room shut. The windows and the ceilings had turned black from the smoke.

"The smoke from the candles is holy. It protects my house. It protects me," she said to me one day.

Santa Lagring was fond of children, though they loved to make fun of her. She would call to them and ask them in for some sweet sticky rice or whatever it was she had prepared that day. Once, Ligaya and Celia went to her house. They were curious children, wanting to see Lagring's altar. They said she had asked them to kneel in front of her altar and make a wish. But Alfonso discouraged them from going often or staying long. "It is not healthy . . . all that smoke."

But the smoke-filled room did not seem to affect

Santa Lagring who spent hours praying in there. Maybe Our Lady and all the *santos* did protect her, for even the landlady's threats to evict her were never carried out. Perhaps she feared the saints would punish her. So Lagring stayed on.

In our street, the girls were very popular. Especially Ligaya who everyone thought was a beauty. Often, we had the neighbourhood children come and play. Thelma, your mama, used to say, "There's never a moment of silence in this house." I didn't mind because I liked the sounds we all made. It was a happy home.

But if I had known then that he would die so young and leave me to care for all the children myself, I would not have had so many of them. But you never know these things. While you are happy, you do not think of sadness, you do not think of it all ending, you do not think of death.

I almost lost him twice, you know; twice he almost died.

We were in Pasig when Clark Field was bombed. It was also the day the Japanese bombed Pearl Harbour. I did not even know where that was.

"In Hawaii," Alfonso told me. "It is where the Americans have their fleet of ships." It sounded so far away. But when I heard they had bombed Clark Field, I was frightened. It was close to us, only a few hours away from Manila, less than a day's journey.

It was the Feast Day of the Immaculate Conception.

The eighth of December. We had left Manila in the morning for Pasig, where Alfonso's friend Nanding, to whose child he was godfather, had invited us for lunch. He said he would roast a suckling pig in his backyard and Alfonso could not resist that. *Lechon* was his favourite dish. He loved the taste of crackling. He sat with the men in the backyard on a long bench and table, drinking beer and shelling fresh oysters, then dipping them in vinegar. The men laughed and told yarns, while the women sat inside listening to Nanding's wife explain how she prepared the goat meat to make her delicious *kilawing kambing*.

Suddenly, Nanding shushed everyone, telling us to keep silent as he turned up the radio. Clark Field had been destroyed. The Japanese had attacked. The announcer said in an excited voice that almost the entire US Air Force in the islands had been wiped out. The field had been bombed from end to end. The Japanese had swooped down and blown up the aircraft on the ground. Our pilots had no time to get in the planes. Many people died and many more were injured. We would not be able to fight the Japanese bombers. The Philippines had no air defence.

There was silence for a while, then everyone started talking at the same time. Lydia, Nanding's wife, made the sign of the cross. I said a silent prayer. There had been much talk of war in the past for war had been going on in other parts of the world, but far away—it would never come near us. There was war in Europe. The Germans were invading other nations. There was war in Asia too.

In China, the Japanese had been fighting a long time. But all this did not concern me. I did not ask about it. I only listened as Alfonso and his friends spoke about it. No one ever imagines he or she will live through a war. It is something that happens to other people. But now, it was just hours away from where we lived, less for a plane carrying bombs. We left soon after, the food uneaten, everyone rushing home.

"We must buy food as soon as we get home," Alfonso said.

The trip home was slow compared to our earlier journey to Pasig. It seemed as though everyone had heard the news at the same time and was heading home. When we finally arrived in Manila, we were greeted by so much confusion. The motorbus we rode had to pull aside to make way for military trucks that thundered through the streets one after another.

"Will they be able to defend us?" I asked Alfonso, who shrugged. He did not think so.

"We were caught unprepared," he said, "and I do not think we have enough men to fight."

Just then, an elderly man sitting in front of us turned around and said, "It will not be easy. My son is in the army. There are only 75,000 Filipinos and maybe 12,000 Americans. And most of our boys are young and inexperienced. In all, there are maybe only 20,000 regulars. In a war, those numbers are small. And with no planes to defend us from the air, it will be like suicide.

"The Japanese armed forces number three million.

Man to man alone, they can take on the armies of several Asian countries combined. And these men are not green-horns. They are battle-hardened soldiers. They have fired their weapons and killed men. Many of our boys have never killed at all. They are innocents. In China, the Japanese have been fighting since 1933. With thousands of troops stationed in Manchuria. The toughest conditions will not frighten them. Their military is stronger and better equipped than ours. They have been arming themselves for years. Do not forget to take into account their discipline. Military might springs from discipline and Japanese soldiers live and breathe by the code of Bushido. So fighting for them is tied to their honour. When you consider all this you can see what our soldiers are faced with. Our poor boys who have only been playing at being soldiers."

Alfonso squeezed my hands but it did not take away the fear I felt on hearing the old man's words. I tried to keep calm and not let my fear show through. I looked out of the bus window with the children. In the streets there was much running and jostling. You could feel the panic. It was as if the whole of Manila, all its citizens, had run out in the street. There were people frantically trying to go in all directions.

"Where is everybody rushing to?" asked Paolo.

"Out of Manila," the elderly man said. "If you are wise, you too will leave soon."

I looked at Alfonso and saw him nod.

Suddenly, a dozen car horns blared long and loud.

The cars had taken over the streets again after the military trucks had passed. Their drivers ignored all traffic signals.

The moment we arrived home, Alfonso asked Ligaya to help the maid pack the children's clothes. "Not too much, Ligaya, for it is food and medicine we will need most," he instructed her.

Once inside our room, he took out all the money he had and began counting it. "We must go out and buy food. Forget fresh food, buy canned things. They will last. It is too bad I did not keep more money in the house . . . if only we had some warning. The banks, you know, will not be open for a while. All accounts will be frozen."

I reached out and smoothed out the frown lines on his forehead. Then I got up from the bed and walked to the dresser and opened the bottom drawer. There, under a pile of envelopes, I lifted a box secured by a rubber band. It was an old box that had once contained expensive imported chocolates. A present from Alfonso. I had kept it because I loved its beautiful gold foil trimming. I slipped the band from the box and opened the lid. Inside was a thick pile of bills. I took these out of the box and walked back to him. I handed him the money without saying a word.

"What is this?" he said, looking at the money that now lay in his hand.

"Food money."

They were all crisp new bills I had saved through the

years. Every time Alfonso gave me money for the house, I would separate the new bills, thinking it a waste to spend them. So I had kept the bills in the box, liking their crispness, their newness, their clean smell, never thinking one day they would be used to buy food to fill the stomachs of a family of eight throughout a war.

"Oh, Emma," laughed Alfonso, "Emma . . . you and your new bills!" He gave me a big hug, all the time laughing loudly, then pulling away to look at me, then at the bills, then laughing once more. It would be a long time before we would be as carefree again.

WE TOOK ALL THE money we had and bought all the food we could get. The shops were full of frantic people. There was much shouting and pushing. We bought several *cavans* of rice and sacks of sweet potatoes. I stocked up on sugar and condensed milk and as much toilet paper as I could find. I hoarded canned food like Spam and Spanish sardines, going from one shop to another. We paid a young boy to help us carry the load in his pushcart. I told Alfonso we should buy everything we could with the money we had. It was better to buy too much than to find we did not have enough. So we bought and bought. In fact, when the war ended three years later, we still had some tins of sardines left.

It did not take long for the shelves in the stores to be emptied for everyone who had money had the same idea. The store owners made the most of our panic buying. You could pay ten pesos for something one moment and find that the price for the same item had gone up just an hour later. It made me angry but there was no point haggling. The person next to you would just grab it and hand over her money. It was wiser to just buy without complaining. The shopkeepers never did such brisk business. Their luck would not last long, though, for later there would be much looting.

"The old man was right. When the Japanese come, it will be safer outside the city," Alfonso said. "Taytay . . . we must head for Taytay."

Just then we heard a long wailing sound. Everyone in the streets began to run. Alfonso grabbed my arm and dragged me with him. I followed without questioning. All I knew was we were in danger. We ran with the crowd. A child stumbled and her slipper came off. But her mother would not stop, she simply lifted her off the ground and ran. Finally, out of breath, we found ourselves crouching against the concrete wall of a low building. There was little else that could shield us. A little girl began to cry. Her mother put her hand over the child's mouth, as if fearing her voice would travel upwards and give us away to the enemy above. Everyone raised their heads to peer at the sky. We waited. No planes came. Then the air-raid siren went on again, signalling it was safe to come out. We headed for the house.

"What will we do, Emma?" My neighbour met me with tears in her eyes. "We have just come from the shipping offices. There are no ships. They have cancelled all the regular services because the army needs them. I must go home to Leyte. Manila will be bombed to pieces and we will all die."

"Have you tried Tutuban Station?" I asked her. "Maybe you can go by rail, then take a connecting boat?"

"We lined up for two hours at Tutuban but could not get near a ticket window. There must be thousands of people there."

"Then you must go to the hills—Antipolo—it is not as far from Manila as the provinces, but it will still be safer, at least you will have a better chance," advised Alfonso.

The news over the radio gave us little comfort as we learned of the Japanese bombings all over the country. That night, the skies glowed from the fires in the distance.

Two days later, the news was even grimmer. Cavite Naval Yard was hit by the Japanese. First the planes, and now the ships were gone as well. It seemed hopeless. I said a silent prayer for my aunt and uncle who lived in Cavite. God will take care of them, I kept telling myself. Now, I must think of my own family.

Already, there was some looting. The warehouses at the docks and railways had been forced open by people frantic to get their hands on food and medicine. A neighbour of ours came home with an armload of goods she said had been given to a crowd by three Americans who had opened up a warehouse. One of the Americans said to them he couldn't take them so the locals might as well have them. Better them than the enemy. So she came home with rolls of plastic, some spools of wire and yards of gauze. She didn't know what to do with them. I asked her for some of the gauze. Maybe it would come in handy one day.

When the real looting began—we were gone by then—shopkeepers found themselves helpless against the crowds. This happened as the Americans were retreating and panic spread throughout the city. Even the cold storage at the foot of Quiapo bridge was broken into. But I think it was the Chinese who suffered most. Looting was no longer just an act of desperation, it was also caused by hatred and jealousy. You see, the Chinese were never really liked by the Filipinos. They were envied. They owned stores and property and were shrewd at business. They were also moneylenders.

I would often tell Alfonso he was the only Chinese not born with a sharp business sense which is why we would never be rich. He would say, "At least our neighbours like us." What he said was true. We lived much like our neighbours, so when the looting began our home was left untouched even though we were not in Manila to protect it. Most of the shops and houses that were broken into belonged to the Chinese.

The Spaniards did not suffer as much. Filipinos disliked the Chinese more than they did the Spaniards. The Spaniards they feared and envied; the Chinese they hated and envied. Two different things. Many of the Spaniards owned businesses and vast haciendas that employed Filipinos, and many were in the law profession. They were not to be crossed. Most of us saw them as belonging to a different class. After all, they had ruled the country for several hundred years.

Within days the situation in Manila deteriorated. "We must leave tomorrow," Alfonso said.

So we loaded all our things; some clothes, not much, for it was not clothes that we would need most, but foodstuff. We did not know how long we would have to live in the hills, so our survival would depend on food more than anything. We loaded the food we had bought into the small truck—it was more like a pick-up with wooden sides—that Alfonso had hired for two hundred pesos to take us to Taytay. Two hundred pesos was a lot of money then but we had no choice. It was old and dirty and had been used to carry sand and gravel by a friend of Alfonso who made deliveries to construction sites.

The other families on our street also packed their things and locked up their homes. Except for the widow Lagring. As the truck we rode moved down the street, I saw her looking out of her front window. Lagring had refused to leave her *santos* behind. I prayed they would protect her from the Japanese army that was headed towards Manila.

The roads leading out of the city were full of *calesas*, *carromatas*, *carretelas* drawn by tired-looking horses, overloaded buses that ran on charcoal and which broke down easily, and hundreds of carts pushed by men and women. I saw women with bundles of clothing over their heads walking alongside their children who struggled with heavy packs, some carrying their chickens with them. A boy of perhaps ten carried his pet dog, and a man had two piglets in a wooden cage set on a small pushcart. At least, his family would have meat to eat.

It seemed like everyone was leaving Manila and I remember thinking the Japanese would come and find no one there. I had this picture in my mind of Manila, all dark and deserted, the streets silent, a ghost city.

The trip was slow. We would not get there till nightfall. It was too late to find a place to sleep so we slept in the small truck that night. In the morning, we moved further up into the hills and Alfonso joined a group of men in clearing a small area. Armed with sharp *bolos* and saws, they felled trees, bamboo trees, *ipil-ipils* and hacked at the thick shrubs, while the women and children gathered firewood for cooking. The men put together some makeshift huts of nipa that families moved into by the end of the day. The huts were spaced out carefully so that a few trees stood between each hut to provide cover from above. Our hut had a thatched roof and stood on big bamboo poles. Inside, there was only one partition. The outside section was where we sat when people came to talk. It was where we ate and spent the day. The inside section was where we all slept at night. When it was too warm, some of us would sleep in the outer room. The first few nights we found sleep impossible, for the hills were not a silent place. Crickets and frogs and all sorts of things buzzed and chirped in the evening. It had a sound of its own. And the mosquitos were all over us every night. The children would wake every morning and compare the size and number of bites from the night before. But we were lucky to have our own hut for those who did not make it to the hills had to seek shelter with the rice farmers below.

A shallow brook flowed about two hundred feet away. Alfonso put a pole through the wire handles he made for two big empty cooking oil containers. One on each end of the pole. He and the boys carried water, making three trips, from the brook to our hut every morning. The water was then poured into a big metal drum that stood inside a small square nipa enclosure a few feet from our hut. Here, we washed ourselves, scooping up water with a *tabo*, a small plastic bowl, pouring it over our heads and our bodies. To save on soap, we walked by the brook, searching for a good pumice stone and, on finding one, used this to rub the dirt and dead skin off our bodies.

Every morning, with the help of the older girls, I would gather up our dirty clothes. Together we would join a group of women and walk to the brook where we squatted as we washed our clothes. Soap was in short supply, so after a few weeks we had to make do with simply soaking the clothes in water and rubbing and squeezing them with our hands, and beating them with a small wooden clothes bat. While we worked, we told stories and swapped gossip and discussed the war. After we had got used to our new surroundings, it felt as though we had simply moved to a new neighbourhood and made new friends. This was how we spent our life in the hills while we waited for the Japanese to enter Manila.

As the Japanese advanced and the Americans retreated there was much burning. Both sides took turns setting gasoline depots on fire. In Manila itself the Americans burned the Pandacan gasoline depots so the Japanese could not use the fuel. In Iloilo City it was the Japanese who bombed the gasoline depots. The smoke could be seen tens of miles away. The skies turned red then black and stayed that way for as long as four days.

Copper was important for the Japanese. To make ammunitions. Baguio in the north, as you know, is rich in copper ore. The Americans did not want to leave this to the Japanese so they wasted it. They got rid of it by pouring the copper down the hills.

Before Christmas Day, General Douglas MacArthur declared Manila an "open city." The buildings and the streets, they say, were ablaze with lights when the Japanese soldiers came. It was the signal that there would be no resistance. The people who stayed behind thought this would be enough to save them, and the city. But the Japanese dropped their bombs just the same. Santo Domingo Church fell along with Santa Rosa and the Letran College.

On December 28, we listened to President Roosevelt himself speak over a short-wave radio. I remember his words well. He said, "I give to the people of the Philippines my solemn pledge that their freedom will be redeemed and their independence established." He promised us that America would stand behind us in this war.

Every new family that joined us in the hills brought fresh news about the city. So we learned of the convoys moving from the south to the north, over the Calumpit bridges. They were heading for Bataan. On hearing this, the men broke into a long discussion. They talked endlessly of battle plans and what they thought our men should do, and what it was MacArthur was thinking.

A few nights after Christmas, the sound of explosions, though muted by the distance, still reached us in the hills. I glanced at Alfonso who had sat up straight at the sound of them, gazing into the dark, his eyes glittering.

"They have done it," he said.

"More bombings."

He shook his head. "The bridges . . . it must be the bridges. They are gone."

Sensing my need for an explanation, he continued, "We talked about it just this morning . . . that our men have no other choice but to blow up the Calumpit bridges. I think that is what we are hearing this minute."

In the distance, the deafening explosions continued. The children stuffed their ears with cotton balls. "They cannot turn back now," Alfonso said.

"But they are safe then . . . in Bataan."

"No. They have simply bought themselves time. There, the Japanese cannot send more ground troops after them, but they will still be vulnerable by air. Help from outside—from the Allied Forces—must come soon. Because with the bridges gone, our men cannot cross back, no fresh supplies can reach them. They have cut themselves off. The jungles around them will only provide temporary shelter. When the bombs start dropping, they will have to fight, not just the enemy, but burning trees and shrubs as well."

Later, we would hear just how unprepared the army was. Many of the soldiers did not even have proper helmets and wore dried coconut husks instead. Many had to scavenge for arms with which to defend themselves and their country. Those that had guns and rifles to fire found these did not work at all. They had no proper shoes to walk the long miles. And no coats to keep them warm as they stood watch on the hills. Many of them, some as young as seventeen, shivered through the cold nights. The communication lines did not work, so many soldiers did not know where they were supposed to go and what they were supposed to do. There was much confusion. Within days they would come to know hunger. After only a week in Bataan, they were already on half rations. When the food was finished and fresh supplies could not reach them, the members of the cavalry had to shoot their horses and eat them.

JANUARY 2, 1942. THAT date is carved deeply in my generation's mind. We were not there when it happened but we felt the pain just the same. For it was the day Manila fell.

The Japanese turned the University of Santo Tomas into an internment camp for the Americans. They were rounded up without warning—men, women and young children—and they were given no time to pack their things.

I remember Alfonso saying bitterly, "Our oldest university, a prison camp! How the Japanese show disrespect. Why, Santo Tomas is even older than Harvard in America." Alfonso was a graduate of Santo Tomas.

The Japanese showed cruelty as well. They hated the Americans so much, it did not matter that they were mere civilians. For six months they were given no food. They had to rely on their Filipino friends for survival. In one part of the camp was a fence. Here, the Americans were allowed to accept food and clothes from the Filipinos. It was a great sacrifice for the people to give food when food was scarce, but many went just the same with little parcels of food, and whatever clothing they could spare.

It was many, many more weeks before we returned to Manila. For while the Americans and our men fought on, there was hope.

At night, we would gather in one of the huts where one of the men had a radio. Here, we listened to the news of the battle.

"People of the Philippines. You are listening to the 'Voice of Freedom' from the battle fronts of Bataan," was how it always began. At first the news gave us hope, but as the Japanese increased the force of their attack, the news became worse and worse.

"By now, food and water, medicine and ammunition will be almost gone. If the jungle itself does not defeat them with disease, Japanese bombs will get them," one of the men said gloomily one night.

Then Quezon and his staff were secretly taken by submarine from Corregidor to safety in the south. A few weeks later, MacArthur followed. They would head for Australia.

"He has left us. What will happen to us?" I said, expressing what every Filipino felt. MacArthur was the leader of our army, we had put our trust in him, believing he would defend us.

Then, over the radio, we heard him make a promise. He said, "I shall return." Over the next three years, while we suffered under a harsh Japanese rule, we found comfort in remembering those three words. We believed he would keep his promise. We needed to believe. But his leaving left us feeling alone and frightened, like a child that had been orphaned or abandoned. As you know, we would have to wait a long time to be liberated.

Among some of the people there was a feeling that we had been betrayed. Alfonso for one said, "I do not understand why President Roosevelt cannot liberate the islands first. He is committing his forces to Europe. And we have to suffer at the hands of the Japanese while we wait."

What followed was the continuous bombing of the Bataan Peninsula and Corregidor. All day long and all through the night the explosions could be heard. Lying in our nipa shack we could hear the loud bombardment in the distance. Sleep was impossible.

"The Japanese have planes. They can mark our troops' positions during the day. Then drop their bombs on them at night," said the men who gathered to listen to the news. "With all these explosions, most of the trees and shrubs would have been burnt off. There will be few treetops left to hide the men, even the Malinta tunnels where they are said to be hiding cannot withstand so much force."

After fourteen weeks of fighting, Bataan fell.

"It won't be long now," Alfonso told me, "Corregidor will follow."

THE WAITING WAS HARDEST to bear. I found the long days of sitting and waiting difficult. If there had been the possibility of winning the fight against the Japanese, we could at least have waited with hope in our hearts. But as things stood, all we could expect was news of the fall of Manila.

I just wanted it to be over. I wanted the killing of our soldiers to stop. I wanted to leave the hills and return home. Do not think I was brave. I was filled with fear. I imagined the worst whenever I thought of life under the Japanese. But I was sick of waiting for the end.

How I envied the children. While older people filled the long hours worrying about the future, they filled their lives with ordinary childish concerns. Life touched them so lightly.

It is true that in the beginning, the girls—Ligaya, Celia and Laura—complained about the many discomforts they had to suffer. But they eventually accepted our new living conditions. Laura, who had refused to sleep on a mat laid out on the bamboo floor, eventually got used to it and stopped asking for her child's cot. As for the boys, the joy they got out of playing in the hills made up for the hard task of carrying water from the stream to our hut. In no time at all, the children were their old selves again—meaning the three girls sided with each other against the boys. There is one incident I will never forget.

The scream was loud and shrill. Then Ligaya's, Celia's and Laura's voices rang out. Scolding. Paolo's cries filled the hut and a second later, Miguel joined in. The three girls were fighting with their brothers again. Alfonso and I went to see what was going on. We had been out walking.

On the floor of the hut was a broken glass jar. Its contents, which had spilled on the bamboo floor, made me shudder. The girls had been cleaning the inner room where we slept when Celia had found the jar under a pile of Paolo's crumpled clothes. She lifted it, then dropped it in her shock.

The story then poured out of Paolo's mouth. Inside the jar, Paolo had secretly kept two field mice that he and Miguel had caught one day. They were to be the boys' pets. But the mice had died from lack of food, air and space. The boys then agreed they would not bury the mice. They wanted to see the bones. The skeletons. So they kept the jar hidden and forgot about it for a week. When Celia had picked up the jar, the mice had by then rotted away and maggots crawled all over the decomposing bodies. The boys looked at this with disgust yet could not hide their curiosity.

"How did the worms get inside when the holes on the lid are so small?" they asked Alfonso.

"Who cares!" Ligaya interrupted before Alfonso could explain. "All I know is we're not cleaning this up!" she said, speaking for her sisters while looking meaningfully at Paolo.

"But Celia should . . . she was the one who broke my jar," Paolo reasoned.

Alfonso spoke then. "You two boys have to clean it up. You should not have kept them in the jar and left them inside the hut."

The boys grumbled and made sounds to express their disgust as they got some twigs and broad leaves to use in cleaning up the mess. I boiled water and poured it over the soiled area. When they were through, the boys dug a hole in the bush and finally buried their pets.

A MONTH LATER, THE news we had been dreading came. "This is the 'Voice of Freedom.' Corregidor will surrender at noon today. This is our last broadcast." The 13,000 men who defended Corregidor surrendered at last. They were weak and sick and their guns had been silenced.

"The Japanese have a free hand now."

"Not in the provinces, not in the hills and mountains. There they will meet with some fighting. There is talk of resistance, Emma, many of the men have chosen to keep fighting . . . as guerrillas. A few American soldiers and thousands of Filipinos have taken to the hills. They have refused to surrender."

"Of what use will they be, with no leader, no guns, no food?"

"On their own, they will not be able to defeat the Japanese. But they can hurt them in many little ways. Sabotage their operations. Ambush their men. And they can gather important information. The Americans will need all the information they can get to plan their return. And our men have an edge. They know the land. The jungles and the forests will hide them. The villagers will help them. But to the Japanese, the land itself will be an enemy. And, I believe, those in the hills will fare better than those who have become prisoners."

Alfonso's words were prophetic. Those who survived the fall of Bataan soon wished they had perished in the jungles instead. In April, the Bataan Death March began. Later, when it was all over, Alfonso would tell me the horrible facts he had learned.

"Seventy thousand men in all . . . Americans and Filipinos . . . in poor health, hungry and thirsty, sick with malaria, suffering from dysentery, infected sores, all weak and hardly able to walk. They made them march sixty-five long miles in the heat. They marched from

Mariveles all the way to San Fernando. Those who fell were kicked, clubbed, stabbed, shot."

One time, the reports said, three hundred and fifty Filipino soldiers were bayoneted and beheaded in two hours. Prisoners were forced to bury alive their weak or wounded fellow-prisoners, in graves they had just dug themselves. As the soil fell, some prisoners tried to crawl their way out of their graves.

The prisoners were crammed into airless boxcars that took them to Capas, and from there forced to march another eight miles to Camp O'Donnell. They were not fed the first week. In the end, only 54,000 reached the camp alive. Some 7,000 had died on the way. The rest escaped to the surrounding jungles to join the guerrillas.

WE MADE OUR WAY back to Manila soon after Bataan fell. By then we knew the Japanese were here to stay. It was time to return and pick up the pieces of our lives. At first I was reluctant to return. I feared the Japanese. But Alfonso believed that it would be all right. He said, "The Japanese are now in power so the number of atrocities they commit will begin to lessen. When you think about it carefully you will see that war is bad in the beginning and towards the end—the fighting is strongest then and people forget they are human beings and act like vicious animals. The time in between we will be able to live through if we are careful."

Like us, other families began returning to Manila.

Already, some of the houses on our street had been opened by the time we returned. Lagring was there to welcome everyone back. Each of us, in our own way, was thankful she had suffered no harm.

A surprise of another kind was awaiting us. We ourselves had little to do with the Japanese before the war. But there were many Japanese in Manila in those days. Not as many as the Chinese but still, there were several thousands of them in Manila and many more in the other cities. They owned little businesses, some worked in big offices as ordinary employees. The people soon discovered who their Japanese neighbours and workmates really were. They were members of the Japanese military. Many were officers and others were spies. It was only then that we realised how long the Japanese had been planning this invasion. In the mines of Baguio, they had intelligence officers pretending to be mine workers. They gathered information about the rich copper deposits. They were very smart those Japanese and we were very blind.

The Japanese had set up a puppet government. They told us Asia must be for the Asians. But deep down the people despised them. Cursed them. Another hundred years of American rule would have been better than this. Even the Spaniards had not been as cruel. When Alfonso heard people say such things he would reply that we were all foolish to think this way. He said, "We have short memories. The Japanese rule now so it is their actions we remember. But the Spaniards were just as bad.

And the Americans, too. You all look surprised, but really they are all the same. Why should one country rule over another? The Spaniards, the Americans and the Japanese have no business here. This is not a Filipino war. Did you ever think about that? What has this war to do with us?"

But worse than the Japanese, Alfonso said, were people who turned traitor to their own kind. He meant the collaborators. It was a new word to us, but even the children learned that word. Many accused Laurel of being a collaborator when he became president of the Japanese puppet government. But as I told Alfonso then, "Do not judge him harshly. No one has ever pointed a gun at you, so you do not know yet what you would do to stay alive or save your family. Not everyone can be a hero."

There were heroes though. Like Jose Abad Santos who was Chief Justice under President Quezon. He chose to stay behind in Corregidor when Quezon escaped to the south then on to Australia. He was caught in May. The Japanese ordered him to collaborate and join their puppet government. He refused. A Japanese firing squad was called in and they executed him. Abad Santos was a hero to the many people who chose to resist rather than join the enemy. And we needed heroes in those days.

Ordinary people defied the Japanese in their own way. In little acts that allowed them to show their spirit. What they did was often lost to the Japanese who did not understand they were being insulted or made fun of, but it gave the people some sense of satisfaction, no matter how small. Like the time when a parade was called after the Japanese took over and the puppet government was established. During the parade, attended by all the political collaborators who stood in line with the Japanese high command, a Filipino band came marching in. On approaching the officials, they played a tune recognised by the Filipino crowd but not by the Japanese. It was the *Stars and Stripes* that they played. There was much secret laughter amongst the ordinary folk gathered there to watch the marchers go by. The Japanese stood at attention throughout. To the Filipinos it was a battle hymn filled with hope.

After establishing themselves in Manila, the Japanese began their propaganda movement. They spoke of Asia being for the Asians. That we had to be proud Asians. They did not like how much the Americans influenced us. Filipino writers who wrote in English began to write in Tagalog. They had little choice. There were only two official languages—Japanese, which was being taught in the schools, and Tagalog. Local entertainment was very popular. The Japanese produced many propaganda movies using popular Filipino stars.

"I do not trust them. Anyone who can commit the kind of cruelties they have cannot be trusted, there is a flaw in their character . . . the Japanese, they are like animals," Alfonso told me angrily one time. But thoughts like this were never said out in the open. Everyone had grown careful. Outwardly, we did as we were told in order to stay out of trouble. We learned to bow to the Japanese, in the way they wanted us to.

If you asked me to name the things I remember most about the war, bowing would be one of them. The Japanese insisted you bow to them. It was an important act of respect. Do you know that if you were on a bus travelling somewhere, every time the bus approached a sentry point all the passengers had to get off the bus, line up in front of the sentry and bow, then reboard the bus and travel on until the next checkpoint, then do the same thing all over again? Why, between Muntinglupa and Manila there were maybe five to six sentry points. It was enough to discourage people from moving around.

Alfonso and I spent a long time teaching the children how to bow. "You bow this low, at least fifteen degrees, watch me . . . Then count to five, count slowly, before lifting your head, and never, never look a Japanese soldier in the eye. They will see that as a challenge. And do not show disgust or disrespect. It is not a time for pride. When this is over and we have survived, then you can be proud," we told the boys. Paolo and Miguel gave us much to worry about as they took delight in making fun of the Japanese, imitating their bow-legged walk and their halting language, shouting "Hai!"

Our life became harder with time. Whereas we lived in comfort before, we now lived carefully. One of the first things we did on our return to Manila was to dig up the little back garden. Ligaya, Celia and I pulled out the flowering shrubs—the rosals and champacas, the sun tans, the gumamela, they all went. Laura, who was very young then, did not understand why we were doing this. She was gathering the flowers that lay scattered on the ground, saying, "Bad Mama! Pull flowers . . . spank you!" From now on there would be little colour in our life. It was only then, to be honest, that we stopped to appreciate the plants growing in our backyard. Before the Occupation, the boys used the place to play in and I went there only to hang out the washing. But as we kneeled on the ground and turned the soil over and began planting vegetables, we suddenly cherished those plants and their flowers. It had taken a cruel war to make us stop and look at the little things in our life. I remember Ligaya saying then, "When this is all over, I will have a garden filled with flowers. I will always be surrounded by flowers."

The only thing that we left alone was the old guava tree. It had been here when we moved in and it would become a source of medicine for us. As the war progressed, our diet became more and more limited, so we did not have the vitamins our body needed. It was common to sprout boils. Miguel and Paolo were especially prone to them. Maybe because boys play in all sorts of places and come home with all kinds of germs. But I remember them always with boils on their bodies. The guava leaves were the only medicine I could give them. I would let the leaves simmer in water while Alfonso put the point of a pin in fire to make sure it was clean. Then he would pierce the boil while the boys yelled out in pain. I would wash the boil with the water. The powder from guava leaves helped hasten the healing. But the powder stung badly. With tears brimming in their eyes the boys would promise to keep clean and not play in dirty places. But they never kept their word.

The most important thing that happened on our return was the closing of Alfonso's business.

"There is no way the Japanese will let me continue. These spare parts can be used to build short-wave radio equipment that can be used against them, so they will take all of this away."

The business he had slowly built over the years was gone. He took what he could home. We cleared out the small back room and stored radio parts and electrical supplies there, hoping one day they would provide him with the means to earn a living again. But that was not to be.

COLLABORATORS. INFORMERS. THERE WERE many of them in those years. No one knew any more who their friends were. No one knew who to trust. So I do not know who it was that informed on Alfonso, who it was that betrayed him.

What he did, you see, was a crime. Hiding those things in the back room. Dangerous equipment. They could have executed him for it. Why they did not I can only guess.

This is what happened.

We were having lunch when the Japanese came. There was a loud knock on the door and I got up to open it. A Japanese officer stood there. Short and thin and sickly looking in spite of his sun-darkened skin. He ordered me to step aside as he and his men marched into the house. By then, Alfonso knew something was wrong for there was no mistaking that the voices coming from the front door belonged to the Japanese.

The children who were still sitting around the dining table stared in silence. I did not dare look at Alfonso. The officer walked past the dining room and went straight to the back room. He knew exactly where to go. He pointed to the lock, indicating to Alfonso that he wanted it opened.

They took everything away. And just when I thought, all of us thought, they would make Alfonso go with them, the officer ordered his men to leave. At the door, he did something strange. He tilted his head, as if to take his leave politely.

Maybe it was because God heard our prayers; maybe it was because I was pregnant then with Mia and seeing me as I opened the door, and seeing the children when he entered the house—so many and so young—he could not make himself take husband and father away. Anyone could see we lived on so little, the food on the table so meagre, that without a man in the house we would suffer.

He returned again, the Japanese officer, after that day. He showed up late one morning, close to midday. I opened the door and found him standing there with a small parcel in his hand. I quickly bowed. And he, too, bowed his head slightly in greeting. Then he held out the parcel. I stared at it, not understanding, so he pushed it into my hands. I asked him to come inside. Alfonso was out but the children were home. Paolo and Miguel, who were playing on the floor, stared at him. He smiled at them and pointed to the parcel in my hands then at the boys. I opened it. He had brought us powdered eggs. I showed the boys. "Say thank you. Bow to him and say thank you."

I set a place for him but he waved his hand, signalling he wouldn't eat. I think he knew how little we had and how far I had to make it go. The children loved the powdered eggs. He smiled and nodded as they wolfed it down, leaving their plates so clean, they looked as if they'd been washed.

After the meal, he sat and played with the boys. But both sides said little. Language was a problem. We spoke with our hands. The boys pointing at their toys, showing him how they played. The girls were nervous and shy and watched him from a polite distance.

When he took his leave after playing with the boys, they told him, with their hands, to come again. Later, when Alfonso came home, I told him of the visit and the gift of powdered eggs. Alfonso was at first fearful but later, after getting to know the man better, he realised he was missing his family and home. Still Alfonso told us it would be wiser to keep our distance. He never got rid of his dislike for the Japanese.

The Japanese officer came several times during those three years. The boys looked forward to his visits. Once, he sat and drew for them. And another time he showed the girls how to fold paper and turn it into flowers, birds, boats and frogs.

Every now and then, I would see on his face a look of longing . . . as if he was somewhere else, far away, home again. I think the children reminded him of his own. I do not know what happened to him after the war. We lost touch. I do not know if he survived it. But I like to think he made it home, that he returned to his family, safe and secure, growing old, like me, in peace.

EVERY ACT OF KINDNESS in those times had its shadow. An act of cruelty. It was how things were with the Japanese. Suddenly, except for the collaborators, most people found themselves equal: we were all treated badly. The wealthy Spanish businessmen found themselves controlled by the Japanese. They had to continue with their business but had little means to pay their employees. Some Spaniards who had offices in Manila paid their employees with the produce of their haciendas in the provinces. In some ways this was better because food was hard to come by. Many big houses were taken over by the Japanese. They lived in them or turned them into their headquarters.

The Chinese suffered in a different way. Because of the Japanese war in China, many of the local Chinese had to face the Kempeitei. Those who were suspected of supporting the government in the mainland—and it did not matter if they were pro-Kuomintang or pro-Mao—were arrested and executed. In order to survive, many wealthy Chinese became collaborators. They even set up a chamber of commerce that supported Japanese policies.

Like many others, Alfonso was to have a taste of Japanese cruelty. The second time the Japanese came, they took him away. They took him in front of the children. I feared he would be taken to Fort Santiago in Intramuros. If that had happened, he would have been tortured and killed. Hundreds of innocent men and women had vanished behind those prison walls. Since the Spaniards built it, the fort has been a sad place. The Japanese made it evil.

But Alfonso was not taken to the fort. Instead they made him join a line-up. He was taken for identification. There was still a chance that he would not be executed. To sow fear, the Japanese often picked people out and threatened them with death if they did not inform on their neighbours, their friends, their own blood. The Japanese wanted to know who was against them, who supported the guerrillas, who had relatives fighting in the hills, who did anything suspicious. Then they rounded up people— civilians, innocent men. They lined them up and brought in the informer who pointed out the guilty. Most of the time the informers did not really possess any information, but it was safer to pretend to know something. So they pointed at someone, anyone, to save their own lives.

Alfonso was one of the men that stood in a line that day. When they took him away Ligaya and I began frantically looking for help. But we never knew where the Japanese officer who befriended us was stationed. We didn't know where to find him. So Ligaya and I had only each other and our prayers. We stood and watched, holding our breath as they brought the men in. Pale with fear, Alfonso walked into the crowded square. The man behind him stumbled. A Japanese soldier barked at him. And as the man struggled to his feet, the soldier hit him on the side with the butt of a rifle. He was lucky. It could have been the point of a bayonet.

Then they brought the informer in. I strained my eyes to identify him but he had a bag over his head to hide his face and all I could go by were his clothes and tattered slippers. I could not tell whether he was a friend, a neighbour, someone we knew.

He stood there while we all waited. He pointed his finger and moved it along the line of men standing in front of him. Meanwhile Alfonso stood with eyes staring ahead of him, dazed, seeing nothing. I could not tell whether he had gone past Alfonso or was still on him when he finally pointed. Ligaya's hand, which clasped mine, had dug deep into my palm with her nails. But I did not feel the pain until later.

A soldier came forward and with his rifle hit the man beside Alfonso on the shoulder. Pushing him forward, away from the line. He screamed, and pleaded and begged, crying over and over, "I am innocent! This is a mistake." They executed him on the spot. Do you know how a man dies when he is beheaded? I will tell you. This is what they did to him. They tied his hands behind his back and forced him to kneel. By then he was no longer struggling. I think he just wanted it to be over. The soldier took out his sword and raised it, then swooped down. The head rolled off the man's neck and the blood, how the blood spurted from the vein. You could see the exposed vein, like a tube out of which blood kept spurting. The head rolled to a stop a few feet away from the body and its eyes stared out at the crowd. The body, lying in the pool of blood, twitched for another minute, then stopped. It reminded me of the chickens I used to kill in the back of the house. You had to hang onto the body because sometimes there was still a lot of life in it and it got away from you, this headless chicken spurting blood as it flew about.

Ligaya and I rushed to Alfonso. We hugged him, held his hands, not believing he was free. The poor soul who stood next to him had died but I did not care. Alfonso had escaped.

I lit a candle when we got home.

After that, we stayed indoors most of the time. It was safer. Besides, Mia was born soon after. Alfonso and I tried our best to give the children what they needed, but it was hard with him having lost his business. Few people did well during the Occupation, the collaborators mainly.

Alfonso took to the road to try to make a living. Like

many people he learned to engage in buying and selling and bartering. This was hard work and involved much travelling. I insisted he keep within Manila, only making trips to the nearby towns of Laguna when it was necessary. He would buy whatever he could get his hands on and trade with this. He would buy used clothing and barter that for mosquito nets then exchange those for blankets. On a lucky day he dealt in canned food or candies or even cigarettes. One of the most prized commodities was soap. It was precious and as good as real money, if not better, so when he could end the day with bars of soap, it was a good day.

It was hard work because he had to carry a lot of the things himself, walking most of the time. The heat was merciless, and without real shoes, only *bakyas*, walking was made even more difficult. Have you ever tried walking for long in those wooden clogs? They torture your feet.

When I knew he was going far I would stand by the window at the end of the day, returning often to see if he was walking down our street on his way home. I would not feel at ease until he returned. In those times many people never had the chance to say goodbye to one another. You just never knew when it was going to be the last time you saw someone. They walked out of the door and did not return. I know many people who tell me things like, "That morning my father got on the bus was the last I ever saw of him. I don't know what happened to him or how he died. All I know is that he never returned."

So I would wait by the window for Alfonso's return. Because of how afraid I always was when he went on these trips, he would only go when our pantry was close to empty. I usually insisted he stay home and the children stay home. God was merciful, for though we had to tighten our belts, we never went hungry. But the boys, when they think back to that time, say, "We were never ever full though."

There was a shortage of rice. When the war began, the Philippines was used as a military outpost and a source of raw materials. But as the war dragged on, food became scarce and the Japanese began to use the country as a source of food. The Japanese confiscated most of the rice harvest to feed its army and civilians. So rice became a precious commodity that could only be bought on the black market. The price of rice rose from one hundred pesos for a *cavan* to 7,500 pesos. By the end of 1944, a *cavan* of rice cost 12,000. Maize became a cheaper substitute but even that was hard to come by.

We had a neighbour who owned a cock. A fighting cock which he would groom carefully every day. He no longer went to cockfights, you understand; cockfighting was not something poor people went to and during the war we were all poor. Every *centavo,* every *peso* was saved for food. So we could not understand why he refused to give up his cock.

"It is his pet. He would rather see us starve than kill his cock to feed his family!" his wife Lupita complained to all of us in the neighbourhood.

"He sleeps with it downstairs!" she said. "He is afraid that if he leaves it outside someone will come and steal it then eat it. He sleeps downstairs. I told him I will not have it in my bedroom. So now he sleeps on his own in the *sala* with a short rope tied to the cock's leg on one end and the other end tied to his wrist. If I did not think it would kill him or he kill me, I would have cooked it long ago. The children have not had meat for such a long time. He says the meat is tough. But I don't care."

That cock survived the war. How it escaped the Japanese I do not know for they loved chicken. They would kill it and dip it in vinegar and eat it raw. It makes me sick just thinking about it. Like barbarians they were sometimes.

If food was hard to get hold of, medicine was impossible. One did not have to die from battle wounds. Without medicine, the simplest illness became grave enough to kill.

With the price of things on the black market costing thousands and thousands, there were not enough pesos to go around. The Japanese had to print their own money. We called it "Mickey Mouse Money." To buy a banana, you paid with a satchelful of it. It was worthless after the war.

One time when we had little rice and corn left, I was forced to do something I had hoped I would never have to. I sold my jewellery. I did not have much you must understand, for my parents were not wealthy and Mama did not have much to give me when I married. All I had was a pair of pearl earrings which had been handed down from my grandmother, and a ring with tiny diamonds set in white gold. The only other piece was a locket on a gold chain, the heart-shaped locket Alfonso gave me when he was courting me. Yes . . . yes, it was the piece I gave to you when Marla was born. I had taken it with me to sell but could not bear to part with it. In the end, it was the only thing of value or meaning that I could give to you. Giving it to you was my way then of letting you have something from your father Alfonso. You still have it? You have kept it? I am happy for at least it was worth going hungry for. It would have bought some food in those days.

I left early that morning and walked to Quiapo where I knew I would find some pawn shops. I told Alfonso I was going to visit Thelma. During the war, we saw each other every now and then. Thelma tried to help me when she could but I did not like to ask. So I pawned my jewellery knowing I could never get it back. I had hoped to keep it to pass on to Ligaya and the girls for it had come from my mama and my grandmother.

I did not tell Alfonso what I had done. I did not get much for my jewellery, only two sacks of corn. When Alfonso asked where they had come from, I lied to him saying Thelma had given them to us. He did not like that because he felt Thelma and Raoul had enough problems of their own. The Japanese had moved into Raoul's parents' home and Raoul, refusing to work for the Japanese army, had shut down his construction business during the Occupation. But Alfonso would have liked it less had he known I had parted with my jewellery so I kept the truth from him.

The war was a time of lack except when it came to stories of cruelty. There were plenty of those. Of women being raped, their breasts criss-crossed with bayonet points; of men being tortured, their hands tied behind their backs as they were stabbed over and over again. Often, acts of cruelty were committed for the shallowest reasons, like old people and children being slapped and made to grovel on the ground for not bowing before a soldier in the proper way.

It was wiser to keep out of people's way. "Stay home," we told the girls. "Keep out of trouble," we warned the boys. "And always bow, remember to bow with respect when you see someone in uniform." This was how we lived and behaved during that time. We watched what we said and what we did and we waited.

THREE YEARS LATER, THINGS began to turn bad for the Japanese. Guerrilla resistance became stronger. And there was talk—secret talk—that somehow the Americans had been arming them, that guns and ammunition had found their way across the seas, that American and Filipino agents had returned to the islands by submarine and were now working with the guerrillas. We knew the rumours were true because the cruelties the Japanese committed increased—when something went wrong with their army, they took it out on the people.

The whispers grew louder as people became bolder. Then whispers became open talk. The Japanese could not hide the movement of their troops. They were moving them out of Manila and transporting them south. At first, our eyes and our minds were focused on Mindanao. But news came and suddenly Leyte in the Visayas became the heart of our talk. There, they began to say, he would return. MacArthur was coming to Leyte.

One day a neighbour called me aside. "I have something to show you but you must not ask questions for I do not know how the person who gave it to me came by this." From inside her bag, she pulled out a crumpled cigarette pack. On it was a message. "I shall return," it said, and at the bottom was a signature I could not make out. But the name of the person to whom the signature belonged appeared just below this. It read, "General Douglas MacArthur." I gave it back to her without saying a word, but I wanted to cry then. Later, a friend would whisper to Alfonso that he had seen a matchbook with the same message.

Then the news came. The Americans had sailed into Leyte Gulf. In the safety of our home, we said a silent prayer and celebrated. We followed their progress, keeping our ears open. But the fighting was slow. For not only did they have to retake towns and hills held by the enemy, they had to fight the weather as well. It rained and rained in the Visayas where the fighting was happening.

Where roads used to be now flowed rivers of mud. Soldiers on foot and even powerful tanks were helpless in the pouring rain. The delay cost thousands of lives. And the people had to wait longer for liberation. Then, finally, they took Ormoc and Carigara on the west coast. And one day in October of 1944, the miracle we had prayed so long for happened at last.

I had just picked some string beans from my little vegetable patch in the back of the house. The beans, eggplant, tomatoes, and onions we planted had gone a long way to feeding us. Though the backyard was small, and the soil not good, we were lucky to have it at all. The vegetables that grew there allowed the children to have some variety in their food. They were tired of eating the same thing every day. Rice with corn. Rice with sweet potatoes. Rice with sardines. I had just carried a tray of beans to the kitchen when Paolo rushed in. "He has landed. He has come back!" he shouted to me, jumping about excitedly as he said the words.

I did not know what Paolo was talking about until Alfonso rushed in. "Emma, Emma, it has happened! MacArthur has returned. He is now in Leyte!"

On the east coast of Leyte, MacArthur had stepped off a boat and waded through the water until he stood on Philippine soil again. There, he said, "People of the Philippines, I have returned."

"Rally to me," he called to us.

True to his word, he had come back to free us, bringing with him over five hundred warships and over

200,000 men. In Tacloban, the American flag was raised. MacArthur set up his headquarters there and directed the fight to regain Leyte. All over the country, 250,000 guerrillas, on hearing his rallying call, emerged from hiding and began to harass the enemy from all sides. We knew then that it was just a matter of time before the Japanese would be defeated.

We followed the fighting huddled around the radio. "The Philippine Hour Broadcast" told us of the American and Allied Forces' successful encounters against the Japanese army. And when it was not safe to listen to the radio, news reached us through secretly distributed pamphlets and through word of mouth. So we knew when MacArthur took Lingayan Gulf. And we secretly celebrated the American attack on Mindoro where they began to build airstrips. Their victories came one after another. It was not too long before Clark Field and Calumpit fell. The Americans were moving closer and closer to Manila, and the Japanese began to panic. We knew it would soon be time to leave the city once more.

We returned to Taytay. It was, like that first journey, a long and arduous one. But this time, we travelled with hope. News of the Americans approaching had spread. Liberation was near.

"When we next return," Alfonso told the children, "we will be a free people once more."

In Taytay the people fleeing the city set up numerous evacuation camps which quickly filled with thousands of families. At the evacuation camp where we lived, the men would gather at night around a short-wave radio and listen to the "Voice of Freedom." We fed on messages promising liberty. I prayed it would come before our food ran out. The rice we had brought with us was disappearing before my eyes. To make it last longer, I started mixing rice with sweet potatoes. And once, trying to save more, I made a rice gruel. More water, less rice. It was a mistake. The gruel was less filling so everyone had at least three bowls each.

Out there in the hills where we waited, our lives were not always filled with fear. The open air, the trees and the hills had their own kind of beauty. Some nights when there was a break in the fighting, we could hear the crickets chirp and the frogs in the fields croak. After the children had fallen asleep, Alfonso and I would sit outside on a tree stump, saying little, just looking up at the sky—or what we could see of it, for the trees were so dense even the moon often stayed hidden. There was a spot we liked going to where we could gaze up at a piece of sky framed by the leaves of trees.

One clear night, Alfonso stood just under this spot and stretched his arms upward. "Look," he told me, "you can almost reach out and pick a star."

The stars seemed closer out in the open. Like pieces of diamonds that had fallen from a pouch, scattered against a black silk cloth, waiting to be picked. On a night like this, it was hard to believe a war was going on.

Then the battle to reclaim Manila began. The people who arrived after us said the Japanese were blowing up all their military installations, and bridges leading to the city were being destroyed to slow the American advance. There was no water supply. No electricity. The Americans, too, they said, had started strafing Manila. At first, MacArthur had prohibited air attacks because many civilians would die. Manila, at that time, had 700,000 people living in it. But the Japanese were proving hard to defeat. The fighting had gone on for longer than the Americans expected. In the end, the General ordered the bombings to begin. By the end of the war, there would be 100,000 dead civilians in Manila.

Sometimes the fighting happened in the skies above us. The children, especially the boys, could not be kept in our hut. They would join the men, going a fair distance, crouching under thick shrubs, to watch the dogfights light up the night sky. It was scary yet exciting. An adventure to them. The skies would fill with the sounds of gunfire, and quick bursts of light as Japanese and American planes fired at each other overhead. When a plane exploded, it was like fireworks on New Year's Eve.

Once the Americans dropped a bomb on an evacuation camp, thinking it was a Japanese hideaway. It was the one next to us. Only a rice field separated the two camps. The explosion rang so loud, my ears felt as though they would burst. Then trees and dry shrubs caught fire and the men from our side ran across to help put out the flames before they burned through the hillside. When the fire died down, we brought the wounded over to our camp. Among them was a young girl, around seventeen. Her thigh was almost completely blown off. It was dangling, with just a few inches of flesh connecting it to the rest of her body. The skin was all curled up around the cut area, like someone had folded it up the way you push up the sleeve of a shirt.

There was no doctor and no medicine and we had nothing to give her to numb the pain. We boiled water and cleaned a sharp knife. One of the men cut off the connecting piece of flesh. She screamed and screamed as I held her down. We wrapped her thigh with a coarse sackcloth, the ones we used to keep rice in, I do not even know if it was clean. When it was over, I ran outside and vomited. Someone dug a hole in the bush and buried her leg. Two days later, we buried the girl.

BEFORE THE WAR ENDED, I was to see the guerrillas take their revenge on an informer. The Japanese had many informers who led them to the hiding places of guerrilla commanders or revealed the identity of their sympathisers. These men and women were then tortured and beheaded. By torture I mean their "water cure." It is hard to understand how someone can enjoy watching another person suffer, but there were many Japanese soldiers who enjoyed torturing people. They would make a prisoner lie down and then force water into his mouth using a water hose which ran for ten minutes or more. He would be bloated with water in no time and he would feel his stomach swell, then they would put a plank of wood on his stomach and ride it like a seesaw. The other thing they sometimes did was to drop a heavy object on his stomach. The victim would not even be able to scream from the pain because when this pressure was applied to his stomach, water and blood rushed out of his mouth. The victim doesn't die but the pain and weakness he suffers for many days after may leave him wishing for death.

The guerrillas would hit back. Not at the Japanese but at the Filipino informers. They soon learned that if you killed one Japanese, they would take the life of a dozen innocent people. So it was the informers they hunted down. I saw one executed in an open field.

The men dragged him into the camp just before noon one day. I was with the womenfolk sitting on the steps of a nipa hut where we often gathered. Celia was with me. I was braiding her hair which I had just finished combing in search of lice. We had long run out of soap and keeping clean was impossible. We washed in streams when we could. And when we could find no water or had none to spare for bathing, we simply scratched ourselves to sleep. Lice were a problem: in the tropical heat the eggs hatched quickly. We would take turns picking the lice out of each other's hair. As I said, I had just done Celia's hair and was braiding it while one of the women talked on, when suddenly, three of the men in our camp burst from the thick bushes with a man in tow. You must understand the men in the camp were guerrilla sympathisers and there were at least half a dozen who were themselves guerrillas.

The man they had captured was gagged, blindfolded and had his hands tied behind his back. He made no attempt to plead for mercy. He did not deny their accusations. His captors said he had betrayed three guerrilla sympathisers and his betrayal had resulted in the execution of all three along with their families. They had followed him around and saw him admitted into the Japanese headquarters on several occasions. Now they would punish him.

They waited for dusk. When the sun finally went down behind the mountains they took him out into the field where they were joined by two more men who came with four *carabaos*. We followed them. Just the adults—the children were too young to witness the next scene. We stood in the shadows of the trees and shrubs, the men pushed the informer down to the ground and they proceeded to tie his limbs to the animals. One limb to each beast of burden. Then they each took a bamboo stick and hit the animals on the back to make them move. The *carabaos* at first moved at the same pace towards the same direction dragging the man with them. But only for a while. Soon, two of them moved sideways and we heard, even from a distance, the snapping sounds of bones that had been pulled apart. The *carabaos* tore every limb from his body. But from the man himself, not a cry was heard. They had kept him gagged. When it was all over and the field was streaked with blood, they untied his parts from the animals. He was not buried. They hung the parts from several trees. A warning to other traitors of the fate that awaited them. For many weeks after I saw that man quartered by *carabaos*, I would suddenly hear that awful snapping sound in my mind. And do you know something? I still remember it to this day! It's a short, sharp sound.

Soon after this Manila went up in flames. At night the skies were an angry red and orange. The fiery glow was visible for as far as fifty miles. And in the day, a dark film covered the sky as black palls of smoke travelled up from the flaming city below. The people who had remained in Manila had been asked by the Americans to move as they cleared the southern half of the city. The whole northern port area was ablaze for many days.

"They demolished many buildings, to create fire-breaks," explained one late-comer to the camp. This was not supposed to have happened, you must understand; it was not meant to be. The Japanese under Yamashita had intended to do as the Americans did at the start of the war. They were going to make Manila an "open city." That is why many people remained in their homes as the Japanese retreated to the mountains and General Yamashita headed for Baguio. But before they could all leave, MacArthur sent his men to Manila. They arrived too early. In Manila, there were still Japanese sailors and marines under Admiral Iwabachi. Thousands of them could not leave for there were no ships. So the two sides met and turned the city into a battlefield.

"The Japanese have retreated. They are holed up in Intramuros," said another man who had just come from the city. "All day long, we would hear the sound of rifle fire and machine guns."

The Americans closed in on Intramuros. The Japanese fought on, refusing to surrender. The people who thought the city would be spared found themselves caught between the fighting soldiers. It was a slow process that caused much destruction. The Japanese torched many homes. Sometimes whole blocks of residences went up in smoke. The Japanese were not afraid to die but when they did die they would take many innocent lives with them. The survivors would remember one thing—how they kept running here then running there, for wherever they ran they would meet more soldiers.

Desperate people lose the thing that makes them human beings. They lose their heart. Anger and hate fill them so that they act like animals. That is the only explanation I can think of for what happened at the De La Salle College. The Japanese herded forty-one people, many of them priests, into a room and lined them against a wall. One soldier to each prisoner. Then they plunged their bayonets into the neck or chest of their prisoners. The lucky ones died soon after, but many still lived. They lay on the floor slowly bleeding away, taking several days to die. Meanwhile, they had to pretend to be dead. The Japanese checked on them. They were devious. They put a glass of water next to each body. Then they left. They would return every day to check whether the water had been touched. If it had, the wounded would soon be lifeless. Those who had survived had to drink from the glass of those who had died, then crawl back to their spot. Blood which had slowly seeped out of the survivors' wounds had caked on the floor so that their original positions were outlined by the dried blood. This allowed them to return to their spots undetected. One man, however, was caught before he could crawl back to his place. The Japanese soldier who found him quickly ended his life with the point of a bayonet. The ordeal of the remaining survivors would not end until a week after the day of the massacre when members of the liberation forces arrived. Of the forty-one in the group, only a dozen or so would live to tell their tale.

The blood of the victims seeped deep into the floors and the walls where it had splattered. If you go to De La Salle today you will see the bloodstains through the paint. The walls have been painted over many times in the last forty years but the stains still show through. It is as if the people who died refuse to be forgotten. In that group there were sixteen priests. Do you still wonder why we are not allowed to forget?

The battle to retake Manila took longer than we expected. The Japanese were vicious fighters and the liberation forces met with very strong resistance from them. I despaired that the war would ever end. Like everyone else I wanted to return home to Manila. Lying next to Alfonso one night I asked, "How much longer can they fight?"

"Longer than any army in the world, I think," Alfonso answered. "You must remember, these people have war in their blood. They will die fighting. To them, it is the honourable way. To surrender means to lose face. Their kamikaze pilots should give you an idea as to what they are willing to do to win a war."

You know the expression, *"Masamang damo, mahirap mamatay?"* It's true of the Japanese. They were like bad grass, stubborn weeds that were hard to kill.

But all things end. Even when you think they never will. In March, the Americans won Manila back and the Japanese surrendered at last. So we returned to Manila two weeks later when things had calmed down.

Three of the houses on one end of our street had burnt down. Their black remains lay on the ground. The only parts left standing were the soot-covered stone steps that led up to nowhere. Against a leaning beam, I saw what looked like a charred arm. There was no body in sight. The fire had been caused by the retreating Japanese soldiers. All over the city, fighting had broken out and spread rapidly, and thousands of civilians were killed in the cross-fire. Our street had not been spared. But miraculously the fire had stopped right before Lagring's house, as if an invisible wall had prevented the flames from spreading. After the fire had broken out, when screaming women and children ran for their lives, Lagring had locked herself inside her altar room. When the fire had died down, the people returned to see if anything was left of their homes. Some of them then forced their way into Lagring's house. They found her on her knees praying. She had been praying since the fighting began. Though her eyes were open, she did not see them. Neither did she hear them call her name. They lifted her and laid her down on the bed. She woke three days later.

Looking around me, I learned that there is no going back. Nothing is ever the same again. We all have to move on. I learned this when we saw what had been done to Manila. We all cried. Alfonso was pale and tears slowly rolled down his face. All around us was rubble.

Intramuros, which had stood for over three hundred years since the time of the Spaniards, was gone. The ancient walls barely stood. Where bombs had not exploded, tanks had breached its thick walls. Three years of Japanese rule did not produce a tenth of the destruction the Americans made in their fight to retake Manila.

"Next to Dresden, this is the worst damaged city of the war," Alfonso said to the children one time.

What is the price of freedom? We were free again, but out city had died. For many of my generation, Manila ceased to exist. Our homes still stood but all the familiar places we loved were no longer there. The city you see today is not the Manila I knew. It is hard to be the one left behind.

LIFE IS CRUEL AT times and offers no explanation for its cruelty. Alfonso was given his life twice when he should have lost it. And it was taken away from him when he should have lived.

I could not see a reason back then as to why he should

survive the war only to die in peacetime. I have stopped asking for a reason. It is the way life is. Like a wheel that turns, sometimes it misses you, sometimes it crushes you. At times life gives and at times it takes away. And each day you wake up and breathe and live is but another day's reprieve from death.

We did not stay long in Manila. Only long enough to pack all our things. Alfonso decided to move the family to Olongapo.

"I want to begin again."

"Why there?"

"I have friends there. It is where I first lived when my father and I came from China. There I will know how to begin again."

Alfonso wanted to start a new business but not in Manila. He no longer had the heart to build a business here. Besides, we no longer had the money to buy the equipment he would need, the Japanese had seen to that.

"In Olongapo, Lucio and I can start an ice plant. There is no ice plant there. And I can get it started without a lot of capital."

So we moved to Olongapo. The older girls, specially Ligaya, were unhappy. The boys did not mind—it was a new place to discover. Mia does not even remember the move.

In a way, I was glad to leave Manila. For everywhere I looked, I saw only signs of destruction. Shanties appeared where streets used to be. People squatted where they could. The air smelled for there was no working drainage. Even water itself was scarce. And there was the stench of death. In the evenings, the dark hid the ugliness, but daylight forced us to live in a nightmare.

Looking with sad eyes at the rutted streets and damaged buildings we passed as we left Manila, Alfonso said, "The dead are lucky. They do not have to live with memories of what has been."

ONCE IN OLONGAPO, ALFONSO immediately worked on his plans.

"Out in the swamps, you do not know what you could catch," I kept warning him. He would not stop. Not until he came down with malaria. But even that did not kill him. It is strange that it was his heart that finally failed him. Heart attack. Does our heart attack us? A good heart? Alfonso was a man with a good heart. It is strange that his good heart killed him.

We had not been in Olongapo long when he died, just over six months. The ice plant had not even opened. In the end, Lucio, Alfonso's partner, lost interest in the whole thing and sold it.

When Alfonso died he left me with very little money. I did not know how I could provide for six children and a child yet unborn. Alfonso also left me homeless. We did not own the roof over our heads. If we owned a house, my choices would have been different.

I was very frightened then. There was only enough for a few months' rent. I would not have managed had

Thelma not been there. Which is why, you must understand, I could not say no to her after all that she had done
for me.

Thelma was five years older than me. She was the eldest, and I, the third of four children. As she grew older,
Thelma managed us, the younger ones, while Mama
took care of the house. Mama did not like wielding the
rod, preferring to use her words to discipline us, so we
pushed her, which we couldn't do to Thelma. She was
more like our papa. One sharp look from her did more
to silence us than a hundred warnings from Mama. We
feared her, but we also trusted her. She was fair. When
we fought, she decided who was right and who was
wrong, who could have this and who could have that,
and who had to give up something, and whose turn it
was to play or do the chores.

It was to her that I turned for help when Alfonso died.
I did not ask. She was just there. After the funeral, Raoul
returned to Manila. Thelma stayed with me a few days
longer.

Between her and Ligaya they kept things going. Ligaya
had returned from Manila by then but she was too
young—only fifteen—to run the house. Besides, what
happened between her and her papa would have made
his death very painful for her. To this day, we have never
discussed it, but maybe now she will talk about it to you.

The night after the funeral, Thelma slept with me in
the room Alfonso and I shared. But even my brave sister
would not sleep on his side of the bed. She slept on a cot.

I lay in bed but could not sleep for crying. Silently, I let the tears fall down my eyes and drank them when they touched my lips. I was like the woman in the story, the one my grandmother who was full of stories told me when I was a little girl.

She said once there was a man who stood on an old wooden bridge. On one side was his wife, and on the other side an old man.

"Come," said the old man, "come with me."

As the man took a step forward, his wife cried out, "Don't go." The man hesitated.

"It is time to go," the old man said to him, "this cannot wait."

The man understood and turned to follow him. His wife began to cry, burying her face in her hands. The old man turned and spoke these words to her: "Do not shed tears, woman, for the child will know sorrow."

The woman, you see, was with child. When she heard the old man's words she held back her tears. She watched her husband walk across the bridge in silence. But that night as she lay in bed and felt the empty space where he used to sleep, the tears she had held back broke through the gates of her eyes. First one tear, followed by another, until they rushed down her face. She touched them with her tongue and drank them in.

The tears formed a river, and she could no longer stop its flow, so it was that it ran down her womb as a river flows into an ocean. Her unborn child woke, stung by the change in the water. So before the child was born, it knew of its mother's sorrow.

So you see how it is, Caridad, how you are the child of my sorrow, my poor daughter born with my tears.

YOU ARRIVED BEFORE YOUR time. The first rush of pain woke me in the middle of the night. I remember thinking, "It cannot be . . . it is too soon." So I did not wake Ligaya who was sleeping with me. Thelma made sure one of the children would stay with me after she had gone. The younger ones were afraid to. Ligaya said she would.

When the pain came once more, I realised you were going to be born almost a month early. I feared for you. Women have always been told babies born in their eighth month cannot survive. I could not deny the pain any longer. How I wished Thelma was there.

So I stood up and made my way to Ligaya's cot. She must have sensed my approach for she opened her eyes before I even spoke. "It's time?" she asked. All I could do was nod. Ligaya jumped up and dressed as I returned to my bed.

"Boil water!" I heard her shout to one of the girls. Laura came to stay with me as the boys hovered outside the door. The front door slammed shut. I knew Ligaya was racing out into the night to fetch the *komadrona*, the midwife who lived nearby.

The waters broke soon after.

You were in such a hurry. By the time they arrived, your head was already out.

"This one's in a rush," the komadrona said. I bore down once more and the rest of you slipped out. Ligaya cut the cord and tied it. She was the one who said, "It's a girl, Mama."

I wept. Oh, how frightened I was. All I could think of was how impossible everything was, that I would not manage to feed another mouth, and I kept asking Alfonso how he could have left me like this.

The komadrona wrapped you in a blanket and handed you to me. I held your feet, then your hands, and counted. I did this with all my children. I made sure all your toes and your fingers were there. By this time, the other children had come inside to have a look at the new baby.

"What are you going to call her, Mama?" someone asked.

I thought for a while then said, "Caridad . . . I will call her Caridad."

"Why Caridad, Mama?" Ligaya wanted to know.

"Because it means 'charity,' and she will need a lot of it in this life."

THELMA RETURNED TWO DAYS later. It was to become a regular thing. She would come for a few days and return to Manila before the weekend. She said Raoul did not mind and she made sure his needs and the house were attended to during her absence.

So Thelma cooked for the children. I still had a maid then who washed and ironed the clothes, but she would go by the end of the month. The money was running low.

We never discussed it. Thelma refused to do so when I tried to thank her after finding the money she had left in the drawer where I kept the baby's clothes. She knew I would not miss it there. She helped me many times in those months.

I did not like taking money from her but I am ashamed to say I was relieved she was there to help. I would not have been able to keep us going on my own.

I had never worked in my life, never earned a living. It was something women did not do unless they came from a poor family. Then it would have meant working in a shop or, worse, as a servant. Though my parents were not wealthy, we did not have to work. We lived at home until we married. By then, our husbands provided for us.

When Alfonso died I had no means of making money. But even Thelma did not know how bad things were. My pride would not let me admit how needy I was. Not even to Ligaya who was the eldest did I tell the truth, not even when it was her piano that she loved so much that I sold to pay the rent. It shames me that I did not have the courage to tell her.

THE PIANO WAS A birthday present from Alfonso. It arrived on the morning of Ligaya's fifth birthday.

"It's too costly a present for a child," I told him.

"But the others can use it, too, when they're older," he said, reasoning with me.

There was no swaying him. Right from the day she was born, he had set his heart on her learning to play. Soon after her fifth birthday Ligaya began taking lessons. She had a gift and learned quickly. By the time she was ten, we hired a second piano teacher for her.

"To teach her pieces to perform," Alfonso explained to everyone.

Ligaya shared his dream. She wanted to be a pianist. The year before Alfonso died, she told him she was going to music school in Manila.

But I ended those dreams.

THE PIANO LESSONS WENT first. I waited for the teacher to arrive. Mrs. Buencamino, I still remember her name. She came once a week and had been doing so since we came to live in Olongapo. We were fortunate to find her in that small town.

Ligaya was upstairs minding the baby. I was glad she was not there when I spoke to the teacher. Mrs. Buencamino arrived earlier than usual to extend her sympathies. I spoke to her softly by the doorway.

"I am sorry," I said, "but Ligaya will not be taking lessons any more."

I did not have to say more. She understood. It was not hard to see that without a man in the house the little luxuries we once enjoyed we could no longer have.

"I am sorry to hear that," she said, "for Ligaya has a lot of promise. Maybe when things get better . . ."

"Yes . . . when things get better."

To Ligaya I said, "I told Mrs. Buencamino we are in mourning so you will not be taking lessons."

She nodded, not saying anything, just continuing to rock you in her arms. But the look in her eyes said she knew the truth.

That night I counted what little money I had left. No matter how many times I counted it, the amount did not change. Finally, I sold the piano. Nothing will ever make me forget that day. It was the day I failed Alfonso. The day Ligaya and all the children learned to fear tomorrow.

Ligaya never forgave me. It was not that she did not understand. One can understand but that does not take the pain away. If I had been stronger and more capable, like Thelma, my children would not have had to give up so much. But I did not have Thelma's strength.

When Thelma returned and found the piano missing, she became angry with me.

"Why did you not tell me?"

I kept silent.

"You know I would have helped you."

How could I tell her my pride had a bitter taste, that deep down I resented having to take from her. She would have thought me proud and ungrateful.

But it was too late for pride. Pride would not have saved me then or fed and clothed my children or put a

roof over their heads. So when she asked me, I had little
choice but to say yes.

NOT AT ONCE. NOT even in those moments of desperation could I bring myself to do it. Not even with all the
assurance from her that it would be the best thing for
everyone.

"Think about it. . . . You do not have to give me an
answer now. Just think about it."

She asked for you. Alfonso's child who saw with his
eyes. The last but undying part of our life together.

"I will take care of her as if she were my own. Why,
you are my flesh and blood, and she is too. Besides, you
know how much Raoul and I have always wanted a
child." Your mama had been married many years but she
and your papa never had any children. So Thelma asked
for you.

But how can a mother give up her child? I could not
do it but neither could I find a solution to my situation.

"Have you spoken to Ligaya about it?"

I shook my head. I did not even have the courage to
tell her about the piano, how could I tell her about this?

I tried to buy time. But Thelma was insistent, the
missing piano told her how weak my position was.

"You do not have much time, Emma. You cannot
manage on your own much longer."

I finally said, "Give me a few more days. I will tell
you . . . I will decide before you leave."

———

I OPENED MY EYES and saw Alfonso standing over the bed gazing down at me. He did not speak, just kept gazing at me. I sat up. An immense sense of relief passed over me.

"Alfonso . . . 'Fonso . . . Where have you been?" I said. He remained silent. "I have been so worried; I did not know how I would manage. But oh, now I know it was just a bad dream, now everything will be all right again."

Throwing back my blanket, I quickly got up and put my slippers on. "Just stay there, don't go away," I said, "I'll wake the children. They will be so glad to see you."

But Alfonso turned and walked towards the baby's crib. He lifted the mosquito net that was draped over it and looked down at the baby.

"Oh, you haven't seen her yet. . . . She is so pretty, Alfonso, a bit like Ligaya. Everyone says she has your eyes, even Thelma thinks so. I called her Caridad . . . I hope you like her name."

He bent and picked the baby up. Giving me one last look, he turned to leave the room, the sleeping child in his arms.

"Where are you going, 'Fonso? Where are you taking her? 'Fonso . . . you will wake her. 'Fonso . . . 'Fonso . . ."

He ignored me. I could not move. I realised then I was frozen, as if my feet had been nailed to the floor. I called and called until I woke with a start.

I was soaked in sweat. A dream, that was all it was.

Then my heart . . . for a second, my heart stopped as
the dream returned to me, as I remembered. I walked
very quickly across the room to the crib and threw the
mosquito net back.

The blanket covered the baby's face . . . your face.

How long it had been there I don't know. How it got
there I cannot tell. You were always a quiet sleeper. You
didn't toss and turn like the boys when they were small.
Besides, I always tucked the blanket snugly under the pillows on the side of the crib.

I reached out and touched your face. You were warm.
I moved my hand over your chest and felt it rise and fall.
Only then did I breathe.

I made a promise, a pledge. I made a pact with your
father. "Don't take her," I said, "please don't take her
away. I promise you I will give her the best care there is.
I swear she will never want for anything . . . that all the
children will never go without. Just don't take her."

The next day, Thelma took you to Manila.

LIGAYA

"How many of us grow up,

I wonder, to live the life

we imagined?"

SHE LOOKS AT ME with my father's eyes. She has the same look. The same way of tilting her head ever so slightly as she looks at you and listens. They are not striking eyes like my mother's. It is Mia who has Mama's eyes. Dark, glittering and alive. Papa's eyes were thinking eyes filled with quiet thoughts. They spoke softly. Her eyes have that same look, as though they are deep in thought, but what she is thinking I have no way of knowing.

"Can I come and see you tomorrow?" she asked on the phone.

"Yes, come . . . stay for lunch."

She hesitates then says, "The afternoon will be better, if you don't mind."

I understand. Lunch could be awkward—we would have to sit for a long time and talk. But in the afternoon, we can be at ease, and leaving is easier.

So I show her around the house as she has not been to this one. We have lived here only in the last five years, moving after she had left for Sydney. But even before then, we had little to do with each other. The years be-tween us kept us apart, but it is not as big a rift as that caused by the past.

I look at her, searching for what belongs to us. How much of her remains, apart from my father's eyes, to our side? Is there any part of her that belongs to my mother? I wonder if, like me, Mama searched for a trace of her-self in this child she gave away. Or is she all lost to us? Has Tia Thelma claimed all of her?

That there is Tia Thelma in her cannot be denied. It is in her bearing. She has a sense of ease that says life has been kind to her. That she has not known hardships, gone with-out, or looked to tomorrow with fear. And her hands. Our hands reveal so much about us. I do not mean the lines on her palm. I mean her hands. They have that pampered look about them. Well-cared-for tapered fingers with neatly shaped nails. These are not hands that have known lean times. Not like the times the rest of us lived through.

Looking at me now you would not see those years. But that is often how it is when we look at someone. We see what they are today, at this moment in time; we see them separate from their past. So if you were to look at me now, you would think as my friends think, and say as they say, "You have so much, you are so lucky."

And they are not wrong for what they see are the four cars, the big house, the maids, the jewellery, the holi-days. The signs of plenty. I do not tell them that all this is but a measure of what I once went without. They will not understand. But that is how it is.

I want my children to know only plenty.

"You spoil them," my husband says.

"We won't be here with them forever, Enrique; we won't know how life will treat them when we are gone. So while they have us, we must give them all we can. At least they will have had this."

He shakes his head and explains once more, "They must learn to work for things so when we're gone they can stand on their own. It is a good thing to teach them. To know a little hardship is not bad, it will make them stronger, more independent. You of all people should know that."

I do not listen. And I do not explain. How do I tell my husband, "I want them never to go without so they may live their dreams, be what they want, marry whom they love?"

I never realised my dreams for I have made many compromises in my life. I look at my life now and compare it to how I first thought it would be. I see little resemblance between the two. How many of us grow up, I wonder, to live the life we imagined?

I WANTED THE FAIRY tale. It was how I wanted to live my life, like a fairy tale. Make a wish and see it come true. And the best part was the part that said, "and they lived happily ever after."

It wasn't that my life, our life, when my father was alive was perfect. But all things were possible. I could have what

I wanted if I worked for it. I could go to music school if I practised long and hard. I could do well in school if I studied. I could have a new dress if I helped around the house. When Papa died, the possibilities, the chance of shaping my life the way I wanted it to be, were taken away from me.

I learned to trade dreams for security. My fingers tapped on typewriter keys, tapping out letters instead of music. There were moments when I wondered if he could see me from wherever he was; could he see me, his daughter that he named Ligaya, for happiness? Did he know I had forgotten what the word meant? Did he know of my anger? It is only now that I realise how angry I was. I did not want the burden he left me. I wish my mother had been stronger. It is like a curse, being the firstborn; though I was loved first and best, I suffered most, I carried the heaviest load.

Does he think me weak? I often ask myself. Does he think me weak for having given up in the end? Tired of the burden of mouths to feed, of living in a poor neighbourhood, of buying wornout clothes from women who had tired of wearing them, I compromised my life. I married where my heart was not. Would he understand? Weighing all that I have now against all that I wanted then, would he say I had made a wise choice?

"Marry only for love," Papa used to say to me, "like me and your mama, we married for love."

Does he know that when I had to choose between

two, I chose the one who could lighten my burden, the one who could share it, help carry it?

"I do not love you," I told Enrique the day he asked me to marry him.

"I know," he said softly, adding that it did not matter for he loved me just the same. "And I will help you . . . I will help your family. And as for love, it is enough that you like me; at least you like me, don't you?"

He asked so simply, so sincerely, my Enrique. Yes, I felt a liking for him.

"That is enough to go by. It is enough to begin with. You see, Ligaya, love and passion are well and good while they last, but in the end what matters is whether you like the person you are with. Friendship and companionship matter more. They are the things that last. And if in the end we learn to be friends, I will be content."

So I married a man I liked. In many ways, I have grown to care for him. A quiet sort of caring, a kind of loving. There is little of the passion my parents shared, which even as a child I could feel, in looks they exchanged across a room, or hands that found each other, and knees that touched. But there is peace and calm in my life. We have made a home and raised three children together, and as Enrique said so long ago, we have a sense of companionship.

But I will tell her none of this. For this does not concern her. This is long after her. Instead, I will tell her about the time before her and the time soon after she came. These parts, they belong to her.

———

I TAKE HER FOR a stroll through the garden. It is this that I love best, better than the inside of the house. I love this better than all the paintings and the little curios picked from all the places we have been. I love this even better than the baby grand that sits in the corner of the lounge room, a gift from Enrique and the children on my last birthday.

Of all that I have today, it is this garden that I cherish most. For here, the passing of the seasons gives me over and over again a sense of constancy. I know when each plant will bloom, and they never fail me. Every time a flower appears, I am reassured once more.

This garden is my pride. It is where I have sown my passion and reaped my reward in hundreds of blossoms. It fills my life with colours which drive away the darkness of that small room that knew no morning light, so many years ago, in another life.

"This is the best spot to view it." I guide her to the high ledge. "Here, stand on this rock and you can see everything."

She gazes in silence, turning her eyes to feast on the scene before her, around her, and above her. Finally, she turns to me and says, "It is a sea . . . a sea of orchids."

And I look with new eyes at my garden. The driftwoods covered with purple terrets, the walls lined with oncidiums that form rivulets of yellow, and trunks of palm trees with swirls of wild white dendrobiums. I see my garden as she describes it, a sea that washes us with waves of colour. So perhaps I will see the past through her eyes as well, and see it differently, without pain at last.

———

I HATED LIVING IN Olongapo. You have been there so you know what I mean when I say there is nothing there. But imagine it just after the war, after Liberation. It was worse. A dry dusty patch of baked brown dirt that passed itself off as a town. A place where the sun lived, so you could smell its heat every time you breathed, inhaling it deep inside you so it lived in every cell of your body.

Nothing ever happened in Olongapo and its one main road lined with dilapidated shops. You could walk its length in a few minutes and say you'd seen the town. It was a much smaller place in those days. The town, as you know, was something that grew from the American naval base in Subic. At the time we lived there it hadn't spread out as far as it has today. It had not yet become a city of bars and nightclubs. There was a bit of that maybe, but not as blatant as it is now with prostitutes making up a big portion of the workforce. It was not yet a city of sin. The pimps and their whores came much later when the US servicemen grew in number and the local businessmen decided to open up the clubs and disco joints. When we lived there it was simply a town filled with people trying to pick up the pieces of their lives. A nothing place trying to become something. So my heart sank when Papa told us we were leaving Manila forever, that we were moving to Olongapo to live.

"Why? Why do we have to go there?"

"I can start a new business there, *hija*, it will be easier than trying to make a living in Manila. Just look around you, there is nothing left of this city or my business."

So shortly after our return to Manila, we moved again. We took everything this time. Our clothes—if you could call the rags we wore clothes—the furniture, boxes of books, and my piano we loaded into a small truck Papa hired for the move. In Olongapo, Papa had found an old two-storey house, the bottom of which had once been a *sari-sari* store. So we moved into this rickety old place and tried our best to settle into our new life.

I remember the day we moved in. We all sat around the small dark *sala* with our furniture all around us and our dozens of boxes in disarray. We sat without speaking. Everyone was tired from the long, uncomfortable trip. We sat there like lost shell-shocked refugees. It was mid-afternoon and we had not eaten. After a while Mama rose and said, "It is not the best place to call a home but it will look better once we move these boxes out and arrange the furniture." Mama believes that when you are feeling down you must get up and do something. She was forever doing things. When Celia and I would sit and mope as teenagers often do, she would say it was because we were idle. Idle people have time to feel depressed; busy people have no time for wasteful thoughts. So she proceeded to organise us. She assigned the task of clearing the *sala* to Papa and me while she began to unpack the boxes that contained our pots and pans.

"The sooner I find my *kalan*, the sooner we'll get to eat!" So, with the help of Laura and Celia, Mama began work in the kitchen. The boys were assigned the task of flattening the boxes we had emptied to keep them from taking up space. We worked till late in the evening. With the *sala* done, we moved up to the bedrooms and began sorting through our things to look for our sleeping mats, which we laid out on the cots, plumping our pillows that were close to falling apart, airing our blankets, hanging the few clothes we had in the two *aparadors* we shared.

Holding one of our patched dresses, Celia said, "Even if we have no new clothes yet at least we don't have to walk around with *uling* on our face!" I nodded in agreement. If there was one good thing that had happened since the end of the war it was that Mama no longer had to rub soot on our faces every time we went out. During the war, women tried their best to look as ugly as possible so the enemy soldiers wouldn't grab and rape them. Mama, the few times I had gone out with her, wouldn't let me out of the house until she had messed up my hair. I would wear one of her dresses, at least two sizes bigger than what I normally wear, and walk around looking like a *bruja*. Yes, I could have passed for some crazy witch then. It was a relief not to have to go through all that again.

Celia found the crocheted white runner that Mama used to put on top of my piano. I ran downstairs and carefully draped it over the top. And Celia came downstairs with the metronome. We looked at each other and smiled. We looked around us and felt we had put our mark on the place. You have to do that before you can claim something as your own or before something can claim you. At that moment, we both felt better. Mama was right. Busying ourselves had made us feel better.

"Play something," Celia asked me softly.

I pulled the piano stool out and sat down. I opened the lid of the piano and took off the brown felt cover to reveal the keys. Then, after a while, I began to play. I still remember the piece. It was called *Widmung* by Schumann. My teacher said the English title was *Dedication*. It was a soft, gentle piece that was at the same time plaintive and hopeful. It had words to it I no longer recall. I played it because it was the last piece I had been learning before my lessons stopped. I played what I remembered of it until my fingers came to a rest on the keyboard, no longer remembering the next notes.

"Go on, Ligaya." I turned to find Papa standing behind me and my sisters and brothers by the stairs. And Mama with a cooking ladle in her hand sitting on the arm of a chair. Little Mia, sucking her thumb, came forward and clambered on to my lap.

"It's like home now," Miguel broke in. He had a big grin on his face. He wasn't always impossible.

"Yes, just like old times," Laura chirped in.

"Well, finish playing, *hija*," Papa said, getting impatient.

"I can't . . . I don't remember the last bit."

"Well, we have to find you another teacher but until

then we'll dig up your box of piano books and pieces and you can start practising."

Mama interrupted us saying, "Well, if you want to eat you all better wash your hands for I will not have dirty hands on the dinner table!" Everyone's hands were a bit grimy from all the unpacking we had been doing. Dust and ink from the old newspapers we had used to wrap things had rubbed off onto our palms and fingers. So we washed up quickly in the tiny corner room that passed as our toilet and shower. I remember the last thing we did before sitting down to a simple meal of rice with corn and two tins of sardines—*"Sardinas na naman!"* the boys groaned at the sight of the Spanish sardines Mama had put on the table—the last thing we did was hang up our picture of The Last Supper on the wall in the dining room. We bowed our heads and each said a silent prayer. I secretly prayed we would return to Manila soon. And that was how we spent our first day in Olongapo.

PAPA DECIDED TO GO into business operating an ice plant. As I said, Olongapo was such a nothing place it didn't even have an ice plant. Papa believed it was a good business opportunity as he would be the only supplier of ice blocks and cubes. He would not only be able to supply the residents but also the restaurants. At home, using his skills as an electrician, he rigged together a good size cooler for Mama, and this allowed her to do a little business selling *sorbetes*. She and Papa, with some help from us three girls, prepared homemade ice cream on week-ends which we sold during the week. We had three flavours. *Buco*, because coconut was available, *mangga* and *ube*, because mangoes and yam were easy to find as well. Sometimes Mama would just make flavoured ice sticks which were cheaper and were popular with the children in our street. Our little ice-cream business was what kept us going while Papa went about getting the ice plant started.

We hardly saw him in those days. He couldn't wait to get things started. He would leave early, right after break-fast, sometimes rushing out of the door while he still chewed the last mouthful of *pan de sal*. "The sooner I get the electrical lines connected, the sooner we can make some money," he would say when Mama complained.

He worked hard because he had to do most things alone. Lucio, his partner, knew nothing about electrical work. His role was to find the money to set up the busi-ness, but most of it was his anyway. Papa's contribution was his skill. He did all the dirty work. And by dirty I mean walking around in the swamps. He came down with malaria a few months later. Work on the ice plant came to a halt. The fever made him delirious and when it finally broke, it left him weak and thin, thinner than usual. For a time, he stayed home.

"Play the piano for me, *hija*," he would ask when I got home from school. I would play him his favourite pieces. Papa loved Chopin best. So I would play Chopin's *Etudes* to him during the weeks he stayed home.

Papa was never the same after his illness. He started complaining of chest pains. But he was so young, only thirty-nine, that I don't think he, Mama, or any of us ever imagined how bad his condition really was. I certainly didn't or I would not have gone to Manila for the Christmas school holidays.

"WHAT ARE YOU DOING for Christmas?" asked Nina.

Nina was the only friend I had in Olongapo. I met Nina two days after we arrived in the town. Mama had sent me to the corner store to buy a box of matches and a mosquito coil and, as I was waiting to be served, a girl came up to stand next to me.

"You're from Manila," she said, "the family that moved into the Torres's house."

I nodded.

"I'm Nina . . . I live near your house."

"Well, everything here is near each other," I replied, "it's such a small place."

"You don't like it here."

"I miss Manila."

"I've never been there. But you'll get used to this place. I'll show you around if you like. What's your name?"

"Ligaya."

"The teacher at school said someone new would be joining us. I wondered if it was you. Are you coming to our school?"

"Yes . . . with two of my sisters. We start on Monday."

"I'll come and get you and we can walk to school together."

So Nina and I became friends, spending time at her place when we wanted to get away from my brothers and sisters. We would do our homework together in her house in the room off the *sala* where she liked to spend her time. And when tricky maths questions did not occupy us, we sat and browsed through the magazines her mother collected, or listened to the radio. Her father had a gramophone and when no one was about we would take out his 78s and play them. Most of the time we would just turn the radio on and sing along. Our favourite song was *Stardust*. We knew the words by heart. Sometimes we would spend time at our house when I had to practise my piano lessons.

"I wish I could play like you. But I never learned."

"It's not too late," I told her. "Here, I'll show you . . . what I just played was C major. Major chords only use white keys. When you hit the black keys, you're playing minor chords . . ."

Sometimes Nina would sit next to me on the piano seat, her fingers moving awkwardly over the keys.

In the middle of one such lesson she exclaimed in frustration, "I give up! Let's go out."

It was the day I first saw Subic Bay. It's funny how you can live in a town and simply keep within its boundaries. I had never, until that day out with Nina, gone much further than Olongapo's main road or where the houses and shops stopped. It was a Saturday morning and we took some *baon* with us to eat while we went for a walk. Some *pan de sal* which we sprinkled with condensed milk. We set out and were still walking an hour or so later.

"Where are you taking me? There's nothing out here." We had gone maybe two or three miles.

"What would you know? You've never been this far. Don't be *tamad*. You're just lazy. Keep walking."

I was too hot and my feet too tired. I did not feel like looking around me. I walked without seeing.

"Well . . ."

"Well what?" I answered back, sounding cross.

"Don't you think it's pretty?"

I saw it then. The bay before me with its blue, blue waters. To this day I can still see it. Pretty. No, beautiful . . . beautiful like a postcard. From where we stood on the dirt road, we gazed down at the bay's crystal clear waters. The bay moved in and out of sight as we kept walking for it was a winding road that had been carved out of a mountainside. The bay seemed to curve where the road curved, always following it, its waters wrapping around it. Suddenly I forgot the greyness, the blandness of Olongapo. Along the road, we picked the wild flowers that grew in between the rocks. Little yellow blossoms and some purple ones. We stuck them behind our ears. Nina found some twigs which we bent to make a circular frame. And I took off my *bakya* and like a mountain goat stepped onto the rocks that jutted out of the mountainside and reached for more flowers until I had enough to stick between the twigs, filling the gaps to make Nina a floral crown. I put it on her head and we laughed and sang on our way back home. We were thirsty and a little bit hungry for the sweetened *pan de sal* had been consumed hours before. We came back tired, with a layer of dust on our hair, skin and clothes, but we were happy. Me more than her, I think, for she was a very even-tempered girl. But she was happy, too, in having made me laugh so much that day.

When we got home she gave me the crown of flowers I had made for her. "But it's yours," I protested. She shook her head and said, "It's a remembrance . . . it was the first time you saw the bay." I happily took the crown from her and thanked her for the day. We parted and I went into the house. Mama, on seeing me, asked what we had been up to as we had been gone so long and I had returned looking so very brown. I told her we had walked to the bay and how pretty it was, then I ran up to my room and placed the crown on the table in our room by the window, its bright colours a happy contrast against the dark wood. On seeing it, Celia said, "Oh, they are so pretty . . . pity they won't last."

The next morning I woke to find the little flowers had all wilted. Their faded yellow and purple as sad as my room.

"Are you doing anything special this Christmas?" Nina asked me again.

"No, not really . . . but Clarita, my cousin from

Manila, is coming for a visit. She goes back first week of December. I want to go with her. School will be breaking for Christmas anyway."

Nina looked disappointed. I knew she wanted me to be around for Christmas and we had talked about how we would spend the school holidays together. But even if I had grown close to her and enjoyed her company, the chance of going to Manila was hard to say no to.

"You'll miss a week of classes . . . Will your papa let you?"

"I don't know. We'll see . . ."

WE HAD BEEN IN Olongapo almost six months when the time came for my cousin's visit. Clarita had found a job as a salesgirl in one of the downtown shops in Manila. She and I spent many hours talking about her life in the city. I was so hungry for news, for everything I had left behind.

Life was still hard there, she said, and little work had been done to rebuild the city. "There's still so much clearing to be done before any building can start. Rubble all over the place. The streets are full of holes . . . like they've had chicken pox! And thousands of people are still homeless, living in shanties, wearing rags."

"It can't be as bad as here," I said. I told her I wanted to return with her, for a few weeks.

"I'm going back with Clarita," I told Mama.

"You have to ask your papa," she replied, a slight

frown on her face. "He'll worry about you while you're gone, Ligaya."

Papa refused to let me go. But I didn't worry for there was still a week to convince him as Clarita would not be leaving until the following Friday. So every day I tried to make him say yes. Celia and Laura, even my friend Nina, watched with interest. Half wanting me to go and half envying me should I succeed in convincing Papa.

"Where will you stay and who will keep an eye on you?"

"Clarita said I can stay with her. She said Tia Luisa won't mind." Tia Luisa was Mama's cousin.

But Papa refused to give his permission.

"What will you do when Clarita goes back to work?"

"She said I can go with her and help."

"You will just be in the way. And you are not a shop girl. How can that be better than staying here . . . better you stay with your sisters."

"But Papa—" I started again.

"I don't want you to go, Ligaya."

On Thursday night, I packed my bags. Clarita tried to talk me out of going. She was beginning to feel her visit had given rise to this problem.

"Come another time, Ligaya. I'm sure when things are more settled your papa will agree. Besides, Manila is still in such a mess, there won't be that much to see."

"Papa must understand I am no longer a child. He always treats me like one. I'm going to be sixteen in a few months."

"Well, you are his favourite, you know that."

And it was because I knew I was his favoured child that I had the courage to go ahead with my plans.

The following morning, I came down with my little *maleta*. Clarita had gone down ahead of me and was thanking Mama for letting her stay when I entered the lounge room. Seeing me all dressed and the *maleta* in my hand, Mama knew there was little she could do to stop me without causing a scene in front of Clarita.

"Where's Papa?"

Mama motioned with her head. Papa was upstairs, in their room.

"Go and say goodbye," she told me.

I hesitated, then went back up. The door was shut. Papa had not given in. I knocked but he did not answer although I could sense he was awake and had heard. I knocked once more. A little louder. But still he did not ask me in.

"Papa . . . Papa . . . I'm going," I said to the door, "I will be home soon." I waited for a few seconds but he did not reply. So I made my way back down.

"It's only for the Christmas holidays. I will be back before the New Year." I kissed Mama on the cheek and as I turned to go, she held my hand and put a roll of bills in it.

"Pocket money," she explained, "and buy your papa something nice."

Then she handed me a little parcel. "For your Tia Luisa . . . a little something for Christmas . . . You cannot go empty-handed."

I kissed Mama once more, thankful for having some spending money. I did not think then how little she could afford to part with it. As I turned to go, I heard the sound of footsteps on the stairs. Mama and I turned to look, thinking it was Papa, but it was only Celia come to say goodbye.

"Oh, I am so jealous," she said. "I wish I wasn't spending Christmas here, too. It is so unfair."

"Go back to bed," Mama ordered, "and stop talking nonsense."

"I will write to you," I promised her.

Clarita called from outside. The *calesa* had arrived. I quickly climbed in, putting my *maleta* next to hers on the floor. As the *kuchero* snapped his whip to get the horse moving, I looked up towards my parents' bedroom window but there was no sign of Papa. I kept glancing back until the house was no longer in sight.

Soon, though, I was caught up in the excitement of returning to Manila and forgot my parting with Papa. I knew it would not be long before he would forgive me. He never stayed angry with his children, never for long, and never with me.

Most of Manila was still unchanged from the war. Many places still had piles of rubble. Clarita took me around the city. It was a sorry sight. The once-tall buildings and the many churches that marked its skyline had mostly been destroyed. Even the Manila Cathedral had fallen victim to a bomb.

We hailed a *calesa* to take us around. It was a bumpy ride. The streets were rutted, marred with countless gaping potholes. It was hard for the *kuchero* to find a long stretch of unscarred surface for his horse to trot on.

I lived with Clarita's family. Tia Luisa had made me welcome, asking about Papa and Mama and my sisters and brothers. When Clarita went off to work, I would sit in the kitchen and listen to her stories as she went about cooking our meal. Unlike us, her family had braved the fighting and remained in their home.

"*Ay naku!* When it's your time to die, you die. The hills won't hide you from death. That's what I told your Tio Monching. I would rather die in my house than in the hills. Besides, I was not going to let anyone come and loot my house. In the last few weeks, though, we had to run several times. The fighting was happening right here on this street. Look at the window, there, see that spot under the tree? Right there an explosion killed eight people. All of them civilians. Every time fighting reached this place we would run away then return later. All in all, we ran and came back thirteen times. But see how it has turned out, we are all alive still. Not our time yet, you see . . . not our time to go."

Then she pointed to the house next door. "Take the Santoses, the people who used to live there. They hid in the hills. What for? There's no running away from death. In the hills, a bomb was dropped on their hut . . . an American bomb. Dropped by mistake. Only one of them survived . . . a daughter."

"Where is she? What happened to her?"

Tia Luisa shook her head, "Poor thing . . . Gone to live with relatives . . . they took her in. Maybe she's not right in the head. She lost all her hair, they say; all of it, not just on her head. No eyelashes, no eyebrows—all gone from her arms . . . everywhere, if you know what I mean. Dori, who lives two houses away spoke to the cousin. He said it was the shock. The girl walked back to where the hut was after it happened. It had burned down. And everyone was dead. The girl sat among the bodies, arms and legs and faceless heads. She sat staring, not speaking; she still has not uttered a word, so they tell me. Her eyes when they found her were wild and unseeing. A week later, she lost all her hair."

Sometimes I accompanied Clarita to the shop where she worked, learning about different fabrics and how much they cost by the yard. It was such a treat. Seeing so many designs and colours. But the price of things! No wonder people still wore the tattered clothes they used during the war.

One of the things I recall most about the war was the shortage of cotton. The shortage was so bad, farm land that had been used for growing crops was used to grow cotton plants. The Japanese took control of the harvest for their own use—an army of 250,000 had to be clothed—while many local people had to make do with clothes that had become threadbare. Mama, I remember, had patiently mended our clothes over and over again. My brothers' shirts, while we lived in Taytay, had more stitches on them than an embroidered pillowcase. Playing in the bushes and rolling in the dirt did little to keep their clothes in one piece. Celia and I learned to do a lot of fine stitching during those three years.

By the end of the war, I possessed three dresses. Celia only had two. Laura was the only one who had something that looked decent. It was a dress Mama had sewn together using an old tablecloth. As for the rest of us, the only thing that held our clothes together was the patches we had sewn on them.

Now, with the war ended, many still wore their threadbare clothes for most people had little money to spend. Food, medicine and shelter were their main concerns.

The days I spent at the shop were interesting in another way. There the chatter was different. The other salesgirls were the same age as Clarita so I sat and listened to them talk about going out and who liked so and so.

The journey itself, to the shop and home, was a chance to watch people. Although we took the same route every day, the scenery was forever changing because of the people that came and went. Sometimes we travelled by *carretela*, *caromata* or *calesa*. But these modes of transport were on the way out. They were mostly used in the Binondo area where the Chinese lived and did business. The streets there were narrower. One of the changes the war brought was the jeep. After the war there were many surplus army vehicles so the enterprising locals transformed these into *jeepneys*. It was exciting to ride in one. Even in Olongapo when we had just moved there, *jeepneys* were already taking business away from the *kucheros* and their horse-drawn carriages. *Jeepneys* moved faster and were a better way to see the city. It was things like this that I wrote to Celia about in reply to her letter.

I had been in Manila for two weeks or so but there was still no word from Papa. Only a long letter filled with a hundred questions from Celia. Two years younger than me, she was old enough to remember Manila and our old life. In her letter she would tell me how she envied me for being back in the city.

I bought Papa a shirt in one of the downtown shops. It had eaten away most of the money Mama had given me, but I knew it would please him and it would make up for my leaving.

THE TELEGRAM ARRIVED ON a Saturday morning, missing me by just a few minutes. It was Clarita's day off and we had gone to the Luneta for a walk. The park was nothing like it used to be. The lawns were scarred where the tanks had passed. We could still make out the deep grooves even though the grass had grown over them. It became a kind of game we played, the spotting of places where tanks had crossed and trenches had been dug.

Later, we made our way to Intramuros. Here the sense of desolation was overpowering. If only the Japanese had made their last stand elsewhere, its massive tufa walls that ran five miles long might have been left standing.

I had come here once, before the war, on a school excursion. Our history teacher had pointed out the original seven gates of this one-hundred-and-fifty-acre ancient citadel. In the old days, the gates were secured at night when the drawbridges across the surrounding moat were raised and bolted. Later, of course, the moat was drained and the drawbridges lowered permanently when Intramuros, with its residences, schools, monasteries, convents and churches, was no longer confined to just the Spaniards and *mestizos*. Our teacher told us twelve churches once stood inside these walls. And that the walls at their base measured forty feet thick, and rose sixteen feet high.

But Intramuros was no more. Six days of pattern bombing by the Americans had reduced eighty per cent of Manila to dust. War cares little, you see, for historic monuments or human life. Both the Americans and the Japanese would prove this many times before the end of the war. The Japanese, facing defeat, helped to complete the destruction of the city the Americans had begun with their air attacks. As they retreated, the Japanese went on a destruction spree—firing churches, blowing up ammunition dumps and gas depots, and taking life after innocent life.

"Four thousand hostages were kept here. Only 3,000 were released," Clarita told me as we walked through the rubble of Intramuros. "They were kept inside two churches, mostly children and women. Later, the bodies of the missing thousand were found. The men. Hands tied behind their backs. Bayonet wounds marked their rotting bodies. They were stacked up in the dungeons of Fort Santiago. In the Powder Magazine Chamber alone, they found six hundred burnt bodies. Several priests were said to have been buried alive."

Clarita told me of buried treasure too. Gold was better than money during the war. If you had gold you could trade on the black market or buy goods that were hard to find, like medicine. Because trading in precious metals was widespread during the war, the Japanese were able to amass a big hoard of gold. What they couldn't get through black market trading they simply confiscated. They took valuables in gold and gems from ordinary citizens, banks and businesses. Churches and temples were not safe from their greed. The war became an opportunity for them to strip the helpless citizens of the nations they conquered of everything. After the war, people referred to the Japanese war loot, which had been accumulated over ten years of conquest all over Asia, as Yamashita's Gold. But it was more than just gold. They say the treasure included gems, precious stones worth a kingdom. Only a small part of this loot made it to Japan. The war was nearing its end and the Japanese faced defeat, so a great portion of this war treasure collected throughout Asia was still in Manila, awaiting shipment to Tokyo. But the Japanese had to retreat in a hurry. They had no choice but to bury it, hide it in Manila and its surrounding provinces.

The rumours were aplenty. Some tell stories of truck convoys transporting part of the treasure to the mountains up north in Baguio or to Teresa just a short distance from Manila where it was then hidden in tunnels or caves. Other reports claim that coral reefs were blasted open to make room for gold bullion of different sizes and markings, as well as great quantities of jewellery studded with gems. These sites were then covered with coral and concrete. But the worst tale I was to hear during my visit to Manila was how prisoners were forced to dig pits and tunnels running several miles long right under Fort Santiago where they buried part of Yamashita's Gold . . . and where they themselves were entombed alive. I can imagine them, those poor Filipino, British, Australian and American soldiers, frantically digging and burying treasure, then realising they were digging their own graves. The Japanese, afraid that the men would reveal where the loot had been buried, sealed them in with their secret. Their spirits hover over this ill-gotten treasure. Will they ever find peace?

Clarita and I walked around Fort Santiago in Intramuros but did not attempt to explore inside. The rubble that covered it was enough to discourage us. But the thing that kept me away was a sense of evil. Some places breed evil. And to me, the Fort built on Rajah Sulayman's original stockade inside Intramuros was one such place. Little did this local chieftain know that the land he sold to the Spaniards would become the site of so much human carnage. Every occupying power had made this stone fortress its headquarters. It was a place of death. Overlooking the harbour and the river mouth, its dungeons were below high tide level. During the Spanish times, many prisoners, chained to the lower dungeons, screamed for help as the tide rose and seeped into their cells, only to be silenced by a watery death.

Tired after all our walking, and by the sad sight of so much destruction, we returned home at midday. It was then that Tia Luisa handed me the telegram.

"Come home. Papa is not well." It had been sent by Mama.

I packed my clothes along with the *pasalubongs* I had bought for my family. I remember folding Papa's shirt carefully, thinking, "This will make him feel better."

Early the following morning, Clarita accompanied me to the station. "I'll come back as soon as Papa is better," I said.

As the bus pulled away from the station, she shouted to me, "Merry Christmas."

I waved goodbye to her. It was the twenty-second of December.

I ARRIVED IN OLONGAPO by midday and hailed a *calesa* for the ride to our house. Everywhere, *parols* could be seen hanging from windows. As the *calesa* rounded the corner and travelled up our street, I could see children running, playing, and laughing. It felt like Christmas. As we passed the *sari-sari* store, Aling Ana, who ran it, waved to me. I waved back, smiling at her. Manila was forgotten by now and as the *calesa* drew closer to our house, a feeling of excitement and anticipation came over me. I could not wait to get home. I was surprised at how much I had missed everyone.

It was good timing. I would be with everyone to celebrate Christmas Eve. Not only that, I would also be able to join them for the last two *Misa de Gallo*. Mama always woke us up to go to the predawn masses—the rooster masses some call them. Nine days in a row till Christmas Eve she would come into our rooms while it was still dark and shake our feet till we woke. Sleepy-eyed and grumbling and cold, we would all trudge to the neighbourhood church joined by a multitude of early risers who, like us, had dressed hastily and were now rushing down the street hoping to make it on time for the start of the mass. Nine days we would do this, egged on by the promise of a delicious reward on Christmas Eve when Mama would lay out a midnight feast—*noche buena*—and we would all sit around the table to celebrate the birth of Jesus.

We had not celebrated Christmas or the New Year in this way for the last three years. Oh, how could I even have considered spending Christmas in Manila! How thoughtless of me. I was glad now to be coming home. How I looked forward to sitting around the table with Mama and Papa. I hoped he felt better; perhaps I would arrive home and find him fully recovered. I wanted to be surrounded by Celia's chatter and Laura's questions and the boys with their silly games as we feasted on Mama's Christmas dishes.

I imagined the food laid out on the dining table with the white tablecloth Mama herself crocheted many years ago. She kept this in her wooden *baul* at the foot of her bed and would take it out only on special occasions. I can see and taste in my mind the platters of food she would prepare for *noche buena*. She always had sweet sticky food so luck would stick to us. Of course there would be *jalea de ube*. Except for the time during the war, no Christmas has ever passed in our house without a plate of this purple *ube* yam pudding on our table. Mama made the best *ube* in Manila. And the best *puto bumbong*! I can see her stuffing the purple *pirurutong* rice in narrow bamboo tubes to steam. When it is ready to serve, I will sweeten it by sprinkling brown sugar on top. Mama also makes *bibingka* during Christmas Eve, and always only her special recipe with *carabao* cream cheese, salted duck egg and subtly burnt white sugar. Christmas to me also meant eating *pastillas de leche* to my heart and stomach's content. Mama says it is fattening, but I don't care. I will have as much as I like. And *keso de bola*, surely no Christmas is complete without this wonderful cheese.

Just then, I looked up, for even from that distance our house was almost visible. Thoughts of food were replaced by another Christmas image. I wondered if Papa had bought a new *parol* to hang this year. Our old lantern had fallen to bits the year before. I doubted if it had made the trip to Olongapo with the rest of our things. I was sure Papa would have a new one this year. Papa always prided himself for having the nicest *parol* in our street. One time, while we still lived in Manila, he came home with a very plain-looking *parol*.

"Alfonso, why did you not buy a nicer one?" Mama had asked on seeing the plain white one Papa had chosen.

"It will be the nicest one on our street once I finish working on it," he replied with a twinkle in his eyes. He was like a young boy, excited about a secret project. At night he would lay the *parol* out on the dining table and work on it. He bought different colour cellophane sheets which he cut into fine strips. He attached these to the tips of the lantern so they fell like tassels. Then he cut the center out and replaced it with another colour cellophane. He loved doing things with his hands.

"There is nothing left of that *parol* except the frame," Mama said to him as he worked on in silence.

"Oh, that was what I wanted, just the frame, which is why I chose the one with the simplest design. I couldn't find one I really wanted so I am decorating it myself," he told me and Mama. Three nights later, he finished working on the *parol*. It was covered in a multitude of colours. It was the prettiest lantern in our street.

"It is the Star of Bethlehem," he explained to me. I was perhaps six or seven then. "We put it up to celebrate the birth of the Baby Jesus. It will lead the Three Wise Men—the Magi—to the place where he will be born."

Papa had put a coloured bulb inside our lantern. "Now,

switch it on, Ligaya, so the Wise Men will see it shine from afar. We must make sure they find their way."

So I grew up thinking of life and of birth and of joy whenever I saw these lanterns hung out every Christmas.

I strained my eyes to see what he had chosen, I looked towards our window but saw nothing . . . no *parol*. Maybe he had put the Christmas lantern on the upper window, my parents' bedroom window. My eyes travelled up but what I saw was the flickering of many candles. Even from where I sat in the *calesa*, I could see their tiny flames winking against the noonday sun. I knew then I was too late. My papa had died.

The *calesa* stopped in front of the house and I took my *maleta* down along with my parcels. Then I entered the house. I entered on my knees.

You know the pilgrims and penitents who go to the church in Quiapo in Manila every Friday, arriving in droves to pray to the image of the Black Nazarene? They go to the altar on their knees. So I, too, knelt and walked on my knees across the *sala*, all the way to the dining room, and up the flight of wooden stairs, like the penitents who begged for forgiveness, for healing.

Mama said he was not angry with me. No, he wanted to see me, but he was not angry.

"That is not your papa's way," she kept telling me as I sobbed against her breast. I believed her because Papa loved me; I know he loved me too much to remain angry. And he would not want me to go on thinking that he was. But just the same, I wish . . . how I wish we had not parted badly.

I wish now I had spent more time with him, spoken to him more, hoarded his words to last me a lifetime. I wish I had stood longer by his door that morning I left for Manila, stood there and stubbornly knocked until he opened the door, or that I had turned the doorknob and let myself in. At least then I would have been able to say goodbye to him. I have many wishes. Always in hindsight I have many wishes. But none as great as this . . . I wish I had been able to say, "Sorry. I'm sorry."

YOU WERE BORN A few weeks later. I cut the cord. Did my mother tell you that? I was the one that cut the cord. You were a quiet baby. I remember the two boys and Mia when they were babies, they were not as quiet. Specially Paolo; he used to cry all night. I used to think he must have had the biggest pair of lungs. But you were quiet, as if you knew that Mama could not take any more.

I used to come and watch you so Mama could have a rest, or go to church—she went to pray often in those days. I used to hum to you as I carried you but you would not remember that. All those times that I was up in the room with you, Mama could have spoken to me but she did not.

Mama kept many things to herself, maybe because she did not want us to worry. All I remember is that Tia Thelma came often. Mama needed her in those days. But she should have told me. I was the eldest. She should have let me know. But she kept me in the dark about how bad things were. I did not know until I came home and found the piano gone.

You know how some things are more than what they are. Like I look at this ring here and to me it is more than just a ring. It is my marriage. And if I were to lose it I would think it a bad sign. I never take this ring off. Never. It was like that with the piano. It meant more than what it was. It was mine, you know. It was my piano. I still remember the day it was given to me.

I was five that day.

"What are you giving me for my birthday? What's my gift?" I kept asking Papa and Mama the night before. But Papa just laughed. He loved to keep me guessing, knowing I was dying to know, that I couldn't wait to find out.

"Is it a doll?"

"A tea set?"

He kept shaking his head. "You can't guess and you can't find it in the house, so you must be patient," he said. "Tomorrow when you wake up it will be here."

"Tell me the first letter, what letter does it start with."

"You like surprises, Ligaya?"

I nodded.

"Then you must wait or it will no longer be a surprise, eh?"

Mama got me into bed early, which was a feat in itself as I disliked going up to my room when I knew they were still downstairs.

"The sooner you sleep, the sooner tomorrow will come," she told me as I very obediently got in under the sheets.

I woke early. For a moment I lay in bed just watching the soft morning light come through the curtains. It was something I always liked, the light against the fabric, seeping through to cast a rosy glow over my bedroom walls. But suddenly I remembered it was the morning of my birthday.

Mama was awake—I could hear sounds coming from the kitchen below. I knew she would be downstairs preparing all my favourite dishes. It was always like this on a birthday. If it was Papa's birthday, she cooked all his favourites. Today was mine so I knew she'd make *leche flan* and *macapuno* because she knew I liked having my cream caramel topped with the sweet coconut preserve she made.

A vehicle pulled up in front of the house. Even from my room I could hear the loud sputtering of the engine. The front door opened and I heard Papa's voice followed by other voices, louder, rougher. I jumped out of bed, sensing something interesting was about to happen.

I ran barefoot, still wearing my bedclothes, into my parents' room. I slid the window open so I could see down to the street below. Standing on tiptoe, I saw an old delivery truck parked in front of the house; a man stood at the rear with outstretched hands as someone unseen, from inside, handed him a wooden plank. This they laid against the edge of the vehicle on one end, while the other rested on the ground. Papa came into view then. Standing by, watching them at work. Then, with much grunting, shouting and encouragement, they slid this thing down. Slowly it emerged. A piano . . . my piano . . . my birthday present.

By then, Celia, too, had run into the room. But being smaller than me, she could not see.

"What is it? What is down there?" I did not answer her, just turned and ran down the stairs. I could hear her following close behind.

I entered the *sala* just as the men pushed the piano into the house. Papa and Mama, hearing our approach, turned to look at us.

"Ahhh . . . Ligaya, what big eyes you have!" Papa jokingly said. But all I could think of was how wonderful, how beautiful, how this was the best birthday gift in the whole world.

I approached the piano then and lifted the lid with Papa's help. I lifted the piece of long velvet cloth that covered it, revealing ivory white keys and gleaming black keys that shone in a row. I can still feel them under my fingers. Smooth and cool to the touch at first, then warming slowly as if they were a part of me.

Then wonder gave way to childish exuberance as I played my first loud crashing discordant chord. Celia joined in soon after. And together, our four little hands filled the house with sound.

Mama had her hands to her ears and she turned to

Papa, shouting to be heard over the noise we were making. "I think, Alfonso, this was not a very good idea."

I STILL REMEMBER THAT piano. On each end of it was a little lamp with a small light bulb. In the evening, I would turn them on and they would cast a soft glow over the keys. I loved playing at night. It seemed every note sounded richer, purer, as it hung in the air.

Every time I lifted the lid of the piano, it was like opening a door to a different world. I didn't mind the hours I spent practising my lessons. Not like Celia or Laura who did not take long before losing all interest, preferring to play outside with the kids next door.

I practised every day. By the time I was ten, Papa hired a second teacher for me. "The other one teaches you exercises; you need someone to teach you pieces."

This second teacher was a tall and lean woman—a spinster with a long face—who was in her fifties. She was as good and demanding a teacher as she was strange. The first day she came, she told Papa she would work with me for an hour before deciding whether or not I would be accepted as a pupil. Both Papa and I were taken aback as we had not known I would be tested first or that a teacher would even dream of turning down a student and the money her tuition would bring.

"I do not want to waste my time on untalented pupils. A person who plays the piano must provide his or her listeners with some amount of pleasure. But when parents push untalented children to play, they are not only painful to listen to but quite painful to teach as well."

After saying this, she sent Papa out of the room. I stood there and watched as she took a foot-long wooden stick out of her big black handbag and put it on the piano ledge over the keys. She reached into her bag once more and this time brought out a small wind-up alarm clock. Just before the lesson started, she wound the clock and put it on top of the piano. Then she told me to open my piano piece to the first page. After I had done this, she reached out for her wooden stick and said, "Now, let's see what you can do. Play." She began to beat time with her stick so I began to play, all the while trying to ignore the loud tick, tick, ticking sound of her alarm clock. It was a shaky start but after a few minutes, I settled down and thought I was doing well until suddenly her wooden stick struck my right little finger.

"Leave that finger pointed down. These are piano keys. You are not sitting here holding a dainty tea cup." That was how I discovered what her stick was for.

I continued playing, stopping only whenever she interrupted to correct my playing. Once she told me, "Eh, did you think I was deaf, girl? You need not play so loud. That section is marked *pianissimo*. Play softly . . . I can hear you quite well even when you play softly." Another time she cried, "Stop! Stop! Stop! Can you not read? The notation says *calmato*. Why are you rushing?"

Another time, her hand swooped down and grabbed hold of mine. She did not let go. "You are not a machine.

So do not play mechanically, especially when it says *tempo rubato*. When you see these two words, you play with a different feeling. Not from the heart but from a deeper place, you understand? *Rubato* must be played from here." She released my hand and moved hers below my ribcage, curled her hand into a fist, then pressed down on me. "Feel that. This is where *rubato* is played from— from the gut. From this place, the power rises to your shoulder and flows down to your arms, through your fingers, then onto the keys. *Tempo rubato* is played to your body's time, not to the mechanical time of a metronome. Do you understand what I'm saying?"

I played and she corrected me. This went on until, suddenly, the alarm clock went off. I jerked my head up at the loud ringing sound. She opened her bag then and put her stick back in. An hour had passed. The lesson had come to an end.

"Where is your father? Send him in."

Papa, an anxious look on his face, entered the *sala* once more. The teacher looked him in the face and said with a nod of her head, "She will do." And with that, she informed me she would see me at exactly the same time on the same day next week.

So from this strange, uncompromising teacher, I learned to play Liszt's *Liebestraum*, Debussy's *Claire de Lune*, Chopin's *Polonaise in A Flat*, and Sibelius's *Finlandia*. She taught me to create sweet, gentle, romantic sounds and strong, raging passions with my fingers. The hour she spent teaching me always flew by and I learned to mark my progress by the number of times her stick descended on my hand.

When the Japanese came, my lessons stopped for a while. Then they resumed, but not in a regular way. Food was our family's priority. But I didn't mind because the piano was there and I could play on my own. In the back of my mind, I always thought, "When this is all over, when the war is over, everything will go back to the way it was."

In Olongapo, Papa found a piano teacher, Mrs. Buencamino was her name, so I began taking lessons again. When Papa died and the lessons had to stop for good, I consoled myself, saying, "It's all right, you still have the piano."

Looking back now, I can understand why Mama didn't tell me. But at the time it happened, all I could feel was anger. I thought then it was Mama I was angry with, but later I realised I was angry at everything and everyone. It was as if life had singled me out, unfairly; everything I loved was being taken from me.

It started out like any other day. I got up in the morning and helped make breakfast. Then I walked to school. Nothing really good or bad happened during the day. You know how on some days one thing after another goes wrong so you are not surprised at all when one more thing happens. Well, this was not a day like that. On this day, I was taken by surprise.

I remember walking into the *sala* with my school bag and, like every day after school, heading for the stairs. Then I looked back. Something was not right.

Where my piano had been was now just empty space. I stood there for a second, a minute, maybe longer, and I knew without even having to ask, I knew. But still I wanted to hear it from her, I wanted her to say it to my face, but more than anything, I wanted her to know how angry I was.

I climbed the stairs to her room. Each step loud and deliberate. I did not race up in a rage, I took each step slowly, I wanted her to know I was coming.

She was waiting for me. She had left her door wide open. I stood by the doorway and looked at her. I did not speak. She did not look up. She had you in her arms, against her breast as you fed. She knew I was there.

"I sold it," she said, her eyes never meeting mine. "I sold it because we needed the money."

How futile anger is when you cannot vent it. I turned and left the room. Downstairs I stood in the middle of the *sala*. Then I began. I dragged the chairs around; the tables and the shelves I dragged across the polished floors, not caring that I left streaks on the tiles. Beads of perspiration formed on my forehead as I moved the furniture around, this way, that way, stopping only when the room no longer resembled its old self.

I walked out of the house. I headed towards Nina's house. Like most days, the front door was left open and I walked in unannounced. I walked towards the back room where I knew she would be. It was used as an informal room so it was here we often sat and chatted, as we did our homework.

"Nina . . ." I called to her so she would know who was approaching.

"In here."

The room looked different. I smiled, some of the tension leaving my body. Nina's mother had been rearranging the furniture as well. My eyes scanned the room from one wall to another with curiosity, noting where a chair once stood, where a table had been moved, where a lamp now rested. My eyes travelled from one piece of furniture to another until they came to rest on my friend. But where her favourite chair used to be now stood something else. My piano. And on its stool sat Nina.

I did not say anything. She looked at me with eyes that seemed to apologise, that looked sad and embarrassed.

"Your mama asked if we would like it . . . I thought you knew. Please . . . you can always come and play here."

I walked out of her house, shame and hurt all mixed together inside me. I felt she had betrayed me. I never went back to her house again. And I never spent much time with her after that day.

As I dressed to go to bed that night, Celia came to me with something wrapped in an old shirt.

"Here," she said, "I saw it standing on the little table downstairs. They must have removed it from the top of the piano, then forgot about it. I kept it . . . I thought you might want to keep this at least."

It was my metronome. Papa had given it to me the day I began my piano lessons.

"Thank you," I told Celia. Then I wrapped it up again and kept it in a drawer, under my clothes. It was not just the loss of the piano that I mourned. It was the loss of my old life too. When the piano went, I realised how bad things were. It was the day that I learned to fear.

If I had been older I might have handled things differently. But at fifteen, I knew only one way. To remain silent. As if by not talking about it, our problem would go away. If I had asked Mama, together we might have found a way. But I didn't. She must have wanted to have me to talk to, but I would not give her the chance. I was too afraid of knowing more.

Maybe if we had found a way to talk about the situation, in the end we would have made different choices. She would have known how I felt and in knowing she might have chosen differently. I do not mean the piano, for though the piano mattered in those angry moments, later on it ceased to be important. I mean in the matter concerning you . . . if she had had me to turn to, instead of Tia Thelma, what happened would not have happened.

Tia Thelma came often. And I never asked why. To me it was just that she was Mama's eldest sister and Mama needed her, so she came.

I did not think she wanted something, that she had plans. Maybe I am being too harsh; Mama says I am never fair when it comes to Tia Thelma, but it is hard to change a thought that is deep in your mind. For after it all happened, I thought she had planned it all. That although she helped us—I cannot deny that—she wanted something in return.

She wanted you. But it was too late when I realised that . . . you were gone.

I DID NOT KNOW until I had come home from school what it was that Mama had done. I came home and found her sitting in the *sala*. I thought nothing of it as I went upstairs. Maybe Celia or Laura was with you. Sometimes they stayed with you so Mama could have a rest.

I turned the corner to my room. It was then I noticed the emptiness that lay beyond the open door. And the quiet. I looked inside. The room was suddenly big again. Uncluttered. No baby things, no clothes, no little toys, no crib. But unlike the time with the piano, I did not remain silent.

Celia came out of the bedroom we shared just as I was about to go back downstairs.

"Ligaya . . . Ligaya . . . don't . . ."

I pushed her arm away and rushed down the stairs.

I said many awful things to Mama. I shouted at her, my anger finally finding an outlet. All my anger, all the sad, awful, painful, hateful feelings finally poured out of me.

"Where is she? Where is the baby? . . . What did you do with her?"

"I gave her away, Ligaya . . . to your Tia Thelma."

"Why?"

"Can you not see I cannot do anything more for her . . . We have nothing . . . I have nothing to offer her. Your Tia Thelma will give her everything she will ever need . . . She will raise her as her own, love her."

"How can you give your child away?" I screamed at her, "Your own blood! . . . What kind of a mother are you? . . . You're weak and because you are weak, she will never know us, she will never know her father . . . Papa will never forgive you!"

Mama said nothing. She looked tired and defeated. And I remember her eyes. They glistened. I had hurt her and I had wanted to.

Angry words, once out of your mouth, march on and you cannot call them back. There was a lot of anger inside me. Like bad cells, my anger grew and spread and turned into madness. So when I came home and found you gone, I said many ugly things in madness. The same madness that made me do what I did next.

I did not sleep that night. When the skies lightened with the first signs of dawn, I rose quietly and quickly began to change. Celia, who slept next to me, woke. Rubbing the sleep from her eyes, she turned to see me dressing.

"Where are you going, Ligaya?"

"Sssh . . . you will wake the others."

She sat up and watched me.

"Are you mad? Mama will be furious when she finds out you've left the house. You're not running away, are you?"

"I'll be gone long before she wakes."

"Gone where? . . . Ligaya, where are you going?"

"To Manila. I am going to get her back."

Celia stared at me.

"But . . . but Tia Thelma has her."

"I'll tell her to give the baby back."

Then I went and got my purse and counted my money. I hoped it would be enough. I put my purse in my skirt pocket and made for the door.

"Say you did not see me leave . . . that you don't know anything."

Celia pulled me back.

"Here," she said, pushing some change into my hands, the little money she had, "take this just in case . . . you may need more."

Before I could say anything, she pushed me out of the door. "Go, quick . . . before Mama wakes. And, Ligaya, good luck."

I went down the steps on my bare feet, putting my shoes on only when I reached the front door. Opening that door was more difficult than getting out of my bedroom, for the door squeaked and Mama's room lay right above. It was not a time for being faint-hearted. Rather than opening it slowly and letting it squeak every inch of the way, I swung it open with one sudden move. I was out of the house. Then, with the same force, I swung it towards me, stopping only before the lock clicked into place. This I did gently. With the door shut behind me, I ran towards the bus station.

I took the first bus leaving for Manila. As I sat there waiting impatiently for it to depart, I tried to calm myself, saying over and over again that Mama would not wake for another hour. And even if she had heard me, she would still need to dress. And she would have to get the truth out of my sisters before she could find me. Celia, I hoped, would say she didn't know of my plans. If she did not wilt under Mama's questioning, I would leave Olongapo safely.

The engine of the bus came alive, loud and sputtering as the driver started it. I sat there in silence, willing the engine to warm up, willing the driver to go, to get the bus moving. After a few minutes, the bus moved forward with a jerk. I gazed out of my window, searching for a familiar face, my mother's face, knowing if she was coming, it would be from that direction.

A *calesa* came into view but it was impossible to see its passenger. So whether it was a man or a woman I could not tell. The *kuchero* raised his whip and snapped it in quick succession against the side bar. The *calesa* gathered speed as the horse's hooves bore down on the road. The man's voice rang out. "Wait!" The bus driver turned his head and, catching sight of the racing *calesa*, slammed his foot on the brakes. The bus came to a halt in the middle of the street.

"Please, please don't let it be Mama," I silently pleaded.

The sounds from outside the bus were dulled by the rumbling of the bus engine. And though I dared not look, I strained my ears to catch the voices from outside, but all I could hear was the *kuchero*'s voice. A few moments later, the sound of someone boarding the bus could be heard. I looked down at the floor but out of the corner of my eye I could just make out the figure of a woman approaching the back of the bus where I sat frozen.

She stopped right where I was. I looked up to see her heave a heavy bag on the rack over my head. She smiled at me apologetically before taking the seat next to mine. I smiled at her weakly. The bus then jerked forward, finally making its way up the street, heading for the road to Manila.

THE HOUSE IN SANTA Cruz was not difficult to find. I had been there several times with Mama. It was one of the bigger houses on the street. A big wooden, creamy-coloured house surrounded by flowering shrubs. You entered through an ornate grille gate painted white. Following a paved path, you reached a central set of tiled steps that led up to a front verandah. Here, you could sit on a cane chair and gaze down at the small front garden.

Inside was a spacious *sala* at least twice the size of ours in Olongapo. The floorboards were different, too. They were wider and somehow gleamed with a richness ours never seemed to have. The ceiling was higher and the lights more ornate. The windows were decorated with iron grilles that curved out at the bottom and had rows of pot plants sitting on them. It was this that I liked best whenever I was outside looking in: the pot plants with their rich foliage curled around the intricate grillework.

But the darkness I did not like. Tia Thelma's house was big and dark. I liked houses that were bright and airy for light to me spelt a happy mood. Like our house. I always compared this house to ours. This was a sad house. She had taken the baby to fill it with laughter.

I heard footsteps on the stairs and I instantly felt my chest tighten. I waited for her. No longer feeling as confident as when I first sneaked out of the house at dawn.

"Ligaya," she greeted me, a wary look in her eyes, "why are you here? Does your mother know you are here?"

Ignoring her questions, I said, "I have come to take her back . . . I have come to take the baby."

"Sit down, Ligaya, sit down and we'll talk about it. Have you eaten at all? I'll have Rosa make you something."

I remained standing, refusing to be swayed by her apparent kindness. "I don't want anything . . . Just give me the baby and I shall leave."

She sighed. "Ligaya, Emma probably did not explain the situation to you . . . so let me talk to you about it."

"There's nothing to talk about, I am taking her back. Mama had no right to give her away, she is our sister, she is Papa's child."

"Your mama and I discussed this, Ligaya. It is what is best for everyone concerned."

"I was not asked."

"It is not for you to decide . . . It is your mother's decision."

"Mama does not know anything. She is weak."

"How can you say that? Can you not see how hard things have been for her?"

"Weak . . . she's weak . . . She let you take the baby."

She put her hand on my shoulder but I pushed it away. Then I made for the stairs. She ran after me but I reached the top first. I flung the first door open but it was empty.

"Ligaya, what do you think you're doing?"

The maid, hearing the commotion in the hall, emerged from the main bedroom, the baby in her arms.

I quickened my steps and moved towards her. She twisted away from my reach and Tia Thelma came from behind, grabbing me and trying not to raise her voice. She kept saying, "Stop it, Ligaya, please stop it."

But anger and frustration gave me a strength I did not know I possessed. Afraid that the baby would be hurt, the maid, looking helpless, surrendered her to me.

"Get out of my way!" I shouted at both of them. "I am taking her back and you can't stop me."

You began to cry. Just a soft whimper. I turned to go with you in my arms. I had reached the door when Tia Thelma said, "Take her then and she will starve."

"We will manage."

She laughed.

She was shrewd and I was stupid. If I had only ignored her and walked out of the house, I would have succeeded in getting you back. But I stopped and that was all she needed.

"Manage? How do you think you will manage? There is nothing else to sell, Ligaya."

"We have managed so far . . . just leave us alone."

"If I had done that, you would have starved long ago. There would have been no food on the table. If I were to leave you alone, you would have no roof over your head. You look at me with disbelief, go ask your mother.

"And your sister, you want her back? Take her. But ask yourself this. What will you feed her? How will you clothe her? What life can you give her? Remember this day and how much she could have had. Remember, too, how much all of you could have gained."

"What do you mean?"

She did not answer.

"What did you mean by that?"

"I had an agreement with your mother, Ligaya, something you were not supposed to know about. But I will tell you, you arrogant child, so you may know the foolishness of your actions. I promised your mother I would take your sister and care for her like my own. I would give her everything. She would inherit all that I have. And in return, I promised to help your mother in whatever way I can. I would help provide for all of you."

"All this for a child?"

"No, there's more. I demand everyone's silence. The child must never know."

I looked at her with disgust. "My mother sold her . . . and you bought her."

"Think of it any way you want," she countered, "it

does not change the fact that I can afford to pay. Now, Ligaya, you have to decide. Will you stick by the agreement I made with your mother or break it, take the child . . . and nothing else."

I stood there with you in my arms, you were crying loudly now, and I did not know how to make you stop, and I did not know what I was supposed to do, or why I ever came in the first place. I asked myself what was right and what was wrong but I no longer knew. Spurred by my anger I was determined to return home with you. But now I wondered what it was I was taking you home to.

I walked slowly towards her, our eyes locked, and I gave you to her.

"Don't think," I told her, saying the words slowly so she would not miss a single syllable, "don't think for a minute that she is yours. You may have paid for her but you cannot keep what is not rightfully yours."

She flinched and I walked out of the room, out of her house, and I swore never to set foot there again.

THE NEXT SEVEN YEARS of my life I would not wish on anybody. We moved back to Manila, to an old small dark one-storey apartment near the San Lazaro race tracks. We stayed in this sorry-looking place for the first six years. It had a tiny front room where we sat and ate and a tiny back room where we all slept. Next to this was a narrow kitchen, half the width of that already narrow apartment. The other half was an open area that served as a laundry.

Because our apartment was between other apartments, it had only two windows, one on each end of the unit. They were so small, little light came through, and the interior was always hot and humid. To brighten up the place, Celia and Laura collected calendars with pictures of foreign places. They cut these and pasted them against pieces of cardboard then taped them onto the walls. The only other ornament in the front room was a table lamp; the base was the figure of a dog in a dull, olive green colour with streaks of gold. The dog itself had a chipped nose and the plaster underneath was discoloured. A brass pole ran through the figure of the dog and held the olive green lampshade. Switched on, it cast a sickly green hue over the room.

To make curtains, Mama made us cut up the pages of dozens of old colour magazines she collected from the neighbours. Thousands of three-square-inch pieces of paper sat in a box. Every night for several weeks, we sat in the dark front room and rolled these pieces of paper up. "Tightly, make sure they are rolled tightly," Mama kept saying. Then the boys ran some paste over the edge of the paper as we held the roll between our fingers. We made sure we left a hole in the centre big enough to thread a thin string through. In between each piece of rolled paper was a colored bead. And at the end of each completed string—the length of the curtain—we placed an even bigger round bead. All the strings were then looped onto a curtain rod on one end. A curtain at last. The passage leading to the kitchen had a ten foot curtain of stringed paper. Every time someone walked through, the beads made a soft rustling sound.

It was impossible to sleep in our room. At night, all seven of us crammed into that small windowless bedroom. Even with the door left open, little air found its way in. Mama, Celia, Laura, Mia and I slept on two beds that stood against each other. The boys slept on *kapok* mattresses they unrolled on the floor each night. When the heat became unbearable in summer, they would sleep on the floor in the front room.

We had no money. I never asked Mama how the rent and the bills were paid and where the food came from. Or how we could afford our school fees. And whose idea it was to send me to secretarial school.

I spent six months learning to type and take shorthand. After I completed the course, an old friend of Papa's gave me my first job.

I typed for a living, earning a hundred and twenty pesos a month. I turned everything over to my mother. All I ever got back was my daily fare to and from work. This she gave me each night before I went to bed.

I had few clothes. Two skirts and three blouses. So every evening, I would wash what I had worn that day so it would be dry and ready to wear the day after next. On the rare occasion Mama gave me money to buy something new, I would pay a girlfriend at work for her old clothes. I would sew on a bow here, some buttons there, add a bit of lace maybe, to make it look different. But it did not lessen the shame I felt for having to wear something that had obviously been worn by someone else.

At work, I kept to myself. I could not join the others for lunch when they went out once a week to a restaurant. I could not afford it. Mama always prepared my *baon*. It was never much and of little variety. Rice with salted eggs and tomatoes most of the time. I refuse to have salted eggs today. The sight of them reminds me of those days. In the beginning, the other office girls kept asking me to join them but they eventually tired of asking. They may even have thought I was *suplada* and disliked their company. They never knew how much I envied them as they walked off together while I stayed behind to eat lunch on my own. Poverty made friendship beyond my reach.

Those years taught me to swallow my pride and bite my tongue. One day flowed into the next and there was little that happened to set each day apart. I worked, I came home, I worked.

THERE IS A DREAM I dreamed many times in those years. A nightmare. It came to me the night I came home from the carnival.

It was December. During the Christmas season, they always had rides and games and many stalls at the Luneta. I had gone to the carnival with Celia and Laura. We did not go on many rides as we only had a few pesos between us. Instead, we walked around the park, licking our fingers clean of the sugar that had stuck to them. We'd treated ourselves to a huge pink fluff of cotton candy.

There was loud blaring music which competed with the voices that came through the many megaphones. The men who spoke into them called to the many curious passersby and ogling children, luring them to the many wonders within.

"Come and see the legless woman . . . the spineless man."

"Inside . . . the man with two heads will be shown to you . . . Come and see this amazing man."

"Freak shows," Laura said, making a face.

We walked past a little tent. Celia giggled and pointed to the sign. "Your palms read, your future told in thirty minutes."

She nudged me.

"It's a waste of money," I told her. "Besides, they're all fakes."

"How do you know? Come on, let's go in . . . just for fun."

Laura, always following Celia's lead, said, "We'll all go. But you go first. You're the eldest."

The tent was stuffy. A short, fat candle with melted wax all around it was stuck on a rusty metal lid that stood at the centre of a small table. There were two seats opposite each other.

"Sit down . . . Sit down . . ." the old, toothless

crone said. Her breath was rancid. And when she took my right hand and turned it palm up, I saw the black dirt that lay under her long, unfiled nails, with the chipped red polish.

She pointed to a line on my palm. Tracing it with her finger, she said, "Work . . . you are working?"

I nodded.

"You like working?"

I shrugged.

"You will work and work and work. Pray you learn to like it for it is your life."

Then she grinned at me and I felt myself swallowed into the black gap of her toothless mouth. I remember little of what she said after that.

That night, the dream came to me.

I was in my typing class. And the teacher said, "Very good, Ligaya, very good."

My fingers danced over the keys of my typewriter.

"Look at Ligaya, class, look at Ligaya type."

My fingers flew across the keyboard.

"Ligaya has hands made for typing," she told the class as they all stopped to watch me type.

"Her fingers are nimble and quick like the hands of a pianist. She types like a pianist."

The keys started to make music.

"Did you hear that, class?" The teacher's voice boomed across the room, like a person speaking into a mega-phone. "Ligaya makes music with her fingers on the keyboard."

My fingers gathered speed. And the music became a crazy tune like the music that played when the merry-go-round turned. Only it played faster and faster. And I watched in horror as my hands moved on their own, the fingers tapping away like they were powered by batteries, and I could not make them stop even when my mind screamed at them to Stop! Stop! Stop!

And all the while, the teacher kept telling the class to "Watch Ligaya, see how fast her fingers can go . . ."

Celia shook me awake. "You were typing in your sleep," she said.

THE FORTUNE TELLER DID not lie. For seven years I did nothing but work. The first four years were the hardest, for I was the only one bringing money in. Then Celia started to work part-time while studying accounting at Santo Tomas. Two years later, Laura finished school and found a job. With three incomes, we were finally able to provide for ourselves. Together we took over paying the rent, our bills and the boys' and Mia's school fees. Then we managed to move to a small two-storey apartment. It was old too, but compared to the first one, it was an improvement. The extra level gave us some breathing space.

Then I met Enrique. I was twenty-two. One day, he came to the office where I worked to sign some papers for a property he had just bought from my boss. He wore a dark grey suit that suited his serious look and his quiet manner. I had heard my boss mention his name on many occasions but had never felt any curiosity about him.

"If you'll just take a seat, Mr. Limhengco won't be long . . . he knows you're here," I said to Enrique. But instead of sitting on one of the comfortable armchairs, he stood in front of my desk and asked politely when I had begun working there for he had never seen me before. We talked for a few minutes until my boss came out to lead Enrique into his office. I thought no more of him after that. To me he was just a client.

But Enrique came again a few days later. He began to woo me, coming into the office on one pretext or another. My boss teased me, saying, "Well, Ligaya, I think it was a lucky day when I hired you. At the rate someone keeps coming here, why, I may just sell him a few more properties before he sweeps you off to the altar!"

One morning the phone rang and it was Enrique on the line. I said my boss was in and that I'd put his call through, but he said it wasn't him he wanted to speak to but me. He said he would love to take me out to lunch that day. I felt a sense of panic. I was not dressed to go out to anywhere fancy. He must have sensed my reluctance.

"Have I caught you at an inconvenient time, Ligaya? If so, I apologise."

"Oh, it's . . . it's not that. It's just that I'm not really dressed to . . ."

"To go out to lunch? Why, I don't think the owner of that small restaurant in Escolta will refuse to let you and me in. There's no sign at the door that says black tie and formal gowns only, or is it me you're embarrassed to be seen with? I promise you I'll dress neatly."

I laughed and stammered out my acceptance. "Well, yes . . . I mean . . . yes, I'd love to have lunch with you."

"I'll come for you at five past twelve, is that all right with you?"

I ran to the ladies' room at twelve noon and quickly combed my hair and straightened out my skirt. I kept thinking how unglamorous I looked. No make-up on my face. Not even a touch of lip colour. I was so nervous. I didn't want to embarrass him.

Enrique arrived promptly at five past twelve with a bunch of red roses for me. I turned as red as the petals of the roses for before I could say thank you, the door to Mr. Limhengco's office opened and my boss stepped out. Seeing Enrique standing next to me with me holding a big bunch of flowers, my boss broke into a huge grin. I could feel myself burning in the face. Only Enrique seemed relaxed and unperturbed by everything.

"Well, Ligaya, better put those in a vase before they wilt," said Mr. Limhengco. "Can't have them wilting now can we. There's a spare vase in my office just under the side shelf. Go on, *hija* . . ."

I gave Enrique a glance and rushed off. When I had finished arranging the flowers, I came back to join him and my boss.

"Well, I shall not delay you two. Have a nice lunch and, Ligaya . . ."

"Yes, Mr. Limhengco?"

"I shall be back late so don't rush Enrique here to finish his lunch . . . you two have a nice time."

With that he left. Enrique escorted me out of our office on the seventh floor and as we walked towards the elevators I found myself standing next to my officemates. I could have died right then. For it was easy to see what thoughts were going through their minds. And, as is often the case in life, you don't get what you want when you want it. I wanted the elevator to arrive quickly so Enrique and I could get away from everyone's curious looks, but it took ages coming. Maybe it wasn't as slow as it seemed, but I was counting the seconds. When we finally got into the elevator it was to find ourselves crushed against each other. Enrique stood right behind me. Tall and self-assured, I found his presence comforting. I can't say I was excited about going to lunch with him. He was not only much older but also more worldly. I was terrified of doing something wrong.

"Do you mind if we just walk, Ligaya, it will be quicker than waiting for a ride?" he asked in that deep quiet voice of his.

"No . . . not at all," I replied, glad for the chance to collect myself. It would have been awkward in the taxi. I would not have known what to say.

The restaurant was a small cosy place, not daunting as I had expected it to be. It specialised in seafood. Enrique ordered crabs and prawns and I remember wondering how I could eat the food without making a big mess. Crabs and prawns are so messy to eat. But I need not have worried for when the food came and I picked up my fork and knife, Enrique said, "I don't know about you, Ligaya, but I am using my hands. It's quicker and more fun. And besides, if you insist on eating properly you will take forever and there won't be any left for you!"

I couldn't help laughing. A lot of the tension I was feeling disappeared. I put down my fork and picked up the crab claw he had placed on my plate. I enjoyed my meal. I cannot say, though, that I was able to relax totally. Every time Enrique asked me a question—he asked many questions about me and what I liked doing and about my family and how Mama was and what my sisters were doing and how the boys were—every time I had to answer them I thought carefully, phrasing my words so as not to cause disapproval or censure. It sounds strange, I know, but I wanted his approval. He, in turn, told me about himself, though it was nothing I did not know already. Mr. Limhengco, my boss, often gave me a rundown of the clients we dealt with. So I was aware that Enrique had studied in the States and had a degree in engineering from MIT and was a self-made man who owned a lot of real estate. He was in his early thirties. What was new to me was that he was the second of two sons and that his brother was living in the States. His mother passed away a few years ago and his father, on the death of his wife, moved back to Cebu where he had been born. Enrique had a sister who had three children he loved to spoil. He said he was fond of children and would like to have a family of his own. To that I said nothing, although I could feel my face heat up again.

At the end of our meal, the waiter brought two bowls filled with warm water with a *calamansi* in each. I followed Enrique's example and dipped my fingers in it. He paid for lunch and walked me back to the office. I thanked him politely.

It was the first of many lunches we had together. Mama began to question me as to why I was not eating my *baon* which she prepared for me every morning.

"You must stop working at lunch and eat. Surely, Mr. Limhengco does not expect you to starve yourself."

Not long after this, Mama was to realise what I had been doing for lunch because Enrique brought me home after work one day. I remember how embarrassed I was then. He drove me home in his car and, as we passed the streets of my neighbourhood, it struck me as to how poor the whole place looked. You can live in a place and get so used to it that its ugliness no longer bothers you. But that day I saw the place as if for the first time. I saw it with his eyes. I was very silent in the car and I could feel him glance at me several times. When he finally pulled up in front of our apartment, I thanked him and slowly got out.

"Aren't you going to ask me in?" he said.

I hesitated before answering, "Maybe another time."

"Is it because your mama won't like me?"

"No . . . no, it's not that."

"Because if it is, I don't scare easily, Ligaya," he said with a gentle smile.

In the end, I asked him in. He looked out of place sitting in that dimly lit, small front room in his expensive suit. I imagined how it must have appeared to him. Dark, drab and depressing. But he did not seem to notice.

When Mama came out to meet him, he stood up, greeting her courteously. He spent a long time talking to her. I watched with wonder as he drew Mama out, making her speak with ease, listening to her with genuine interest as she told him of the old days, the neighbourhood, the increasing noise the passing jeeps made. She stayed longer than I expected, then realising the time, quickly excused herself to go and prepare our meal.

"I would ask you to stay for dinner but I have not prepared anything special . . . but if you do not mind a simple meal, you are welcome to stay," Mama said to him.

Enrique thanked her for the invitation but politely declined it, saying his sister expected him at her home for dinner. "Another day then," Mama replied, relieved yet disappointed, like me, that he was leaving.

I did not think he would ask me out again. For if he could not see before how we belonged in different worlds, surely he could not be blind to it now. I appreciated, though, how he had gone out of his way to make everyone feel at ease. In a way, I felt sad I would no longer be seeing him. But the following day, to my surprise, he came to take me to lunch again. And, after that, when he couldn't come, he would call to ask how I was.

The girls in the office began to tease me and look at me with envy. "Ligaya," one of them said to me in the ladies' room, "that's a big fish you've got on the line. Reel him in before he escapes. And in case you're silly enough to let him go, I'll have him."

Then one day, a few weeks after he had first driven me home, Enrique asked if Mama would mind if he came to visit on Sunday.

Mama cooked as she had not cooked in a long time.

"We're having a fiesta, are we?" said the boys on seeing Mama busy in the kitchen.

Enrique arrived an hour before lunch, bringing with him kilos of sweet *lanzones* which were in season and a box of imported chocolates for Mama. He chatted amiably with everyone, and over the meal praised Mama for her cooking. By the end of his visit, he had won everyone over. Before he left, Mia gave him her cheek to kiss—that fussy child, who always wiped her face with the back of her hand every time someone kissed her.

Soon Enrique became a regular addition to our Sunday meals. How Mama took to him. "If only for this reason," Celia said to me one night, "if only to put Mama in a good mood, we should have Enrique come every day."

One Sunday after lunch we piled into his car—a gleaming black Chevy—and Mama and I squeezed into the front passenger seat next to him. How we fitted in I cannot imagine. There was much laughing and screaming but he seemed to enjoy it all. He drove us to Balara where we strolled along the dam walls and gazed down at the water in the reservoir, then he drove us to the University of the Philippines, where the boys attempted to climb the Oblation—you know the one, the statue of the naked man with his arms spread out like wings and his head tilted up towards the sky. Enrique took pictures of us all afternoon.

That night when it was just Mama and me left in the *sala* she said to me, "He is a good man, Ligaya, your papa would have approved of him."

I HAD ANOTHER SUITOR then, you did not know that, did you? Yes, there was someone else who was in love with me.

His name was Leandro. He was a nice man, much younger than Enrique; we were closer in age. He was tall and lean and handsome with a fine moustache like Errol Flynn. We worked in the same office. He was a clerk in the accounts department. All the girls at work had a crush on him. They would find one excuse after another to walk past his desk. So I was flattered that he singled me out. We got on well and he often chatted to me on the way out of the office.

After work one afternoon, he accompanied me home. I introduced him to Mama. She sat with us and asked him questions. She was not rude to him but I could tell she did not like him as much as Enrique. Maybe if Enrique had never come into my life and Mama had never met him, she would have approved of Leandro. That day he came to visit, he did not stay long for it was difficult to talk with Mama sitting there complaining of a headache. He left soon after and though he would visit again every now and then, nothing ever came of it.

Leandro and Enrique knew about each other. But neither ever discussed the other with me. There was one occasion, you see, when Leandro had offered to walk me to my *jeepney* stop after work and Enrique had driven past in his car. Our eyes met and he nodded at me. The next day he rang soon after I arrived at the office and said he would take me home after work. He came promptly at five in the afternoon, but all the way home in his car he never asked about the young man I had been with the afternoon before, the man I had chatted to so animatedly. I still remember how Leandro and I laughed and joked as we walked to the *jeepney* stop in a way I never laughed and joked with Enrique. But Enrique was persistent where Leandro was not. In the end, Leandro left.

Leandro left many things unsaid. He dared not speak. He was aware of who Enrique was. Because he knew he had so much less to offer than my other suitor, Leandro thought himself undeserving of my affection. Oh, if he had only spoken, how the course of my life could have changed! Although I was aware of my responsibilities to my family, I was also a young woman who dreamed of love and romance.

See this medallion I wear on this chain? The silver is slightly tarnished but you can still make out the image of Our Lady of Lourdes. It is a remembrance gift. He gave it to me before he left for the States. There were many unsaid things between us and I often wonder what course my life would have taken had we given voice to them. Leandro left three months before I married Enrique. He did not return. He decided to stay on and live in Chicago, I heard from one of my officemates whom he had written to. We lost touch.

Then, ten years later, I received a surprise phone call from him. He said he wanted to see me, he was on a short visit to Manila. He asked about me, Enrique and the children. Could he meet my family, he asked.

Enrique, the children and I took him out to dinner. We met him at the restaurant. He had presents for the girls. Leandro had not married. In the States he lived alone. Was he lonely for home, I wanted to know. I do not remember if he answered my question.

Lying next to me that night, Enrique said, "Marrying you was the best thing I ever did in my life, Ligaya. I only hope I have not been selfish in doing so. You are happy are you not, Ligaya, you are . . . content?"

I reached out and took his hand and whispered to him, "Yes . . . yes, Enrique, I am. I have never regretted marrying you." I heard him sigh and I wished I knew how to ease his pain. I could not bring myself to say, "Everyone has dreams when they are young but they are just dreams and I do not know if I would be any happier had they come true . . . Leandro was a dream of long ago."

One afternoon, two years after that dinner, I sat in front of my dressing table and cleared out my drawers. I found this medallion in an old silk pouch. A few days later, I received word of his passing. Leandro had died of cancer. Only then did I find out that he had been fighting it even before his visit. The day I heard the news, I took this medallion out. I have worn it ever since. And talking to you now, it has just occurred to me that if I had married him, I would have been widowed early like my mother . . . How similar our lives would have been.

But it was Enrique I married. He changed my life. And my family's. There has been nothing I have wanted for since. And if you asked me now if I could change anything in my life would I change this . . . would I rather be with someone else, all I can say is I would be very sad if Enrique were to disappear from my life. It is funny to realise only at this moment, after being with him for so long, how much I like having him come home to me. I love him, you know, in a warm, quiet way. And look at me, Caridad, at what I have become: a person no longer afraid and haunted by nightmares. He made all this possible.

SO YOU SEE, SURELY you must see, there was no room for a child in those times. One airless, dark apartment. A sad place from which to see the world. Had I not left you with Tia Thelma, you would have grown up in that place, you would have had seven years of nothing.

Though I was angry at Mama and Tia Thelma, they were right in their own way. But I had no way of knowing that until I had lived through those years.

I called Mama weak. But now I realise it takes courage, the ability to bear pain, to give away one's child. In the hospital, when they put Clarise in my arms soon after I gave birth to her, I realised what it was to love a child. And how a part of you must die when you must give that child away. I should tell Mama this. I must remember to tell her so she does not think I still think her weak. I must tell her she was brave.

As for what Tia Thelma did for us, I cannot deny that she provided for us during those years, but then again, it was not as if she did it for nothing. After all, she got you in return. I know I should not be so hard and ungrateful, but that is how I feel. No point hiding it. I have never tried to, I will not start now. Mama says I must forget my differences with Tia Thelma. Maybe she is right. I can't change the past. Nothing can. And this is all I have to say.

THE SUN LIES LOW on the horizon, sinking behind the Marikina Valley in the distance, its red, yellow and orange rays tint the skies in the land of the longest sunset. The afternoon is almost gone. The air is cooler and a soft breeze rustles through the leaves, stirring the crickets awake so they begin their crispy chirping. There is a hint of the moon already, a new moon. I have always found this a strange sight. The impatient moon unable to wait for the sun to leave before taking over the skies.

I am all spent. It is like living those years again in just a few hours. Time, I find, has taken most of the pain away.

In recounting the past to her, I have finally given voice to the many things I have kept inside.

Maybe I can tell my story to my children at last. For every time they have asked, I have always given just the bare facts. "My papa died after the war. We returned to Manila. A few years later, I met your papa." Just the bare facts.

It was not just the pain I feared, you see. It was the shame. I was never sure I acted rightly, that I chose unselfishly. But now that I look at her and how well her life has been, maybe I did the right thing after all.

The truth is, when I returned home without her, I felt I, too, had sold her, exchanged her for the security Tia Thelma had promised. I felt no better than the rest of them, than Mama and Tia Thelma.

She stands to leave. It is late she says and she thanks me for my time. I look at her and I say I hope I have told you all you needed to know. She smiles at me and nods. And there is a look in her eyes. I try to read what her eyes are saying. But it is not until later, after the car has pulled away and I return to my garden, that I understand. It is not with words that I understand, but with a feeling. Her eyes, so like my father's, her eyes spoke with kindness and understanding.

I am forgiven at last.

THELMA

"He cheated . . .

he had another woman."

Tomorrow could not come quickly enough. Tomorrow I was to be married to Raoul. I sat on my bed looking at my wedding *terno* that flowed down from a clothes hanger Mama had hung on to the upper corner of a wardrobe door. It was of the finest silk beautifully hand-embroidered with a floral pattern. My veil was of a thin lace fabric that reached just down to my back. It came from Spain, given to me by my godmother for my wedding. Not too long. Mama said long veils do not bring good luck, they are like the heavy burdens you must drag through life. So I had a short veil.

"And this you wear tomorrow," she said, handing me a necklace with a diamond pendant.

"But the pearls will go better with my *terno*."

"No, no, no . . ." she said with a violent shake of her head, "no pearls . . . pearls are not *suerte*, not lucky for a bride. They bring tears. You must wear this instead. This is a good stone, not big, but a good stone, and feel the chain . . . this is real gold . . . twenty-four carat . . . very heavy. You must look your best to-morrow."

I understood what Mama meant. Tomorrow everyone would be looking at me, everyone from Raoul's side. His relatives and his friends will all be looking to see who it is he has chosen for his bride. They will think me fortu-nate to be marrying so well. Some of them will look at me with envy. I must not shame him. But most impor-tant, I must not shame my parents.

"Sleep early. You don't want dark circles around your eyes. But first, go and say goodnight to your papa. It will be the last time you sleep in his house."

I found him in my parents' bedroom where he liked to retire soon after dinner. He was in bed reading, reclining against his many pillows. When I entered, he looked up and smiled at me, then he removed his eyeglasses and motioned to me to come and sit by him on the bed.

"Ahhh, Thelma . . . tomorrow I will give you away. You will take a new name."

"I will still be your daughter, Papa. And you know I will come often to visit."

He nodded. After a moment he said, "You leave this house tomorrow but you must not forget where you came from. You must remember your family. Do you understand my meaning, Thelma?

"I will tell you how my own father explained it to me when I was only half your age. He said a family is like a house that stands on four poles, and the poles are the members of the family—you and your sisters and brother. If one pole is strong but the others are weak, the house will not stand. Even if three poles are strong but one rots away, the house will fall one day. For the house to stand, all four poles must be strong and straight. So for this family to stand, all of you must do well. It is not enough that you do well. That is my meaning, Thelma. You are marrying well but you must remember your sisters and your brother. When a person is given more, it is so he can give more to others."

"I understand, Papa."

He patted my hand as I bent to give him a kiss on the cheek. Then he took my face between his two hands and kissed me on the forehead.

"God bless you, *hija*."

RAOUL AND I WERE not blessed. The signs were there for all to see that we would not be blessed. The signs were there on the day we wed.

The wedding was held at San Sebastian Church in Manila. You remember the church with the spires? Remember your papa and I used to take you there? I think because he built buildings himself, he found that church interesting.

"Three other churches stood here before this one. All three were damaged by earthquakes. Then they built this. It is the only one of its kind in the country. It was shipped all the way from Belgium in eight ships, in many separate panels of steel—50,000 tons in all—which were put together when they arrived here. It can survive earthquakes better than any other church in the country." He never tired of telling me this. His eyes would shine. He loved saying the words "eight ships, 50,000 tons." To him, facts, numbers, contained magic. They interested him. Your papa was like that. So it was at San Sebastian that we married. I liked the church, too, because it looked like a cathedral but it was not dark like the Manila Cathedral. He explained to me, "It is neo-Gothic in design." He understood these things.

There were over five hundred people at our wedding and even more came to the reception. Your papa, you see, came from a good family. They were in construction and knew many important people. He was also the eldest and the only son. So his parents wanted our wedding to be a big affair.

My wedding was the envy of all my friends, even my sisters. In those days, more than now, people married within their class. The rich married the rich so family fortunes could increase through marriage. It was rare that a wealthy man or woman married someone of a lower class. Most of these marriages were arranged between families and even if they were not, because the small circle of wealthy people kept to themselves they ended up marrying one of their kind. So when people found out I was to marry Raoul, it was news indeed. Mama and Papa were so proud I had made a good match. Of course, my godmother, my Ninang Lorena, says it was because of her that Raoul and I met. She tells the truth for it was to her that Mama turned for help.

Mama thought I would never marry. I was twenty-two and in those days women married as early as seventeen or eighteen, so my parents started to fear I would be an old maid. When Mama mentioned her fears to my Ninang Lorena she promised Mama she would do something about it.

"Do not worry, I will find her someone suitable."

True to her word, she found your papa.

"He's the son of a friend I grew up with. He is intelligent and well-educated. An engineer . . . comes from a good Chinese family. Both parents are from old, wealthy clans. The mother—my friend—her family originally came from central China. Her mother was the daughter of a mandarin, a court official. So my friend was brought up in the old way. She is very Chinese. That is the only thing you must think about carefully—whether Thelma can live in such a household. For she will certainly not be allowed to move out. My friend's husband will not be a problem. He does not meddle in the house. He runs the business . . . and is very shrewd when it comes to money. The family construction business is one of the biggest in Manila. Though he is Chinese, he mixes with many Filipinos and Españols. He is wise enough to realise it is good for business. They mix with all the right people. The son—Raoul—from what I have seen of him is sophisticated, very suave and *guapo* . . . yes, he is handsome. Though quite dark for a Chinese. But that is not bad in a man."

Ninang Lorena was sure my parents would approve of the man she had found for me. After all, he was pure Chinese and had a good background. And though my family had taken on many Filipino ways, my parents still preferred us to marry only into Chinese families. The Spanish were the same, wanting only their own kind. The Filipinos, being more easygoing, were more tolerant of mixed marriages.

My parents trusted Ninang Lorena. They knew she would not introduce someone unless he was from a good family. They showed their interest. And far from being upset by their matchmaking, I found myself curious about this man.

I met him at the fiesta. Ninang Lorena had invited his family to her house that Sunday. Mama arranged for us to visit in the afternoon for some *merienda*. Papa did not come with us for that would be showing too much interest on our part. It was not good to appear too eager.

The night before, I brought out my best dress and my prettiest fan. Mama had bought me a new pair of *sapatilyas* to wear. My hair I washed and brushed till it shone. Mama put it up for me with her *payneta*, a carved ivory piece that shone against my dark hair.

"We must not shame your Ninang," she said, "you must go looking your best."

Raoul had his back turned to us when we entered my godmother's house so he did not see the look that passed between her and Mama. From somewhere, Raoul's mother appeared and was introduced to mine. Then it was my turn. She did not smile, just looked at me, her eyes missing nothing. You know how you carefully check out fish or chicken in the market? That was what she was doing. I did not like that. I returned her gaze. I looked her in the eye. A look of surprise came over her face. She nodded and something like a smile formed on her lips. Then she turned to introduce me to her son.

Raoul did not miss this exchange between his mother and me for when he acknowledged me, his eyes danced with laughter. That soon turned to surprise as well when I boldly sized him up. Then, like his mother had done to me, I nodded to signal that he had passed my inspection.

I felt Mama stiffen next to me. She scolded me all the way home. "How will you ever find a husband if you act like that . . . like . . . like a hussy? You must be shy, say little and behave like a lady. You should never look at a man so boldly, never hold his gaze. You must look away. Now see what you've done. You have shocked his mother and scared him off. They will think I have not taught you well. Even your godmother will think that . . . How can I face your Ninang Lorena again? . . . What will your father say if he ever hears of this?"

"He will be back," I told Mama.

She looked at me with disbelief, shaking her head as if she thought I had gone mad. But I knew he would be back. And don't ask me what made me behave the way I did. I don't know. Perhaps it was my temper. Mama always said I was too fiery, too quick to take offence. Once she said I should have been born a man.

That night, I lay in bed and did not sleep much. I kept thinking about the afternoon just past. And the image of a man with laughter in his eyes.

A week passed with no news of him. And I began to think maybe Mama was right after all, that I had scared him away. That his mother did not think I was a suitable match for her son. That I did not measure up or come from a good family.

Another week came and was almost over when Ninang Lorena sent word to say that Raoul had expressed a wish to pay me a visit. Would my parents mind? Mama pretended indifference but was secretly relieved. My father gave his consent. And I spent another sleepless night thinking about the coming Sunday.

If the first meeting at my godmother's was awkward and embarrassing, it was nothing compared to the visit that followed at my parents' house. Mama and Papa never left the *sala*. I do not know if it was Mama's way of making sure I did not do anything unseemly again, but whatever the reason, we were never allowed a moment alone. Even my sisters suddenly felt it was a good time to read in the *sala* when they never liked reading at all. My brother was worse. Lito did nothing to hide his curiosity. He squatted on the floor in front of Raoul and stared up at him.

After two hours, Raoul took his leave but not before informing my father that he would be back the following Sunday. He did not ask Papa for permission but told him politely of his intentions.

Papa nodded.

Raoul returned week after week to spend an awkward Sunday afternoon with us. Then things began to change. He and Papa began to converse. It was my father that he engaged in long discussions, talking about business and politics, and this went on for weeks.

Later, much later, he would say to people, "It was not Thelma I wooed, but her father."

Then Mama, to my surprise, told him one day, "Come early next Sunday, come for lunch."

When Sunday came, Papa, for the first time, found something else to do and Mama busied herself in the kitchen. Only my sisters and little Lito stayed with us.

The first time Raoul and I went out together, my brother and sisters and our maid Conching came along. I had more chaperones than you can imagine. Raoul had asked Papa and Mama if he could accompany us on our Sunday afternoon *paseo*. Cars were not common in those days. We did a lot of walking. And the afternoon stroll was something we looked forward to. Sunday afternoon was the best time for a *paseo*. It was a very elegant thing to do. Women dressed in their best clothes and shoes and did up their hair. They came out to be admired. There was no rushing about. Everything was done at a leisurely pace. The ladies strolled about the tree-lined streets, and if there was a park nearby you can be sure it was filled with people going for their walk. It was a chance for men and women to meet.

Street vendors plied their goods. The man selling

sorbetes always pushed his little ice-cream cart along the lanes of the small park near our house. He would ring his little bell and cry, "*Sorbetes, sorbetes . . .*" There was much to choose from. There was the man with little packets of *nilagang mani.* I remember Raoul bought my brother, your Tio Lito, a big bag of these peanuts to keep him busy. While he shelled the nuts and ate them he left us alone. My sisters, of course, got their fingers all sticky from the pink, green and yellow cotton candies. Why, even the maid had something from Raoul. On the way home, he bought several kilos of *lanzones* because he knew Papa had a weakness for them.

Raoul's patience would be rewarded. Almost a year after he first met me, he asked Papa for my hand in marriage and Papa gave his consent.

THE RECEPTION WAS AT a big restaurant along Dewey Boulevard. It had glass doors all along one side, the side facing Manila Bay. It is no longer there. They pulled it down many years ago, even before the big hotels went up. Back then, Dewey Boulevard was where the famous restaurants and clubs could be found. Now everyone goes to Makati. Anyway, from the church all the guests headed for the restaurant for the wedding luncheon. It was not a *lauriat.* It was a Western style reception with long tables. Aside from their Chinese relatives and friends, Raoul's parents had invited many of their Filipino and Spanish business friends, so they decided against having a Chinese *lauriat*. The only Chinese touch to it were the red tablecloths.

After the reception we headed for our home. We did not live on our own for many years. We lived in the big house in Paco with his parents. One section of their house had been given to us. We would have our own room, a small study, *sala*, dining area and a small kitchen.

The furnishings were mostly provided by my dowry. Although my parents were not wealthy in the same way Raoul's parents were, we were comfortable. And being the first child to marry, my parents provided me with a respectable dowry. Part of this was in the form of jewellery. Mama gave me a jade pendant, very old, that had belonged to her mother, a pearl ring with matching earrings, and the diamond pendant I wore at my wedding. In this way, they made sure I would be treated well by my new family. I did not come empty-handed.

At Raoul's parents' house, everyone crowded around the dining room where bowls of noodles were brought out. Everyone ate the noodles, which had been cooked in a sweet soup; and with it everyone had an egg, which had been dyed pink, for good luck.

After the meal, we all headed towards our bedroom. And this is where the first sign, the sign that said we would not be blessed, that no child would be given us, was first seen.

"I'll hold the chicken and you hold the bed-cover up," Raoul's sister Vida told one of the guests.

There was much jostling inside the room as everyone

tried to gain a view of what was happening from the doorway. I did not know what was going on.

Seeing my puzzled expression, Raoul explained, "It's one of those old customs . . . They put a fowl under the bed and depending on which end it comes out, they can tell if the first child will be a boy or a girl."

There was much shouting and cheering as Vida shoved the chicken under the bed. The men hooted and whistled as though they were watching a horse race. The women were no better, screaming and yelling and laughing at the top of their voices. With a frightened squawk, the chicken beat its wings and disappeared underneath. Some of the guests crouched down on each side of the bed, coaxing the poor creature to come out.

The shouting and laughter continued for a while but nothing happened. Finally Vida, with hands raising her long skirt, bent and slid her head under the bed.

"Vida, your dress!" my mother-in-law said. But even in those days Vida did as she pleased. After a few moments, she straightened up.

"It's just sitting there, near the wall, doing nothing. It won't come out."

"Here, let me . . . I'll scare it out," someone volunteered, and proceeded to hoot and shoo at the chicken. But it was useless. Soon, the crowd that gathered in the bedroom tired of their little game and began to make their way back to the *sala*.

"Does that mean there won't be any babies?" Vida asked.

"Sssh . . . don't say that." My mother-in-law gave her a sharp look.

Silenced, Vida turned and gave me a guilty look. From behind me, I heard my mother-in-law say, "Of course they'll have babies. She is strong and healthy."

I wonder now whatever happened to that bird.

YOUR PAPA WAS NOT always as you knew him. He was very different when we first married. When I married him, I was very much in love with him but I did not really know him. I was in love with his dark good looks, his eyes and his manner, but it is only when you marry a man and live with him that you begin to know him.

In our first year together there were many good times for he loved to take me out, he loved to go places and eat in nice restaurants. He was a good dancer. He moved well. He insisted I learn to dance. The poor maids! How they suffered when Raoul took it into his head to teach me all the different steps.

"Well, Thelma," your papa announced to me one day, "I am about to turn you into the best dancer in Manila." He began pushing all the chairs and side tables against the walls then ran upstairs to our bathroom and came back down with the talcum powder.

"What are you doing with that?" I asked him.

He grinned at me and I knew he was about to do something naughty. But I was unprepared for what he did next. He took off the cap from the powder container and sprinkled the powder all over the floor. Do you remember those big dark red tiles you still see in old houses? Well, the floor in his parents' house was made of those tiles. The powder went everywhere and much of it settled in the dark grooves between the tiles. *Aaay naku!* How naughty he was. There were no vacuum cleaners in those days. Everything was done by hand. The floors were waxed with a piece of rag. And they were polished with a coconut husk. Very hard work. So when he sprinkled the powder on the floor, he upset the house-maids very much. But your papa, being such a spoilt one, did not think of this. I tried to stop him but he said, "Oh, don't worry. They can just wash it off." I said no more because by then he was busy picking a record with dance music. He put this on the gramophone, and my first dancing lesson began.

The powder on the floor made moving around easy. You could turn and swirl without your feet dragging. So Raoul took me in his arms and taught me many many moves. He was very sure in his movements and could lead anyone. Even me. My feet were very clumsy. And I felt almost shy of him. But he did not seem to mind whenever I took a wrong turn and just laughed when he found me standing on his shoes.

"I bet my toenails have all gone black, Thelma!"

Then he would begin counting again. "One two, one two, one two three . . . now turn!"

Sometimes Vida would join us and I would have a break for she and Raoul would dance together. Brother and sister had the same grace. They would say, "Watch us, Thelma, this is how you should do it." Then it would be my turn again. I had several dancing lessons with Raoul and it was a happy day for the housemaids when Raoul announced I was good enough to be taken out dancing in the nightclubs.

For a while, Saturday night became our dancing night. I would dress carefully and have my hair done and wear one of my many new dresses. We would first dine at the Manila Hotel then go to the clubs along the boulevard area. Raoul liked to move from one place to another. And always, he would be greeted by the doorman, the waiters and the manager. He would always find a friend or an acquaintance wherever we went. I was proud to be seen with him even if at times I felt a little lost. It was all new to me, the going out. But he was very good to be with and he often bought me beautiful presents for no reason at all.

But there were also bad times. Times when I had to wait up for him to come home because he had gone out with his friends. He liked going out with his friends. Like old times, he would say. He called these outings *lakad ng lalaki*—a boys' night out. No wives or girlfriends allowed. Just the men. So I would remind him—nicely—that he was married now. He would laugh it off and say, "Now Thelma, don't be a killjoy." So I would try not to make too much of it, and let him go.

But sometimes he would forget himself, and go out night after night. And I would find myself getting angry. I would then start to ask where it was that he had been and with whom, but he would only tease me saying, "There is no reason to be jealous. We just have a drink or two and catch up with each other or have a game of poker." That was how he explained it away.

During the times I showed I was angry, he would come home early and take me out so I could never stay angry with him for long. But I was not blind. I had come to realise that I had married someone who was used to having his way. He was . . . well, *pabling* . . . a playboy. He used his charm to get his way . . . melt away bad feeling. I found myself saying yes when I meant to say no.

But there was one time, the first time, that I refused to listen to him. I made it clear that I would not be a quiet, forgiving, blind wife. It was the night he said he would be back for dinner, but he did not come home. Then he sent the driver to say that he was going to be late after all. The driver said he had been about to leave the office for home when his friends met him and he had gone off with them. I waited and waited that night in the sitting room upstairs. I sat and imagined everything I would say to him when he came home but every time I looked at the clock another hour had passed and still there was no sign of him. Finally at midnight I got up and went into our room. I locked the door, turned off the light and got into bed. At two in the morning I heard a car pull up in front of our gate. A few minutes later, I heard him make his way up the stairs. I heard him approach our room. The doorknob turned a little as he tried to get in.

"Thelma . . . Thelma . . . Are you asleep? Wake up, Thelma," he called softly so as not to wake everyone in the house. I pulled the blanket over my head and turned my back to the door. Raoul called again and his voice grew more impatient but I refused to get up and open the door. "I know you are awake, Thelma, I'm sorry I am so late. I'll explain it to you if you open the door."

I ignored him. I knew he dared not shout at me and bang on the door at that time of the night. Of course had we been living on our own he would have done just that. For once I was thankful his parents were only a floor below us. Raoul gave up eventually and slept on the sofa outside.

The next morning, I got up and found him fast asleep. He was still in his work clothes. I did not wake him but went downstairs for breakfast. When his father asked why he had not come down yet, I said he was still asleep.

"Asleep? It is almost seven-thirty, what time did he . . ." He did not continue. My mother-in-law had shot him one of her looks. After that we ate our breakfast in silence. That night and for the rest of the week, Raoul came home for dinner.

If Raoul was angry about what I had done, he made sure not to show it. What he did was brush it aside by teasing me, "Thelma . . . Thelma . . . had I known you were such a hard woman I would have run away the first time I met you!"

———

IT WAS NOT EASY living in that big house. It was his parents' house and everyone lived there together. That was the way things were in those days. A tradition people followed. In some families, of course, the younger married sons were allowed to move out of their parents' home but the eldest son always stayed. It was his duty to remain with his parents. And his wife must always bow to his mother's wishes. A mother-in-law holds much power. She rules the family home. So even if we had our own kitchen upstairs, I seldom used it for we always dined downstairs around the big table with everyone else. Everywhere in the house, there were people . . . eyes. So I kept to our part of the house when Raoul went to work. Upstairs, I had walls to hide me. Downstairs, I would have to face Raoul's mother.

She did not go out often. Except for three or four women who came to play mahjong every Sunday, she did not socialise much. Perhaps it was because of her hand. I think she did not like people looking at it. I tried not to look at it myself. My mother-in-law had six fingers on her right hand. Old people believe it is lucky to have a sixth finger so they did not remove it. Hers was a small one that grew at the base of her little finger. I did not notice it the first time I met her. Only later, when Raoul took me to his home for dinner to meet the rest of his family, did I see it. His mother sat and spoke to me. Her hands on her lap. The left hand over the right. But over dinner, as she served Raoul's father some fish, I saw her sixth finger dangle from her hand. It moved a little every time she waved her hand. I quickly looked away, wondering if it was alive, if she could feel with it.

Once, she accidentally brushed her hand against my arm. I felt the touch of that dangling, extra finger. It was warm like the rest of her. I was surprised. I had imagined it to be cold like the tail of a lizard. Maybe because it was pale in colour and looked lifeless.

Watching her play mahjong one afternoon, I saw it flick about and once it bent at a strange angle as her hand moved over the mahjong pieces. I winced, imagining that it hurt. It was good that I was standing behind her or she would have seen me shudder. I excused myself soon after.

Raoul's mother was different from my mama. Mama talked to her maids, sometimes exchanging stories with them, listening to the radio together in the afternoon as the clothes were ironed. So I grew up treating the maids the same way. Raoul and I had a maid of our own in the big house. And having no one to talk to one afternoon, I found myself chatting to her. My mother-in-law, on seeing us, sent the maid out to attend to some chore. Then she gave me my first lesson in running a house.

"Remember to keep your distance. Never mix and gossip with the servants. And never confide in them. You must unlearn your old ways. They will not do. Not in a family like ours. One day, you will be mistress of this house. You will want your servants to respect you. How can you do that when you have allowed them to be familiar with you? Remember what I have taught you."

I had many new things to learn in that first year for I had married into a family very different from my own. It was hard. There were many things I did not know. One time my ignorance was to cause me much embarrassment.

It was the night Raoul's father invited a couple to dinner at a popular Chinese restaurant in Binondo. The man was a wealthy businessman who had just signed a contract with Raoul and his father's company to build a twenty-apartment compound in Blumentritt where he owned a huge block of land that had stood empty for years. To show his gratitude, Raoul's father booked a table for twelve at the restaurant and ordered the most expensive twelve-course banquet. My mother-in-law had asked the chef to prepare some very exotic things not normally on the menu. She told us the soup would be the best.

"Turtle soup. In China, emperors are served turtle soup." I did not tell her I found the thought of eating a turtle very unappealing.

We arrived at the same time as the guests of honour. The restaurant, being a very popular one, was already filled with people. One floor had been booked out for a wedding reception. Waiters and waitresses in white shirts and black pants carrying pots of tea were rushing about. At the reception area, there were many people waiting to be seated and more were arriving. But we did not have to wait long for the manager recognised Raoul's parents. He hurried to greet us and escorted us to our table. He had reserved a corner table for us that was enclosed by two six-feet-high embroidered Chinese screens. They had been specially brought out to give us some privacy. The space was cramped and we all had to squeeze in behind the seats.

My mother-in-law was saying, "Sit down . . . sit down . . . ," so I made to sit on the chair in front of me when she suddenly said, "No . . . no, not there. That seat is not for you!"

I did not know what I had done wrong. Raoul gently touched me on the shoulder and said, "Thelma, here," pulling out another chair two seats away from the one I had been about to sit on. "Next to me."

Meanwhile, the man kept saying to me, "No . . . no . . . it's all right . . . you sit here."

But my mother-in-law kept telling him and his wife, "No, that seat is for you and this is for your *tai-tai*." So finally he and his wife sat down. He on the seat I was going to sit on and she next to him.

"My daughter-in-law, you must excuse her, she does not know these things," said my mother-in-law as she bowed to them.

I could feel the blood rush to my face. Turning to Raoul, I whispered, "What did I do?"

He squeezed my hand and reassured me, saying, "Ignore Mama. It's just one of those old customs she follows. See the platter on the table?"

I looked at the round turning piece in the centre of the table and saw a platter of food. The usual things they serve at the start of a banquet. You know the one with strips of jellyfish, *tsa-sio*, and chicken. That was all that was on the table so I did not understand what he was referring to.

Raoul explained then. "Where the chicken is—where the head is pointing—that is where the guest of honour must sit. But you didn't know that so don't worry about it. Mama doesn't mean anything bad. She just doesn't know what it is you know and don't know."

So as you can see, it was hard having to learn all this. And because I was often unsure of how to act, I had to be careful of what I said and what I did. I was often lonely.

I was thankful for having Vida. She was the only one I could talk to with ease in that house. Your Tia Vida was the eldest girl and the prettiest, and even then she knew it. At seventeen or eighteen, she was closer to my age than to her two younger sisters, so it was with me that she shared her secrets, her many love letters. Vida would often come up to my room after school and stay there till the maid called us down for dinner or until Raoul would come home.

She was a little spoilt like Raoul but she had a good heart and I knew she liked me. She often said a lot of silly things and often, things that she should not have said. But in many ways, it was because she spoke without thinking that I learned what was being said about me.

———

"So when are you two going to make a baby?"

I almost swallowed the hairpins between my lips. I stared at Vida in the mirror. She lay on my bed, on her side, wearing a crown of wire curlers on her head, facing the dressing table mirror. I struggled with the pins, strands of my hair falling down the side of my face, as I tried not to let her question distract me.

"Well, what are you and Raoul waiting for? Don't you want a baby?"

My mouth free of pins at last, I said, "Vida, you must not say things like that."

"Why not? Mama does."

"Does she?"

"I heard her tell Raoul it's eight months already . . . Wow! You've been married that long. Anyway, Raoul told Mama, what's the hurry?

"You two want to wait a while, do you? I know Josie, my cousin, she had a baby early . . . not even nine months. Everyone said Gabriel had made an early deposit—two months early."

"Vida! The things you say!"

"I'm just repeating things I hear Mama say . . . Anyway, Josie had a son so I guess they forgave her."

It was not that Raoul and I were waiting. No, it was just that I did not seem able to fall pregnant.

"Don't worry about it, it is still early days," Raoul reassured me when I told him about my conversation with Vida and how I was beginning to think maybe something was wrong. "Of course you'll have a baby. We will have strong healthy sons and pretty daughters."

One day, after lunch, when the maids had started clearing the table, I stood up and took leave of my mother-in-law. I always returned to my room to take a nap. But that day, as I turned on my way to the stairs, she called me back.

"Thelma . . . your skirt."

I quickly glanced down at my skirt, wondering what was the matter with it. The fabric had a floral print on it. Maroon with some brown and dark green. You had to have an eagle's or hawk's sharp eyes to see a dark spot against its deep colours. My mother-in-law had sharp eyes.

"The back . . . come here, I think you have sat on something. It is soiled." I went towards her, half twisting my body so she could see better.

It was blood. I had not realised it was that time of the month.

My mother-in-law simply pursed her lips and let go of my skirt. After a while, she said, "Every month, it comes? Not too long a time or too short in between? No need to be embarrassed . . . you tell me . . . you have no problem there?"

I told her I bled every month. I was regular. She did not seem satisfied with my answer. Since that incident, I began to watch out for that time of the month. And every time I bled again, I felt disappointed. I began to worry.

A year after we were married, I still had not produced a child. It was then that Raoul's mother decided to do something about my condition.

Do not misunderstand me. She never treated me badly. But I knew she was concerned that I had not become pregnant. It was important that I have a child, a boy, for your papa was an only son. There was no heir to carry the family name.

So my mother-in-law asked the old man to come.

THE OLD MAN CAME one morning. He was like a moving cloud of grey. His hair was greyish white. And his clothes were grey, from his top to his loose pants like pyjamas, like the ones in the pictures you see of people in China. His clothes were of a coarse fabric almost like *katsa*— cheesecloth—except for their colour. It was as if he had stepped out of another time. Earlier, when my mother-in-law told me of his coming visit, I had asked why, what for? She said because he knows, he's an expert.

"At what?"

"Feng shui," she replied, as if those two words explained it all. But seeing the blank look on my face, she said, "He knows about good places and bad places. People come to him from all over Manila, some even from as far away as Cebu and Davao. They ask him how to build their houses, where they should put doors, where windows should face, if it is good luck to plant a tree here or put a pool there. They ask him if a block of land is good,

what shape it should be, whether it should be wide and high in the back and low and narrow in front. This I know—the back should be high, it is like having a mountain guarding your back so no one can attack you from behind. You are strong and protected. Like this land our house stands on. He knows all this."

So she fetched him from Chinatown, or what was Chinatown then, and brought him to the big house in Paco. She took him around the house. He followed her, saying little. But though his words were few, his eyes took in everything, looking here and there, at doors, windows and passageways. Sometimes he would ask where this led to, where that opened to, who slept here, what a certain room was used for. But most of the time it was his eyes that moved, not his lips.

"But why is he looking at my bedroom?"

"Maybe your room is no good . . . so it affects your health . . . your body."

"But I don't feel unwell."

She just shook her head, indicating I did not understand.

It was all so strange to me. Mama herself had taught me some of her beliefs but I had never heard of this before.

After a while, the old man spoke, using Chinese words I did not understand. My Chinese has always been limited to simple expressions. The words spilled out of his mouth, their meaning only understood by my mother-in-law. Then, as quickly as he came, he left.

My mother-in-law called to the maids in her piercing

voice. Her hands waved, and her sixth finger flicked up and down, from side to side, every time she pointed at something. I looked away. She kept giving one command after another, instructing the maids to move this here, and that there, and I wondered if she would realise she had done all this without asking me if I agreed or not.

Finally satisfied that things were as she wanted them, she flopped down onto the corner of my bed to catch her breath. Only then did she explain.

Shaking her head and letting out a deep sigh, she said, "Why did I not know better? I should have known better. This room, the bed, the window . . . all wrong. But now, everything is right." She sighed once more before continuing, "Now it is right, the direction is good."

She patted my hand before leaving the room, as if I was a child that needed to be reassured. "All this time wasted . . . not your fault . . . now it is right."

Maybe if I had believed more, it would have worked its magic. You have to believe, I think, before a thing comes true for you. Like when we say something bad and are told, "Don't say that," because in saying it you show you believe it and then the bad thing comes true. So maybe it was because I did not truly believe that I was disappointed.

My mother-in-law treated me with kindness in the following weeks. At mealtimes, she would insist I have more of this dish and more of that dish. Sometimes telling Raoul to put more on my plate, sometimes passing a plate of food to me herself. It was a kindness that

made me uneasy for a month passed, followed by another, and still I had not become pregnant.

Raoul himself said nothing but worked late most
nights, often not coming home for dinner. So I would
sit at the dinner table with his parents and sisters on
my own.

"Will you be coming home for dinner tonight?" I
asked him one morning as he dressed to go to work.

"Ummm . . . I don't know yet."

"You haven't come home for dinner at all this week."

"There's a lot of work to do, Thelma, it is very busy in
the office."

"But your papa comes home early," I said, "so why
can't you leave when he does?"

"Because I am managing it now. Look, I don't have
time for all these questions, I have to go to work."

"You never have time for anything these days . . . not
for me."

He looked guilty when I said that, guilty yet irritated.
Guilt won out.

"Listen, we'll do something special this weekend. I'll
take you out." He hugged me and left.

We drove up to Baguio for the weekend. At the time,
the only passable road was the old Kennon Road so it
was a long drive. Six hours at least because the road was
not good and, besides, cars then were slower. But just
the same, I loved the trip up to the city of pines. It was
so different from the sweltering heat of the lowlands.
Up in the mountains, you always needed a coat to keep

warm. Many couples used to go there to spend their honeymoon.

We did not stay at a hotel because Raoul's friend lent us his house—a three-bedroom cottage with a garden full of tall pine trees. How I loved waking up to the smell of pine. If I had had my way I would have stayed in the cottage in front of the fireplace and roasted sausages and marshmallows. It is what people do when they're up in Baguio. But Raoul could not bear to stay in for long, so we always went out for lunch and dinner.

One afternoon we drove to the lookout point. Even in those days it was a popular place. Raoul took all the coins he had out of his pocket and I searched through my purse for all of mine and with a handful of coins each we stood near the wooden fence and there they were—the *igorot* children, some as young as three maybe, poised on the rocks ready to catch the coins we showered on them. Many people had joined us as no trip to Baguio is complete without a visit to this place to throw coins down to the children waiting below. Those *igorot* children are as sure-footed as mountain goats. They scramble up and down the mountainside without missing a step.

On our last morning there we went to the market early. I could go to Baguio's market every day and not tire of it. There was always so much to see and I enjoyed haggling with the shopkeepers. Haggling is a game. The best time to go is just when they've opened their shop. They are more likely to give you what you want. *Buena mano.* The first sale of the day is important to them, you know. It is the lucky opening sale. The start of many. But they will not give in until you have played an intricate haggling game. I learned from my mama how to do this. You pick up the item. And watch how you hold it. This is important. It will tell them how much you want it. So you must not look too interested. Then they will ask you if you like it. You inspect it closely. Turning it around several times. You run your hand over it. Complain about the uneven stitching. The coarseness of the fabric. Or if it is a fruit, you say, *"Matamis ba yan? Parang hindi."* You doubt its sweetness. They reassure you it is sweet or fresh or new. Then you say, "How much?" The shopkeeper tells you the price. You make a face and exclaim, *"Susmariosep, ang mahal."* And you make *tawad*. Your first *tawad* must be half the price they first give you. Of course they will say, "No, no that is too low. *Lugi kami d'yan, Misis."* They cry to you that they will lose money at that price. So you walk away. Then maybe when you are, say, ten feet away, they call out to you. They give you a lower price. You say, *"Masyadong mahal."* Still too high. You browse at the things in the next shop. A similar item to what you were looking at before. They call out again. An even lower price. You do not give in. You make a counter offer that is lower than their last offer but higher than the first one you made them. Then you give in but continue to shake your head as you open your purse. The shopkeeper feels good. You feel good.

Raoul did not have much patience to haggle about prices. He kept saying to me, "If you want it, just get it!"

But I would continue haggling just the same. "At the way you bargain with these people, everyone would think I don't give you enough spending money," he commented once. I haggled when I bought bunches of statice flowers to take home with us. I haggled when I bought fresh vegetables and kilos of strawberries. And I haggled before I paid for the woven cotton blankets, and the half-a-dozen *walis* the housemaid had asked me to buy—Baguio brooms are of a very good quality; they can last years even with daily use.

After completing our shopping, we walked across to Session Road and had lunch at Raoul's favourite restaurant. One last meal of the fresh vegetables and sweet and sour pork they specialised in. We sat and ate in silence. There had been many of these silences during that weekend. Sometimes it would just descend on us. Raoul would be laughing and teasing and joking one moment and suddenly he would go away. I mean, he was there with me but not really there. I wondered where his mind was. What thoughts he was thinking. But I did not ask. I did not want to know. I just wanted to enjoy that weekend in Baguio. He did too. We talked of safe things. Not things we would fight about.

After lunch, just as we were leaving the restaurant, someone called out to Raoul, "*Pare* . . . I didn't know you were here! So who's with you, eh?" We turned and I saw a man around the same age as Raoul with a woman; he had his arm around her waist.

"My wife. Thelma, this is . . ." Well, I no longer

remember his name, but Raoul introduced me to his friend and he also knew the woman he was with. The man looked . . . I don't know, maybe a bit surprised. I thought it was perhaps because he had never met me. They spoke for a few more minutes then Raoul said we had to leave. The man nodded to me and we finally got into the car and returned to the cottage to get our things so we could head home.

It did not mean anything to me, that meeting and their conversation. But later when I recalled it, I would wonder if there was something I had missed. I asked myself who else would Raoul have come to Baguio with. Did his friend think he would have been with someone else?

I look back on that weekend in Baguio and think about how I had been so afraid to speak. There were many things I had wanted to say to him. Like was he tired of me? Not that I could have faced the truth. And my fears. I wanted very much to tell him about my fear. But I could not say the ugly, painful words. Barren. Childless. They were words too painful to say but I knew deep down they were true of me.

When we were not fighting, Raoul would tell me he loved me still, but I felt they were empty words for his absence told of his true feelings. My marriage had become an empty shell, much like my womb.

Raoul's parents said little but their looks spoke of their disappointment. Outwardly they treated me well, but their eyes held no warmth. Only Vida had not changed in how she treated me.

Three years after I married, Emma married Alfonso. Before a year was over, they had a child. Ligaya was born. Mama looked at me with sad eyes when I came to see Emma and the baby.

"Thelma . . . Thelma . . . How your Papa and I wish that it was you that had given us this grandchild."

I could not think of anything to say. And it was with a sad longing that I held Ligaya in my arms during her baptism. Alfonso and Emma had asked me to be the godmother at her *binyag*. I bought her a beautiful white baptismal dress with a baby pink thin satin ribbon under the ruffled collar. As the priest poured water over her head in front of the baptismal font, I looked at Raoul. I could not read his eyes.

You cannot imagine how hard I prayed to have a child. I had never been very religious but, like everyone else, I went to church on Sundays for that was how my parents had brought us up. But during those early years with Raoul, I began to pray in earnest. Every Sunday, whether Raoul would come with me or not, I would go to hear mass. Sometimes I would go during the week, in the morning after Raoul had gone to work. I became a familiar face in that church. The priest, whose name was Father Manuel, would see me and nod, and sometimes he would stop and have a few words with me. But no matter how many candles I lit and how many offerings I made, my prayers remained unanswered. Then my mama intervened.

The week after Ligaya's baptism, Mama came to the

house in Paco, a thing she seldom did. Upstairs where I lived, she opened a parcel she had brought with her. It contained a black glazed clay pot.

"This you use for boiling these things," she said. She then opened a paper bag. Inside were three little packets. She opened one of them.

"Chinese medicine?" I said, recognising the dried leaves and twigs she had unwrapped, their strong earthy smell instantly filled the room. "What for?" I asked, puzzled.

"To warm your body. The Chinese doctor says if a woman's body is too cold, she will not conceive. It needs some heat so a baby can live. Try . . . you must at least try it. You have nothing to lose. Boil the packet the first night with three and a half cups of water and when one cup is left, you drink it. Drink while it is still warm. Next morning, you must use the same herbs but boil with just three cups then drink one cup. At night you open a new packet."

"They are always so bitter."

"You silly child, medicine, unless it tastes bitter, is useless . . . it does nothing for you. This is bitter, true, so it is good for you."

So I tried to warm my body with Chinese herbs. Their bitter taste was the last thing I remembered as I went to sleep and their bitter taste was what I started my day with. Their heavy smell filled our kitchen and escaped into our bedroom but Raoul said nothing, asked no questions.

Lately, he had been kinder, coming home to dinner on most nights, spending more time with me, even accompanying me to church some Sundays. Every now and then I would catch him looking at me, as if he had something to say, but he never said it. I was just thankful he was there. His presence reassured me. It seemed, too, that his parents treated me more kindly.

Maybe if I had been thinking less about myself, looking less inside me, I would have known, I would have sensed it. It is like when you are busy thinking and you do not look up until you have walked against a wall—only then do you realise something was ahead of you. I was like that during that time. I heard only my own thoughts which was why I did not hear what I was being told.

"*AMPON,*" VIDA SAID. ADOPT.

I stared at her. The word making little sense to me, as if I had just heard it for the first time.

"*Ampon,*" she said once more. "Would you adopt a child? I mean, have you thought about it?"

"No . . . no," I said, finally understanding what she was talking about.

"Why not? Lots of people adopt. Mama's cousin Mina has an adopted son. Of course, he doesn't know, they never told him. But he is like a real son."

Shaking my head, I told her, "It is not the same."

"Why do you say that?"

"Because it would not be Raoul's son. Not his blood. Different."

"You want only his son. His blood."

"Yes . . . yes, of course."

She said nothing after that, just looked at me for a long time. Later I would recall our conversation. Only later would it make sense to me, on the day Raoul brought home the child.

IT WAS NOT YOU. You did not know that, did you? No, you did not know you were not the first. I did not think Emma would tell you. She would not have felt it was something for her to tell. And neither could Ligaya tell you for she would have been too young to remember.

But there, I have told you now. Before you there was one other—a boy. I have not thought about him in a long, long time. Perhaps because it was so long ago. Or maybe because I did not have him for long.

I WAS THE LAST to know. I was upstairs in our *sala* when I heard the sound of excited voices downstairs. I had heard the sound of the car moments earlier, now it was my mother-in-law's voice I heard, then Vida's, then Raoul's.

"Thelma . . . Thelma . . ." I heard him call from the stairs. He was not shouting but there was a tinge of ex-citement in his voice. He walked in as I was reaching under the sofa with my foot, searching for a missing slipper.

"Wait," I said, giving him a glance. That was when I saw the bundle he held awkwardly in his arms.

I did not have to ask what it was. With one slippered foot and one left bare, I walked towards him, never taking my eyes off the thing he held.

"I did not know how to tell you, Thelma."

He turned his body slightly, tilting his arms towards me so I could see the child.

"It is a boy . . . He is ours . . . That is, if you want him."

A thousand thoughts flashed through my mind, each one fighting to be voiced. I was confused. I did not know which feeling to give in to. To be accepting of this child whom I knew nothing of or to feel angry and humiliated by his presence.

"Thelma . . ." Raoul's voice cut through my many thoughts. From that place deep inside me, I emerged, and saw his face. It was then I saw his eyes clearly. Oh, how Raoul wanted that child. The look in his eyes said how much he wanted me to say yes. There was so much hope there. They held a silent plea, a prayer. How could I have denied him this when I could not give him another in return?

So I nodded. And he slowly put the child in my arms. The baby stirred then settled down. Like most babies, he had a look of peace and contentment about him. Unlike me whose heart and mind were in turmoil.

"He has so much hair . . . how old is he?"

"A week . . . just a week old."

"What's his name? Does he have a name?"

"Angelo . . . I thought we should call him Angelo . . . It's a good name. He looks like an angel."

I gazed at Raoul, surprised at the tone of his voice. And it made me think that maybe this is a good thing after all, this child that has come to us from nowhere.

Later, in bed that night, as I lay snuggled up against him, I asked him, "Raoul, where did you find him? Was it your mother that found him?"

He did not answer me at once. Instead he took me in his arms and kissed me before saying, "Does it matter, Thelma, does it matter at all?"

"I thought it would matter," I replied. "I thought it would be important to you and especially to your mother and father because, well, he will carry the name but he is not yours."

"He is now. You will be his mother because he will know no other. With time, you will learn to love him like your own."

"I wish . . . I had given you a child . . . a son. And there would have been no need to . . ."

"Hush, Thelma. Do not live with 'if only's.' That is the past. This child is here now."

Reassured, I slept peacefully that night.

THE FOLLOWING DAY, WE bought all the baby things we would need: a bed, pillows, sheets, blankets, diapers, bottles, formulas. We turned the small room Raoul used as a study into a nursery. And my mother-in-law found us a *yaya* for the baby. Her name was Lourdes and she was no ordinary *yaya*. She was a trained nurse and cost us a fortune. This child would have only the best, like a true child of the blood.

Our lives revolved around him. Not just mine and Raoul's but everyone's who lived in the big house. In the morning, the men would leave for work but not before they had come in to have a look at him. My mother-in-law, too, often found one excuse or another to come upstairs. I did not mind. For with the coming of the child, many things changed. And it surprised me without end that this proud family should accept him.

My parents were happy for me. They came soon after they heard.

"A beautiful, strong boy child," said Papa as he gazed down at the sleeping baby. "You and Raoul could not have done better."

Raoul laughed.

In the kitchen, away from the men, Mama would tell me, "It is not just this boy that is lucky, it is you as well. You are fortunate they have all taken to him. It is a blessing, Thelma."

I cannot say I thought of him as mine in those early days. He was but a week old when Raoul brought him home and it would be later, many weeks, maybe even months later, before I stopped thinking of him as separate from me. I was more nervous at having to care for him. Unlike a woman who carries a child and sees her body change as the child grows inside her, I did not have this time, nine months, to think of what lay ahead. Suddenly, he was there.

"Do you know where he came from?" I asked my mother-in-law one day as we both sat and watched the child sleep.

"No . . . no."

"A love child . . . or maybe a child his parents could no longer feed, maybe they have many other children."

"Why waste your time thinking about that? He is yours and Raoul's now; he has our name."

I said nothing more. I felt she did not want to be reminded that we knew nothing about him. But it did not stop me thinking, guessing, about who his parents were and what made them give away their child.

As the weeks passed, he made more and more sounds and began to move his arms and legs strongly. My pleasure in his company grew. I liked the gurgling sounds he made, his laughter and his high-pitched squeal of delight at my approach. He learned to recognise my face and my voice, often throwing his arms out as I walked into a room, his eyes and his smile asking me to carry him.

I remember the first time he came to church with me. He wailed at the top of his voice just when the priest had rung the bells and silence was to be observed during the consecration of the bread and wine. Raoul quickly carried him outside, but inside the church I could still hear his lusty cries from the garden. After the mass, Father

Manuel came and met me and Raoul who had Angelo in his arms.

"So this is your little angel, Thelma. God has given him a good pair of lungs."

How that child filled my days! I could tell the time from his cries. When he woke it was a certain time. When he cried out in hunger, I could tell it was so many hours later. He was my clock. My days were no longer spent aimlessly. There was much to do now before Vida's afternoon visit and Raoul's return home. And I finally felt I belonged in the big house. I was mother to this child.

RAOUL AND I SETTLED into our new life. We were growing closer again, spending time together with the child, at last closing the distance, the invisible gap that had been growing between us for some time. And I felt my life expand. Before, I used to wake and wonder how to fill those many hours that seemed to stretch before me. And every day that I rose from my bed I knew it would be the same as the day that had just passed. But with the coming of the child, there were no longer enough hours to do all that had to be done.

It was also in this period that Raoul began to change. His friends saw him less and less in the nightclubs he used to frequent. Raoul had found a new interest. He fell in love with art and became a recognisable face in Manila's many galleries. He began his collection of paintings the year the child came to us. I had never seen him as excited as when he bought his first painting.

He took me to an art gallery in Mabini. Mabini at that time was nothing like it is today. It was where many artists gathered. The famous and the poor struggling ones. Cafes and galleries lined the street, not cheap nightclubs full of shameless women selling themselves to foreigners like today. Writers and painters came to Mabini then and Raoul would soon become one of their patrons. The moment we walked into the gallery, the owner came to greet him. Only then did I learn that Raoul had been there once before and had stayed quite a while. The object of his visit was an oil painting showing a rustic scene by some unknown Mabini artist.

He held it up to me and said, "What do you think, Thelma? Don't you think it will look nice in our sitting area? The colours and the lines are so true."

He could not make up his mind. And it was with great patience that I accompanied him there another two times to look at this piece of work. To tell you the truth, I could not see what he liked about it. I could not face another visit to that gallery. So finally I told Raoul, "As you yourself always say to me, if you want something, buy it, so buy it!"

He laughed. "Is this your revenge, Thelma? It doesn't matter for I will follow your advice."

He was like a little boy excited about a new toy. When we got home he called everyone upstairs to show them the painting. My mother-in-law was like me. She did not look impressed. But Raoul in his enthusiasm was not to be discouraged. That was the beginning of his collection.

There is the story, of course, of how he came by his painting by "The Master" himself. I was with Raoul that day. He had been collecting paintings for some years. We walked into a Mabini gallery and this painting caught his eye. It was by another one of those unknown, struggling Mabini painters. He bought it. I know now how smart he was to have picked that painting. It was an Amorsolo. Amorsolo became very big. As you know, his works are priceless today. You have heard it yourself how he proudly tells people, "My painting by 'The Master,' my Amorsolo, I got it for a song!" Manansala, Baldemor, Francisco and Legaspi, their paintings came later into the house. I could not tell the difference between them but it made him happy and that was enough for me. Why someone would pay a lot of money for these things, I never could understand. But you are like Raoul. You like paintings and one day they will be yours.

Another thing he became interested in was reading. He began to read a lot. Local writers. American poets. European authors. The small table next to his side of the bed was soon piled high with books. And we put a bookshelf in our small sitting area where he then moved the books he had finished reading. What he started he always finished. He was the same with magazines and newspapers. He read everything from beginning to end.

"Much effort went into writing this," he would say to me, "so one must do justice to the writer and read it carefully. Every word has a place in these pages. There is a reason why they are there." He never skipped pages. It was an unforgivable thing to do to a writer. He spoke of them as if they were his friends. And he was, in a way, when you count the number of books in his library—he bought so many he must have helped feed these poor starving writers.

Perhaps he changed because he was older. And his responsibilities in the office made him more responsible at home. But I think what really changed him was the child. I know I could not have done it. The child unlocked something in him. Maybe all sons do that to their fathers. I say unlocked because I do not believe you can become something unless there is a seed of that thing already in you. I think people are made of many parts. Some parts come out early in life and fade with the years, some parts last till we die, and there are those parts that come out later. Something makes them come into the open. And it is just as likely that they could have stayed hidden. In Raoul, it was the good in him that came out in those years. That is why I think the child saved him.

Raoul needed that child to save him. I do not say he changed so much that you could not recognise him. No. Not that way. He remained himself. Playful, teasing, and still enjoying parties and dancing. But it was without selfishness this time. Without that spoilt part of him coming out.

One of the things we began to do was to go out as a family, taking the child with us to the homes of his friends. I made new friends, the wives of men Raoul did business with. Raoul by then had taken control of the whole family business; his father stayed in the background, giving advice only when it was needed. As Raoul's involvement in it grew, he drew me into it as well. I saw a different part of his life. It was all new to me and a little frightening.

When I was with the wives of his business friends, I felt again as I did when I first began living in the big house. As if I was this small person in this very big space and if I did not grow quickly I would be lost or swallowed up by the walls. Those women made me feel like that again. But with time, I felt I would change and be more like them.

I sometimes wondered how they really saw me and what they thought of me, for I often sat with them and said little. Their world, Raoul's other world, was strange to me. So I sat and listened, hoping to learn. They were different, these women. They had a kind of knowing in their eyes. A certain sharpness. And I, with nothing but my simple life behind me, foolishly believed they would welcome me into their circle.

Perhaps I should not curse them for their cruelty for had they not been cruel I would have remained ignorant, stupid and blind. Their unkindness woke me, shook me into knowing the truth at last.

I WILL NEVER FORGET that day. I still remember the sound of it, its every smell. It was a Saturday. Three days earlier, Raoul had said we would be going to a little get-together at Danilo's house. Danilo Santiago was an architect he did a lot of work with. Danilo designed the buildings and Raoul built them.

"It will be a good time for us to discuss the new project," Raoul informed me. Danilo was designing a new block of *accessoria* and he wanted to talk to Raoul about saving on materials, cutting costs.

"You can sit and talk with the other women while we discuss business. It will be good for you and Angelo to go out for the day. You both spend too much time indoors."

So we packed a bag with the baby's things, extra *lampins* to change with in case he needed them, and his formula bottles. We gave Lourdes the day off as I told Raoul I could take care of the child myself.

We arrived around three in the afternoon and found another couple there. Danilo had invited Peping Jimenez and his wife Pilar. Peping had a lumber business and often supplied materials that Raoul needed. I had never met him before but his name was often spoken by Raoul and his father.

Peping's wife Pilar I did not like when I first saw her. She had airs, that woman, and spoke with her head held high. She reminded me of a poodle. A black one. Poodles are ugly dogs to my mind. Expensive but ugly. Like her. She was a Tantoco. A family that belonged to the old rich. Her nails were neatly manicured and on one of her fingers glittered a big diamond. No, she was not vulgar looking, just hard. Attractive in a cold way. The smile never reaching her eyes.

When Danilo's wife Helena introduced us, I felt her look me over while I stood in front of her with the child in my arms, and I felt I did not measure up.

"So . . . this is Raoul's son," she said.

I sat with them for a while, making polite conversation but I was not of their world. They were friends and they spoke of people I knew nothing or very little of, and of things and past times that had little to do with my life. Every now and then, Helena would turn and explain things to me.

The child started to grow restless. I quickly excused myself, glad to get away.

"If he is sleepy," Helena said, "let him sleep in Anita's room."

I escaped with the child. Once in the bedroom, I scolded myself. Stop running away, I said. You married into a good family and you must live up to their expectations. You must try and belong to your husband's world. Talk intelligently. Learn to be with people. Where is your famous courage? The fire your mama said you had too much of? This was how I spoke to myself so when the child once more smiled and laughed, I carried him out again to join the two women I had run away from.

The soft, thick grass muffled my footsteps. And the child, busy gazing around him, made no noise. So as I approached, they continued talking, unaware that the person they spoke so maliciously of would hear every word they said. Their voices drifted towards me.

"She is so naive."

"Blind, you mean."

Peping's wife laughed. "Poor woman . . . Why, the moment I saw the child I knew he was Raoul's. The eyes, the lips . . . the family's face is stamped all over him. It is amazing what Raoul has gotten away with! Who was the mother?"

"Some woman in the office . . . At least, that is what Danilo tells me."

"She's still there?"

"No, no, it's over. He paid her off—the family did—in exchange for the child."

"They know then."

"Of course, you think that dragon of a mother he has would accept the child otherwise?"

I turned and ran back to the house. My insides felt cold and my stomach turned. I rushed to the bathroom and locked the door. I put the child down on the floor then bent over the toilet bowl and vomited. A sour taste filled my mouth and travelled up my nose. I rinsed my mouth but the taste would not go away. Still pale, I opened the door, only to be met by Raoul who had finished his meeting and had come in search of us.

"There you are . . . I was wondering where you'd gone?"

"Did you think I had run off with your son?" I snapped at him. Taken aback by my tone, he looked at me again and noticed my pallor.

"Why did you not tell me your mama is not feeling

well?" he said, taking the child from me. "I think we had better take her home." The child laughed, his eyes lighting up, so like his father's.

I LEFT YOUR PAPA. The next day, I went home to my parents' house. I took nothing with me. Only the clothes I wore and some money. I did not want anything from him. I left the clothes, the gifts, everything he had given me. I left leaving no word.

"Go back," Mama scolded me.

"How can you ask that of me after what he has done?"

"You silly woman, is it not better that the boy is truly his? That you know you are not wasting your love on a stranger's child?"

"He cheated . . . he had another woman."

"You are not the first woman, Thelma, whose husband has gone astray. And if you insist on being stupid, you will also not be the first woman whose husband leaves her. There are many abandoned women around. The important thing is not to become one of them. And in this, you have a choice."

"I cannot forgive him! A mistress! He has not been true."

"And you think that is too much for your pride. Pride is nothing. It will not keep you warm at night. You must understand men—it is nothing to them. They sleep with another but always come home to their wife. That is what is important. That it is to you he returns. If you let him know you know, there is no need to hide any more, no need to come home every night. But if you pretend, swallow your pride and pretend, he will keep coming back. In the end, he may tire of the other, and even if he finds a new one, it does not matter, it is still to you he returns.

"So you must go back. It is good you said nothing. So you can return. If you do not, if you stay away for long, maybe he will find someone else, worse, he will ask the real mother to return, and it will be too late for you. She will take your place."

Mama stood up. "I must cook now. You sit and think about it. Ask yourself what future there is for a woman without a husband. If you go back, Thelma, you have a chance to keep him. Men change, many settle down when they are older. Do you really want to walk away now? Or will you bear it, fight for your husband and his child, and have the chance of a life together?"

After lunch, I kissed Mama goodbye. She patted my hand, saying, "You are not so foolish after all."

So I can say I left your papa and returned to him and he never knew of it. I resumed my life. It was not easy for I wanted to hit out at him and when he talked softly to me I wanted to shout at him that I knew, I knew everything. And for a while I did not want him near me. I could not bear to be touched. I complained I was not well. But I shook myself out of this mood for I knew that the deeper I allowed myself to fall into it, the harder it would be to smile and pretend.

Every time I remembered that overheard conversation, I would push it away saying, "Go. I have no time for remembering." I replaced it with Mama's words. Drowned it with the child's laughter. Found comfort in the sound of the car arriving before dinner, telling me Raoul was home.

In the end it was good that I knew. Sometimes what causes pain eventually gives us strength. Pain has its uses. The knowledge I gained would help me fight for my husband and the child.

If I had not known the truth I do not think I could have acted with the same courage. I would not have been able to act with a clear mind and a heart free of fear, or worse, frozen by anger. Because I knew the truth, in the end, I was prepared for her coming.

SHE CAME ON HIS first birthday. I was in the kitchen downstairs, preparing food for the afternoon. Earlier we had tied the balloons outside. They made a pretty picture as they bobbed up and down in the wind. The maids and I tied them to the back of the garden chairs while Raoul, with the help of the houseboy, tied them onto the branches of trees. Raoul himself had got on a ladder while Isko, the houseboy, held it steady. I can still see them in my mind. Blue, red, yellow, green globes trying to float away, pulling at their strings, straining to go with the wind.

The *yaya* brought the child outside and he laughed and

clapped and screamed with delight every time a balloon touched his face.

"See, he likes the red ones," said my mother-in-law. "He knows it is his birthday." The night before, she had come upstairs, bringing with her a red suit she had bought him to wear on his birthday.

"He must wear something new . . . something red."

So it was in his new red outfit that the *yaya* dressed him that morning.

"Eeeeeeee . . ." he squealed and shrieked with delight. I stood and watched as Raoul grabbed hold of a red balloon and teased him with it, bringing it within his reach then quickly taking it away, then tapping him on the nose when he least expected it.

My father-in-law joined us briefly in the garden. He loved playing with his grandson. "He's not an angel, he's an imp," my father-in-law said, taking out a small red envelope containing money. It was his birthday present to Angelo. The child reached for it. My father-in-law laughed as the child took the envelope and promptly put this in his mouth.

Two days before, he had learned to say something that sounded like "Mama," more like *"uwawa"* it was, but it was good enough for me. When Raoul heard him, he said, "Well, when are you going to say 'Papa'?" The child chuckled in reply.

The guests were due at twelve-thirty. "Go . . . go up and change, I'll finish the cooking," my mother-in-law said, taking the ladle from me.

As I turned to go, one of the maids came in and said, "Ma'am, there is a woman looking for you."

"For me?" asked my mother-in-law.

The maid pointed to me, then asked, "Shall I let her in?"

"Who is it?"

"She would not say . . . just asked to see you."

"Tell her I'll be out in a minute."

I felt uneasy. Maybe my mother-in-law had that feeling, too, a bad feeling that crawls inside you, for she followed me out.

The woman had her back turned to me as she stood outside the front door. She had long dark hair almost reaching down to her waist. She was about my height but thinner, more delicate, and when she turned at the sound of my footsteps I finally saw her face. A Filipina. Younger than me. Her skin was *morena*, a golden brown. Her complexion clear. I guessed her to be in her mid-twenties. She was dressed simply, neatly, and I wished I had gone to change earlier so I would not have had to stand there in my house clothes with my feet in a pair of old slippers and my hair in need of washing.

Her eyes held mine, never wavering, as I said, "What can I do for you?"

"I want my son back," she replied.

Behind me, I heard my mother-in-law gasp. "What are you doing here? Leave . . . leave this instant!" she ordered the woman. To me, she said, "Go and change, Thelma . . . Go up to your room." I did not move.

Raoul must have walked into the *sala* at that moment and, seeing us by the entrance, had come to join us. I did not know he was there until I saw the woman's face change. A look of recognition came into her eyes, a touch of fear that swiftly changed to defiance. I knew Raoul had come.

I turned. His face was dark with anger, unlike my mother-in-law's—her face was expressionless, unreadable. But it gave me a secret satisfaction that both of them, who had conspired so cleverly, had been caught by surprise. Their secret no longer theirs to hide.

"Why have you come here?" Raoul's voice, razor-sharp, cut through the air. I had never heard him use that tone before. The woman flinched but did not back down.

"I want him back."

"Go inside, Thelma. Let me handle this." But for the first time since he knew me, I did not heed his words.

My mother-in-law put her hand on my arm to lead me away. "No," I said, and remained standing there despite Raoul's stormy look and the insistent pressure of his mother's hand.

If he wanted two women in his life, he must learn to deal with their combined fury. Resigned to the fact I would witness the whole thing, and hear every damning word that would soon be said, Raoul led us into the study. The thoughts in his mind I can only guess at but I would like to think that in the time it took to walk from the front door to the study, he realised he stood to lose both me and the child.

The moment he shut the door behind us, Raoul turned to the woman and said in a quiet voice, "You were given what you asked for. Why are you here?"

"I told you, I want the boy back."

"This is his home. He does not know you."

"But he is mine. Not hers. I am his real mother."

"We had an agreement."

A smile formed slowly on her face. "I have changed my mind."

"How much? How much more?"

"What is the child worth to you?" she countered.

"Stop playing games with me, Lisa!"

Her name. When he said her name, something inside me burst and I found my anger at last. It rose inside me, filling my chest then rushing to my head and through my mouth.

"How much do you want?" Raoul asked once more.

But before she could reply, I cut in. "You will not pay her."

They turned to look at me, all three of them, suddenly remembering I was in the room. Their eyes followed me as I flung the door open and walked out of the study. I went up the stairway—each step I climbed in anger—and, reaching the child's room, I opened the door.

The *yaya* held him in her arms, giving him his bottle. I took him from her without a word. Half-asleep, he woke to my touch. And as I came back down the stairs, he laughed and leaned against me, his arms around my neck. It was in this way that I held him as I stepped back into the study.

I thrust him into the woman's arms.

"Take him," I told her, "and leave at once. You are never to set foot in this house again."

"Thelma! Don't!" Raoul and his mother cried in alarm.

I silenced them with a wave of my hand.

"Go," I told the child's mother.

She did not move, the child gazed at her, not liking the stranger that held him, and began to push and squirm.

"Take your son with you. I don't want him, I never wanted him." Then I looked at the three of them and I said, "And there is nothing . . . nothing that I do not already know."

The child began to whimper. He reached for me but I made no move to get him. The woman looked at Raoul with eyes that glistened with hurt and hate, then she thrust the child back into my arms and ran out of the room, eyes brimming with tears.

I, too, left after her. I did not look at Raoul as I carried the child out. The *yaya* hovered by the door and as I walked past, the other maids scattered. I did not stop but headed straight upstairs.

Once there, I shut the door. My knees felt weak as my anger left me. I sat on the bed and hugged him to me. He cooed and gazed with puzzled eyes as I wept.

I heard Raoul's footsteps on the stairs. He opened the door quietly. I did not look up or turn around. He stood there gazing at me, willing me to look at him. I could not. Finally, he gave up.

"I'm sorry," I heard him say before he quietly opened the door and left me in the room with the child.

I feared I would never lose my anger. For weeks Raoul and his family moved around me carefully, watching me with eyes filled with doubt. But the child, in his innocence, continued to laugh and hug me, warming the parts of me that had threatened to go cold. I realised then I had not swallowed my pride, suffered so much humiliation, only to lose what I had fought for.

I could not change the past. What Raoul had done he and I could not undo, although he kept trying to make up for it in many ways. When I showed the first sign of softening, of relenting, he joined me in leaving the past behind.

I think it is like trying to cross a road. You have to keep putting one foot forward to get there. If you leave one foot behind, you cannot move on, you get stuck.

And Mama was right. Because I had stayed to fight, I still had my husband and his child. And though our life was not untainted, it was still a life together. As for the woman, she never came again to the house. And I never asked about her.

A child pulls you forward, too. You see children pulling at their mother's hand? I think they pull at our minds as well. The child pulled and pulled so in the end Raoul and I moved forward.

Maybe the child was in a hurry. Children have a way of knowing things. They are innocent but at the same time wise. Perhaps he knew there was little time.

———

THE CHILD WAS LOSING weight.

"Is he teething?" my mother-in-law asked. "He looks thinner."

"I think it is just the heat. It makes him hot and uncomfortable . . . He does not like to eat."

Lately, the child had shown little interest in his food. He did not reach eagerly for his bottle like he used to. Usually, he would rest his head against the pillow without much fuss, open his mouth and impatiently reach for his bottle. But now his *yaya* and I could not even tempt him with the tasty chicken mash he loved; even the grapes we carefully peeled did not appeal to him. He would have two or three then push our hands away. His eyes grew dull; he slowly wilted before our eyes.

"Colour no good," my mother-in-law commented. I thought it was his pallor she was talking about until I saw her fingering his bracelet, the one she had given him the week Raoul brought him home. It was made of small red-orange coral beads with fine gold links.

"Pale . . . see, the beads are pale . . . that means his body is not healthy. Beads should be deep and rich in colour."

Two days later he began to vomit. I took him to the doctor. She would not let him come home with me. Raoul met me at the hospital and we sat and waited as they took many tests we could not begin to understand. I was scared for I had never liked hospitals. To me, they smelt of sick people and death, and now the child was sick with something they still had to put a name to.

Meningitis. The doctor would tell us the following day. Water in the brain. Sometimes, she said, it affects the mind. Raoul and I listened, trying to make sense of her words.

"Wait and see," we were told.

We lived in that hospital for a week. Raoul's parents sat with us during the day. Mama and Papa came to visit as well. We kept our vigil. I prayed silently. I said to God that I had not asked him for much in my life. I had not prayed for many things. That this was the one thing I so wished for. That after this, I would not ask for anything else; just please to grant me this one wish. I prayed in those many moments of silence that descended in that room, as each of us sat lost in our thoughts. I don't know how the others bargained with God, for surely, like me, they prayed and made promises too.

On the last night, Raoul's mother sat next to me in the hospital room. For the first time since I knew her, she took my hand into her strange hand. I did not draw away. There was comfort in her touch.

It happened very quickly. His head had swelled up. He did not look like the child I knew. And it is not how I wish to remember him. I remember him laughing. Screaming. Holding on to my hands as he learned to walk. My feet moving forward, one at a time, forward, with him leading the way. I remember the child of better days.

We buried him two days later. Our little angel.

Raoul said to me, "I know now that it was wrong the way I had that child, the way I did it. When you want what is not meant for you, you lose it."

"It belongs to the past. Let it stay there." We never spoke of it again.

There was something else I never did again. Not for a long time. I stopped going to church. I stopped praying. I no longer knew how to believe. One day, the maid said a priest had come to the house looking for me. I knew it was Father Manuel from the church I used to go to. I had not stepped inside that church since the day of the child's funeral.

I asked the maid to show him in. And I waited for him to come up the stairs to our sitting room. He asked me how I was and why I had been absent from Sunday mass.

"I no longer believe, Father," I replied, eyes looking directly into his, waiting for his look of disapproval. None came.

"Because the child died?"

I found it hard to breathe. I could feel this rage inside me building up, my chest tightening. I took a deep breath before replying, "I prayed hard; you cannot imagine how hard I prayed, Father. I cannot understand it. It does not make any sense. Why take this child away? What has he done? Was it to punish Raoul for what he did? You know what I mean, I told you once during confession what he did, so was it to punish Raoul? But did God think about me at all, that in punishing my husband he would be making me suffer? Have I not paid my dues? I accepted the child. I forgave my husband. I followed everything your church teaches. And what do I get for it? I get to have my child taken from me. Mine. I made him mine. Do you know how hard that was to do? To make someone else's child yours."

"Parents do not own their children, Thelma."

"He was mine."

"No, he was but a vessel that carried a gift, Thelma. You have received that gift and his purpose in this life has been completed. So he has returned to his true father—God. The child brought you and Raoul together. That is the gift I speak of. And look, even without the child, you are still together. Is that not something to rejoice about?"

"I did not have to lose him."

"So now you punish God by not going to church, Thelma?"

"No, I no longer go because I no longer believe. Do you know, Father, what I believe in? That if I never ask anything of him, he will not expect anything from me. He will not give and he will not take. That was the last thing I told him, this God of yours."

"Thelma, we all need our faith."

"Not me. I do not want to have anything to do with God or the church or anything religious again."

"That may be so now. It may be how you feel. But as you grow older, you will find, all of us find, we need our faith. And when that time comes, you will return to the

church, Thelma. We all arrive at our faith and our good-
ness through a difficult road but we arrive just the same."

"You must not speak for me, Father, it is not blind
anger that makes me say this but experience. The truth is
that there is no God for he does not answer when I call."

Father Manuel took my hand and, looking sad and
tired, rose to take his leave. I walked down the stairs
with him. At the front door, he turned and said to me,
"Thelma, you may find it hard to believe this but, my
child, everything . . . everything that happens in our life
. . . that is God speaking to us."

I didn't argue with him. For no matter how blindly I
think he followed his faith, he was a good and kind man.
And so I let his last words fall on my ears and set in my
memory, there to stay for many years, until the time
came when I found a need to believe again.

"I FOUND A HOUSE for us, Thelma. I think it is time we
moved and made a home of our own."

Raoul told me this a few months after the child died.
And after taking me to have a look at the house to make
sure I too approved of it, Raoul informed his parents that
he and I were moving out of the family home to a house in
Santa Cruz. Raoul's parents did not want us to go but they
understood why we wished to live in a different place.

As I sealed the last box containing our things, my
mother-in-law came into the room and sat on the bed.
She looked tired. Shaking her head slowly, she said, "It

seems like it was only yesterday you moved into this house, yet so much time has passed and so many things have happened. And now you are moving away."

I hesitated then decided to speak. "I will take care of Raoul, if that is what you are worrying about. I will make sure he is comfortable," I said to reassure her. "You may not think he chose well when he married me, but I have learned much through the years from you."

Looking me in the eyes, she gave a small laugh before saying, "You are wrong, Thelma, for I thought my son had picked the right woman when he made you his wife. I remember the day we all met, the day you and Raoul were introduced to each other. I remember how you behaved. It told me you were a strong woman. My son, I knew, would need a strong wife. You look surprised . . . but it is true. I approved of his choice. Did you really believe Raoul could have married anyone I did not approve of? I knew you needed to be taught many things, for you had not been brought up to rule. But I saw you could learn to rule. The other thing I saw was that you would be strong enough to shape him. And you have done that. Raoul, I cannot deny, we spoilt as a child. His father and I could not help spoiling him. So he remained like a rough stone. Precious but unpolished. Had he married a weak woman, he would have remained the spoilt and useless son of wealthy parents. When you see a useless man, look at his wife. You will find a weak woman. A strong and wise woman can shape a man into someone who is strong and wise. Which is why Raoul needed someone

like you. And in the end—I must say this—it is not
Raoul, but I, his mother, who chose well. And now, you
are leaving with him. I am sad but I am not fearful."

I looked up then and, with regret, told her, "But I have
disappointed you. I have not given you a grandchild."

She grasped my hand and said, "That does not change
this . . . that you are a good wife to my son, a good
daughter to me." She stood up, and without another
glance at me, walked out of the room.

Five years later, she would fall from the stairs of the big
house and die. Raoul's father lived another year after her
passing, before succumbing to pneumonia. I was glad of
those few minutes we talked that day. I had made my peace
with her. And as for the house, the Japanese took
it over during the Occupation. But by then, my father-in-
law had passed away. When the Americans fought to retake Manila, the Japanese razed many houses to the ground.
Raoul's parents' home was one of them. The past is gone.

THE HOUSE WE MOVED to was small compared to the
big house. "You could put four of this inside the house in
Paco," Raoul said. But I liked it. I would at last be mistress of my own house. And it was in this house that
Raoul and I learned to live with each other at last. Ours
was a quiet kind of closeness. Not filled with the excitement and fire of when we were younger, but I liked it
better for it seemed that till then we had known no
peace. So I can honestly say I liked the settling down we

finally did. We learned to accept that we would not have children but we would have each other to grow old with. Acceptance gave us peace.

The time Raoul would have given to a child of ours, he put into his work. The family business grew and we had a good life. For many years this was how we lived: Raoul worked and made money, and I made a home for him.

Vida, who had married a few years earlier, had two children by then. I remember Raoul jokingly saying, "She will more than make up for us. My parents will have more grandchildren than they wish for . . . specially if they all turn out like Vida. And on your side, at the rate Emma is making babies, well, no one else need bother."

My desire for a child, felt so strongly by me once that I ached inside, I put away somewhere deep within me. Sometimes, an occasional wistfulness would gently come to me and just as gently blow away. I began to believe one day I would forget it.

This sense of peace and calm stayed with me for a long time. Raoul and I believed our lives would go on this way until we died. But after the war ended, news of Emma would reach me. Emma's husband Alfonso had passed away. I did not know that both Emma's life and mine would change with his passing.

LESS THAN THREE WEEKS after Alfonso's death, you were born. I had just returned to Manila after staying with Emma for a while.

"Do not worry about me, everything is fine here; it is Emma who needs you," Raoul reassured me when we got the news.

I went back to Olongapo a few days later. And I would do so many more times during the following months.

You were a small baby. Tiny. And not at all pretty like Emma's other children. Ligaya—I still remember when I first saw her—was fair and beautiful. You were all wrinkled up, like a little monkey, and you hardly had any hair. Maybe it was because you were born too early but I thought to myself, "A double tragedy, born fatherless and far too ugly for a girl." But then you changed. It is like that with many babies. They change. A few weeks later, you grew fairer and when you opened your eyes, how like Alfonso you looked, and there was a little of Ligaya in you too.

I often carried you then and fed you from a bottle. Emma had very little milk. It was as if she had only tears to shed. So when she had no milk, I would feed you from a bottle for there was no wet nurse to be found. Of all her children, you were the only one she did not feed from her breast for at least six months.

At times, I would help bathe you. But not until you were thirty days old. Emma, too, did not bathe until thirty days after you were born. You were both only wiped with a warm damp cloth. It is to keep mother and child healthy. How Emma could have lasted so long without washing, I cannot imagine, but that is how it was then.

On the thirtieth day, we bathed you. Emma, Ligaya and I. You opened your eyes wide at the first touch of water. Like this . . . with a look of surprise. Then you smiled. And gently kicked. After that we wrapped you in a towel and put your clothes on. I bathed you many more times after that, and fed you, and watched you sleep.

I would go home to the house in Manila, to Raoul, and I would notice the silence. How quiet our house suddenly seemed compared to Emma's. And how uncluttered every room was. No toys and baby things. I began to miss what I had long ago forgotten.

And as I looked at my husband and how hard he worked and how much we had, I began to ask what it was for—and for whom?—all this work and all these things that we had. No one to leave it to. No one to inherit. Ours was a house filled with every comfort, yet there were just the two of us.

These were not good thoughts for they made me restless once more. I could feel the peace in me begin to seep out through my mind, carried by these thoughts.

I did not share these thoughts with Raoul. But they stayed with me. They were more feelings than thoughts so they did not have form yet, not until I returned to Olongapo.

IT WAS THE DAY I returned to find she had sold the piano that I knew how little money there was left. I always knew Alfonso did not leave her much but I did not expect it to run out so soon.

She said very little. She has always been like that, always thinking that if you say nothing, a problem will go away. But I would not remain silent.

"How much do you have left?"

"Very little."

"How little?" I persisted.

After a while, she answered, "Enough for a month, maybe two."

"Have you thought of what you will do? Emma, don't turn away. Look at me . . . You have to be strong now. Alfonso is not here to solve your problems. *You* must solve them and I will help you. You must return with the children to Manila . . . for there is no future here."

"But Alfonso's ice plant?"

"Alfonso is dead and the ice plant is Lucio's . . . if he cares to finish it. So do not expect anything from it. It is not even operating yet. Besides, Lucio has his own family to feed."

"How can I return to Manila, with what? I cannot even provide for this child." She laughed then, a bitter sound. "I named her well, did I not, for she will live off people's charity, my Caridad."

Then, from out of nowhere, I swear I do not know where the thought came from, I said to Emma, "Then give her to me. I will raise her."

I could not believe I had said this until I heard my voice speak the words. But having said them, I found myself holding my breath for her reply. Emma, too, was silent for a moment before she said, "Oh, Thelma,

I cannot give her away . . . she is my child . . . Alfonso's . . ."

"She will have everything she will ever need," I replied. "She will never need people's charity."

Emma wept. I put my arms around her and felt her shake her head, but before she could speak, I said, "No, do not give me an answer now. Think it over."

That night as I lay in the cot beside Emma's bed, I prayed for the first time in many years. The words came to my lips, still remembered. I offered these prayers in exchange for a wish. Maybe God is forgiving and after all this time, would grant me a wish at last.

The next day, as Emma gave the baby a bath, I went down to prepare our meal. There was very little to cook. The pantry was almost empty. There was just enough rice to last a few more days. Three or four eggs. A few teaspoonfuls of sugar and salt. And wrapped in an old newspaper, some pieces of dried fish. I reached for my purse. I would go out and stock up her pantry. But I stopped myself. I put my purse back into my skirt pocket.

It shames me to say this, that at that very moment I realised I had found a way to make her give up the child. I made a decision not to help. It was a cruel thing to do but I had to do it, to make her see she could not manage on her own.

Come mealtime, the children sat around the table and scraped their plates clean. Emma had so little, giving most of her share to the two boys and Mia. The older girls held their tongues but the young ones gave voice to their hunger. I could not eat, having no appetite.

With every passing day, the food in the pantry dwindled. When it was close to empty, Emma counted out her money carefully and asked one of the girls to go and buy more rice and some dried fish. The milk for the baby had also run out so Emma fed her with the little milk from her breast.

She did not ask me for help but I saw the hurt in her eyes. She could not understand how I could stand by and watch her family suffer. But it was necessary, you can see that, can you not?

Two days before I left, I spoke to her once more. This time I said, "Listen to me, Emma, I will not only raise the child as my own but I will bring all of you to Manila and provide for your family until the older children can manage."

"Give me time," she said. "I will give you an answer before you leave."

I don't know what happened, what went on in her mind. Maybe it was the sight of her children hungry or the sound of the baby crying—there was not enough milk from her breast to lull it to sleep—but on the morning I was to leave, she rose, saying nothing, as she quietly went about packing the baby's things.

My heart wept for her but I cannot deny feeling a sense of joy when she handed me the child. I felt whole again.

"You will not regret this, Emma, I promise you."

"Go," she said, "go before the children return from school."

I left, but not before making her promise that you would never be told. And as I left the house with you in my arms, I reached into her pocket where I left money she badly needed.

Mia, who was the only one not at school, said, "Where is the baby going?"

"With me, Mia, I am taking her to Manila. I will take care of her."

"Ahhh." She nodded as if understanding, then waved her hand. "Bye-bye . . . bye," she said.

LIGAYA CAME THE NEXT day, descending like a storm on the house in Santa Cruz. I had not expected her nor was I prepared for the bitterness she would leave behind. Her words were like bile.

It was ugly. We were like two people, each holding a knife, stabbing at each other, no one leaving unhurt. She said many things and so did I. Things better left unsaid.

"Mama sold her and you bought her," she told me in anger. And yes, there is truth to what she said then. I did buy you but, although it was not the right thing to have done then, I like to think of it now as a wrong act that has led to many right things in the end.

For I did keep my promise. I sent for them. And in Manila I provided them with a roof over their heads. I fed them and clothed them and sent them to school until they were finally able to make a life for themselves. Look at them now. They all have good lives. Ligaya in her big house, Celia comfortably married and running an export business, Laura married to a wealthy banker, the two boys with their own companies, and Mia married to Rey who is a good provider.

And Emma, though she does not live a life of luxury, has all that she needs. She has never wanted much. In many ways, she has more than I have. She has her children around her. So I say now it was not such a bad thing what I did then. But because Ligaya and I had no way of seeing this far, we said many things we cannot forget today.

I NEVER TOLD RAOUL the truth of how I took you from Emma. When I came home with the child that day, it was to find him already home. He was in the small room he used as an office. Hearing the front door open, he came out to meet me.

I stood facing him with you in my arms. "I told Emma we will raise her like our own."

Raoul simply nodded but his eyes were not with me. They were far away, looking back into another time.

"Here, why don't you carry her?"

He came closer and gave you his hand first. You eyed him carefully, then curled your fingers around one of his. Gently, he took you into his arms as you gurgled with laughter.

That was when he told me this. He told me, "We must tell her when she grows up." It was the one thing I always remember him saying. And the more I have thought about it since he died, the more it is like a request, or an instruction from him. That is why I keep remembering it. So I finally picked up a pen and wrote to you. "Come home, Caridad, I need to speak to you."

And now you are home. Maybe it is not too late.

CARIDAD

"I have come home to learn

to talk again and to listen."

I RANG JAIME IN Sydney this morning. I rose at five. No point lying in when sleep continued to elude me the way it had done every night since I arrived.

"Information overload" is how Jaime would describe my condition. I toss and turn in bed while my body screams for rest but my mind, in overdrive, refuses to stop as it continues to process all the things I have learned.

Count. I tell myself. Count down, not up. I remember Jaime telling me, "Counting sheep never works because you count up and that keeps you awake. You must count down instead. It gives you a sinking feeling that puts you to sleep." But even that hasn't worked. One night, I tried counting down from fifty to one; the next night, I tried a hundred to one, but I still tossed and turned. Eyes shut, my mind would race and race, then I'd open my eyes and find to my surprise that morning had come.

So at the crack of dawn, I threw the blanket aside and jumped out of bed. I went down to the study and picked up the phone. It would be seven in the morning in Sydney. Jaime would be getting in the shower.

"I'd like to place a long distance call to Sydney, Australia please."

The operator took down the number I recited from memory. And as I waited for the connection to be made, I could feel the pounding of my heart against my chest and throat.

His voice came through, overlapping with mine as it travelled the distance, reaching me a split second later. Did my voice sound like his, like it was passing through a hollow chamber to echo into his ear on the other side?

"Is anything the matter, Caridad? Is Mama all right?"

"She's fine, Jaime."

"Are you sure? Can you talk?"

"Yes . . . she just wanted to see me, talk to me. I'll tell you about it when I get home."

"When are you coming back?"

"Monday morning."

"How is Marla?" I asked, wanting more time to calm my mind and put words to my thoughts. So we talked about Marla for a few more minutes. Then I said, "Jaime, we must talk . . . about us."

There was silence on the other side. Was it from surprise? But I pushed on. The words came rushing out and I wondered if they were coherent, whether they made sense.

"This has gone on too long, Jaime, I want to talk again . . . learn to talk again like we used to." I was close to crying and he sensed this.

"I will pick you up, Caridad . . . Caridad . . . are you there?"

"Yes."

"Now don't cry. We'll sort this out. It'll be all right. Are you listening, Caridad?"

"Yes. But no . . . I mean, don't pick me up. Come to the house later. I just need to settle down . . . but come before Marla gets home."

We said goodbye and I placed the receiver down.

I don't know how to say what I want to say. There are too many things. Feelings. They are difficult to describe. But I must learn to talk the way everyone has talked to me in the last few days. Truthfully giving voice to the most shameful things. And I must learn to listen in turn to all that he will say, even to what is hurtful. I have come home to learn to talk again and to listen.

I have been given a gift. The gift of my past. And with it has come a lesson. I have learned that the telling of the truth—the act—is where the answer lies. It is what I need to do in my own life. It is no easy thing to do. It is an act of courage.

I sit in the study, on the swivel chair my father used to sit on when he was alive, and I wonder what his story would have been if he could be here to tell me. I regret I will never learn from his life. Are there lessons he could have taught me? For I see now that no matter how different our lives may seem, the lessons we need to learn are the same. Every life is about the making of choices. Do we choose to love or hate, resent or forgive, hurt or heal, run or be brave?

Did my father know this? Is this why he wanted me to hear the truth? In that faraway place and time when he first held me, did he sense I would one day lose my way, and only find my way home in his story?

"We must tell her the truth," he told Mama long ago. I can hear him say it, see how he would have looked when he spoke those words. And I smile at the irony of it all. For now it is my turn to speak the truth.

I pull open his drawer. To one side is a neat pile of his blue stationery paper. Next to it, a row of pens. I take a few sheets out and pick one of his pens. I shut the drawer. And I begin to write. "What I want to say is this . . ." I stop to read then I cross it out. I start again. "I don't know how to say this . . ."

I cross it out. Start again. Finally, I cross nothing out. And just write. Go through it later, I tell myself. Somewhere in those words hides the answer.

MIA CAME YESTERDAY TO take me out. She arrived soon after breakfast. A vision in bright apple green.

"At least, you won't lose me in the crowd," she said. "The palace will be packed. The queue is always long. But it's worth the wait. I want to get there early. So later we can shop."

The Malacañang Palace—the presidential residence—in the municipality of San Miguel on the north bank of the Pasig River had become a big public attraction, not just to the tourists who fly into Manila for a few days but to the locals as well.

The name "Malacañang" comes from the Tagalog words *may lakan diyan*, which mean "a noble man lives there."

As a seat of power, it had been hidden from the eyes of the public for over a century. This splendid colonial style mansion, featuring numerous arches, grilles and balconies overlooking the river, was originally built as the residence of a Spanish grandee in 1802, and was later purchased by the government in 1825. Many a Spanish governor used it as a summer residence. Malacañang at that time was considered too far from the city centre.

In 1863, a severe earthquake destroyed the official palace in Intramuros. Malacañang then became the permanent residence of the governor. And after the Spaniards, it became the official residence of the Philippine First Family.

"You know, of course, the people stormed the palace the night Marcos and the rest fled," Mia said. "The marines who had been guarding the approach to the palace left their post in a panic. Earlier the pro-Marcos group had organised a rally to show their support for the First Family. They had even coaxed others to join them with a promise of free food and drink. When the helicopters sent by the US government departed with the president and his entourage, taking them into exile, the crowd that had come to the rally found themselves trapped within the palace grounds. From Mendiola Bridge and all the streets around the area, thousands of people were making their way to Malacañang. The gates broke open from the sheer weight of the crowd. There was no stopping them. Fighting broke out as they went after the people inside. Many innocent people who had simply come for a free meal earlier found themselves accused of being Marcos supporters. A fair bit of looting occurred. Chairs, TV sets, video machines, stereos were taken . . . rooms were stripped. The crowd slashed at the pictures of the First Family. Signs of the family's rushed departure were evident in the open drawers, empty wardrobes and discarded clothes. The main ceremonial hall was littered with official papers and reports. God knows how many important documents were destroyed by the celebrating crowd."

I recalled the news stories I had read in Sydney. They told of a crowd that moved about the palace in a frenzy. Anger mingled with astonishment at the sight of the antique furniture, urns, paintings, tapestries, and jewellery that filled the palace. To the poor who came, this extravagant and lavish lifestyle was not just a far cry from the life they knew, it was an insult of great proportion.

The new president herself had ordered the palace to be opened. "So the people can see for themselves the greed of the Marcos family," was how she explained her decision.

"But Cory uses it only as an office. She has refused to live here," Mia said.

I wonder if it is because there is something in its walls that breeds corruption and causes the abuse of power.

Our tour guide referred to the palace as "a monument to the excesses of twenty years under Marcos."

"It's a depressing place," Mia said. "There are sections that have been left exactly the way the family left them the day they fled."

"Even the shoes?"

"Yes, even the famous shoes."

The First Lady, who had reclaimed land from the sea and built the massive Cultural Centre, the Folk Arts Theatre, the International Film Centre, the Philippine International Convention Centre, and spurred the construction of fourteen luxury hotels for an IMF–World Bank convention in Manila, would not be remembered for the monuments she had created. It is sad and funny and ironical that after a reign of two decades, she would be known for her 3,000 pairs of shoes.

Photographs of the shoes, still standing on their racks, rows and rows of them, mostly new, were splashed all over the pages of many international magazines. The shoes became the symbol of a lifestyle best described by a journalist as "obscene beyond belief."

When an inventory of the goods found in the First Lady's basement dressing room was finally completed, it gave the public more than just 3,000 pairs of shoes to marvel at. It contained an astounding hoard of things no woman could possibly use up in a lifetime: sixty-seven racks of dresses, five hundred black brassieres with their tags still on, 1,000 unopened boxes of stockings, the same number of silk panties and formal gowns, five shelves of Gucci bags, and enough jars of Estée Lauder anti-wrinkle cream to stock a department store cosmetic counter.

The First Lady's bedroom with its thick pile carpet and two queen-size beds housed a king's ransom in antiques and jewellery. And to one side was a small chapel with a statue of the Virgin Mary. It seemed out of place amidst the worldly goods on display.

As the tour guide took us through one of the function rooms, someone whispered behind me, "Is that the famous table?"

"Why?" another voice responded. "Who ate there?"

"Silly! I'm talking about the table where Madam is said to have lined up all her diamonds in a row . . . loose stones, flawless, brilliant white diamonds . . . they reached from one end of the table to another."

Her friend laughed, "Did it sit twelve or twenty-four?"

Mia and I exchanged looks. She, too, had been listening in. Rumour or fact? We will never know. For during Marcos's twenty-year rule, the government controlled the newspapers, radio and television networks. The news they churned out was branded by the public as propaganda. Rumours became a means of telling the other side of the story. The wilder the tale, the greater its hold on the public's imagination. Rumours carried the weight of truth.

Paintings, worth a fortune, lined the walls. My father, who loved art, told me during one of my trips home, "There is a painting, they say, that was too big . . . but the versions vary, some say it is by a European master, others say by our own famous Amorsolo . . . as the story goes, the canvas was too big to fit the wall Madam had intended it for, so she had it trimmed down to size. Hacked into two pieces!" If Papa had been here, he would have searched for that desecrated piece of art among the many that graced the walls.

Finally, the tour ended. I was not reluctant to leave. Mia and I were the first out of the entrance, glad to be outside again where the air seemed free and unpolluted. The palace was fascinating and I would have plenty to tell Marla and Jaime. But as a place, a home, I could not possibly care for it.

We headed towards Makati where I bought Marla the black tops she had asked for and Jaime some Christian Dior cotton shirts to wear to work. Clothes were cheap in Manila. Even designer labels were a bargain compared to Sydney prices. I picked up some clothes for myself, and a bag for Meg.

After two hours of walking we plopped ourselves down on two not very comfortable cafe chairs, our shopping bags on the floor around our tired feet. We both ordered a tall glass of cold, green mango juice that I have become addicted to.

"Good for reducing," Mia said, as she sipped her drink.

Mia has not asked about the last couple of days. It is not her way. Although Mia loves to chatter and gossip about many things, she never pries. I was curious about what she thought.

"You've always known, haven't you?" I finally asked her.

She sucked at her straw and at the same time shook her head. "Not till I was in my teens . . . twelve, thirteen maybe . . . something Celia said struck me so I asked her and she was surprised I didn't know, didn't remember, until we worked out I would not even have been three years old when it all happened."

"So you remember him?"

"Papa, you mean . . . very vaguely. I just remember a lean man, sort of pale, not much else. I must have missed him for a while. Celia said during the funeral I asked after him and that the priest said he had gone away to be with God and I would see him one day. I don't remember any of that. It's not a very nice thing to say but it's true, you don't miss what you don't know or remember much of. I was too young to retain much."

"The time you all returned to Manila . . . do you remember that?"

"That I do . . . but Caridad, it was different for me. I know Mama and my sisters, Ligaya specially, don't like talking about it. They remember it with pain. Even Celia and Laura. But to a child of three, the world looks different. Maybe from their great height, grown-ups see more. But through a child's eyes, that apartment we moved into was a new place to play. A darker world maybe, but still a place for adventure. Later, of course, I would be more aware of what my surroundings were and what it meant. Specially when I had just come home from playing at your house. As I grew older, I realised we were poor, that I wore hand-me-downs, but even that period did not last long for the others had started working and our life gradually became easier. Then, of course, Ligaya married and things changed.

"But what I'm saying is this: it doesn't quite matter how someone else sees things because you will see them differently. My sisters talk about how hard life was because that was how it was for them. But for me, there were good times. I was lucky. Children are lucky . . . their innocence protects them."

I disagreed with her. "I don't think I was ever so accepting . . . I always questioned things."

"Well, now you have all the answers to your questions . . . Do they make all that much difference, really? I mean, do you love someone less or hate someone more because you know their past? Do you love your mother less, or resent mine now that you know everything?"

"No . . . no, I don't. I just understand things better. But it hasn't changed things . . . how I feel about people."

Then Mia leaned closer and said, "Travel light, Caridad. Don't be like Ligaya, she carries too much baggage. Good memories you can take with you. The rest you should get rid of."

"You sound like my friend Meg . . . in Sydney."

I REMEMBER THAT NIGHT in Mama's room. The night she gave me my past. She sat across from me. Silent at last.

Her story all told, like a jug filled to overflowing, finally emptied of every drop of liquid.

After a while, I said to her, "I guess I have always known . . . not the details . . . just a feeling."

"I never told you," she started to speak again, "I was afraid you would not understand. Your Papa Raoul, he used to say it will not make us less in your eyes. But I could not tell him that he himself did not know the whole truth. That the little he knew he saw as harmless. But I knew all. And were I to tell you all, you would think I did wrong.

"But now I can tell you. You have made another life for yourself. If you look at this and turn your back, there is still another life for you. You understand, Caridad?"

I nodded. And I reached out and took her hand, then I leaned across and kissed her on the cheeks.

It is not true that she no longer fears the truth. She still fears it greatly but has found a courage that is so much greater than her fear that now she can tell me the truth.

Was she right and Tia Emma wrong? That no longer matters. Right and wrong are judgments we make on hindsight. But at that moment of choice, we make our decisions in the best way we know how.

THE SILENCE OF THE morning is broken. Mama's voice reaches me from the stairs where I hear her cane go tap, tap, tap as she slowly descends. I put the pen down and read through the papers I have filled with words. They are heavily crossed out here and there. And what has been left alone are the words that best capture my thoughts and feelings.

Own person. Time together. Trapped. Left out. Drift apart. Talk to me. Listen. Lost. Go away. Anger. Scared. Bored. Simplify. Start again. Direction.

I gather the sheets together and fold them. I put them inside the pocket of my robe, keeping them for tonight to think about.

I hear Mama make her way towards the maids' quarters and I imagine the scene as it unfolds. She taps with her cane on their door. Waking them. "Six-thirty and still asleep. Is this how you all behave when I do not come down? Humph, this is laziness I will not tolerate." I pity the new maid whom I imagine to be shaking on bare feet, the sleep still in her eyes, as she opens the door to be greeted by her mistress. I see her staring at the señora with wide eyes.

How they must curse the coming party and wish it were over so the señora would go back to her room and leave them in peace once more. They have all been used to having her up in her bedroom, a world away from them. There is something they do not know though. That the señora will not keep to her room again after today. She has laid her ghosts to rest and will remain downstairs with the living. If they know this, their hearts will sink.

I come out of the study, hearing the sounds of pots and pans clattering against the kitchen stove. Her voice preceding her, Mama emerges. Seeing me, she orders, "Go back to bed. Why are you up so early this morning?" I stay where I am. I do not tell her sleep will be impossible with the racket she is causing.

"Make her breakfast," she tells the young one.

Tap. Tap. Tap. She moves with her cane to the glass door that opens out to the back garden. She pulls the curtain rod and as the curtains part, she peers through the glass.

"Leaves . . . leaves all over the lawn . . . Tell the boy to sweep them all up." The houseboy, too, is to be deprived of his sleep.

The word soon spreads through the servants' quarters. The señora has come down and she is going about with a vengeance. Next, she discovers dust on the furniture and another maid is summoned to run a clean cloth over every bit of surface that has gathered an offending film of dirt.

"Sit down and have breakfast, Mama."

Already on her way to the study, she does not hear me. I sit in the dining room as the young maid brings me my cup of coffee. She smiles shyly at me then scuttles off as she hears the tap, tap, tapping of the cane.

I wonder at Mama's energy. It is as if she has found a new lease on life. Today's gathering infuses her with a purpose she has not felt in a long time.

I offer to help her in the kitchen with the cooking. But she shoos me away.

"Go . . . go shopping with Mia."

I tell her we have already done that.

"Go rest then. This party is for you; you don't have to do anything."

So I wander around the house. Somehow it is different. Then I notice the light. Mama has thrown open all the curtains. And the light streams through the windows, flooding the lounge room with brightness. The walls and the furniture and the paintings soak it all up. Thirstily. Hungrily. They have not seen so much light in a long time.

She comes and stands beside me. "New curtains . . . I must get new ones made, these have faded. And the sofa, too, needs changing. I will ask Mia . . . you leave tomorrow, so I will ask Mia to come pick them out with me."

I listen to her in amazement but she turns to go to the kitchen once more before I can say anything. She continues to surprise.

THEY ARRIVE ALMOST AT the same time. One after the other, the cars come up the driveway, stopping at the front entrance, disgorging yet another family. Mia is first out of the car and gives me and Mama a kiss.

"That colour," Mama says, pointing at her flaming red skirt, "does it not hurt your eyes?"

"It's red enough to flag a bull with," I hear Rey say as he gets out of the front passenger seat.

I am seeing Rey for the first time since I arrived.

"Don't say it," he says, "I have lost my hair and have gained a few inches around the waist."

"What waist?" says a voice that sounds so like Mia. Susan is Marla's age but stands at least two inches taller.

"Look at you . . . you haven't stopped growing," I say to her.

She grins. "And Mama, you must have noticed, is getting smaller."

"Susan says I've shrunk. She says people shrink as they get older," Mia explains. Then she turns and beckons to her son.

"Iggy, come and kiss your Tia Caridad."

I turn to see Mia's son, tall and gangling, all arms and legs, like an octopus. He scowls at Mia for asking him to kiss me. So I give him a kiss instead and watch him turn red as a shrimp.

"What's this?" I ask, patting the black case with a long strap he has slung over his shoulder.

"He's the official photographer assigned to this event."

"Is that what you want to be?"

Before he can answer, Susan cuts in, "Yep! And he'll starve!"

"Shut up!"

"Okay, you two, fight somewhere else," orders Mia.

A Kombi arrives and Celia and Paul get out, followed by their daughter Sara and three fat little buddhas.

"All yours, Sara?"

"One more in here." She pats her tummy, laughing as she sees the look of disbelief on my face.

Celia says, "She's out to break Mama's record."

"No, I'm not. I told Edwin if this is another boy I'm

giving up. So this one had better be a girl! I'd like to dress someone up who doesn't end up looking dirty and scruffy five minutes later!"

"What are you all doing out there? Come inside . . . come inside," Mama calls to everyone.

Just then, Laura and Monching arrive. "You look really well, Caridad," she says, kissing me and giving me a gentle pat on the back.

Paolo and his wife Lana come and I greet them. Then Miguel arrives with someone I have never seen before. I turn quickly to Mia, and she whispers in my ear, "I wrote to you about her . . . remember?"

I recall her long letter about the *querida*, the mistress, who has replaced Marina, his shrewish wife who was three years older than him and whom no one in the family liked. I look doubtfully at this new woman and I wonder what it is he sees in her.

"She is young, of course, and dumb and thinks the world of him. He likes that. Marina, as you know, spent twenty-five long years telling him what to do . . . No, no, you mustn't laugh, Caridad, this is your family, too, remember?"

I look around me and I am amazed, if a bit confused, by all this bustle and chatter. It seems there will be no peace in this house today.

Mama is talking to Laura in the corner and I catch a phrase or two. "The maids today are not like those of long ago . . . Rosa . . . these three together do not measure up to one like Rosa . . ."

Another car arrives. The last one. I glance at Mia, wondering if she, too, is thinking what I am thinking. She breaks into her chat-chat-chat voice, as Marla calls it. Mia does this to dispel awkwardness.

"What took you so long?" she calls out in a loud voice to Ligaya who enters with her husband Enrique, followed behind by Tia Emma who is helped out of the car by Maita, Ligaya's youngest.

Mama, I see from the corner of my eye, is walking towards the door.

"Emma," she calls out, "everyone has been waiting . . . the food is getting cold."

I kiss Tia Emma and she pats my hand.

"I made you some fresh *ube*. You like *ube*, don't you?" She hands me a big jar of sweet yam. "You take it back to Sydney . . . You cannot? Oh, then, you must eat it today. Feel the jar, it is still warm."

Ligaya greets Mama. She stands stiffly and tilts her head but does not kiss her. Mama then surprises us all by taking Ligaya's arm and drawing her into the *sala*, saying, "Where are the other children? Why only one? Which one is this? Ah, the youngest . . ."

Enrique, Ligaya's husband, kisses me on the cheek. I have always liked Enrique. Much older than Ligaya, his hair is mostly grey now, salt and pepper-ish. It gives him a distinguished look.

"Jaime did not come with you?"

"No, it's a busy time of the year and someone has to stay with Marla."

"I hear she is to be a pianist."

"Yes . . . we're really proud of her."

"It's good to be able to play. The girls all play a little, but not like Marla. And, well, only Maita is still at home, and she's never been really interested."

"No one plays? But you have a baby grand."

"That was for Ligaya's birthday. She never really used it . . . but this week, just a few days ago, she sat down and played again."

"I'm glad," I told him. "I'm glad to hear that."

"Caridad . . . Enrique . . . Come and get some food. Eat first then talk later."

"You mean, Tia Thelma, we can't do both at the same time," Enrique teases Mama. And I am reminded of Jaime.

So we all sat and ate as Mama ordered everyone to fill their plates again and again. "Have some more . . . Here, these are fresh prawns . . . Very fresh and juicy . . . Caridad says prawns in Sydney are just half the size of these and not as tasty. Look, these are almost eight inches long!"

"No, not now, later," Mia says, fending off her son who has raised his camera. He takes a shot of her just the same, mouth open, fork raised in mid-air as if about to attack someone.

"But that's the way to take pictures . . . candid, not posed and stiff."

I stand to go to the bathroom. When I come out, Ligaya is waiting for me. A box in her hand.

"I thought Marla would like this," she says.

I take it from her and look inside.

"It is my metronome. Papa gave it to me the day of my first piano lesson. It was left behind when the piano was sold."

I close the box. "Thank you," I tell Ligaya, "thank you . . . It will be a good way to begin telling her."

"You will tell her?"

"It belongs to her, too."

Ligaya nods, saying nothing, then returns to her seat.

Later, when the meal is over, we call to Iggy and insist on the classic posed shot. "There is only one shot left," our photographer haughtily informs us. So we set about organising where to sit and where to stand. Mama and Tia Emma in the centre, me next to Mama, with Mia on my other side. Ligaya next to Tia Emma and Enrique behind her, and Maita next to him and so on.

Young Iggy rolls his eyes, exasperated by our fickle-mindedness as we constantly change our positions. Until finally, refusing to wait a second longer, he presses the button and takes the shot.

We will all receive a copy of that family picture. Mia will send me mine, specially blown up, showing us all in mid-pose, some with smiles that look more like a grimace, some with mouths wide open, others with eyes shut; Mama and Tia Emma with faces turned towards each other as Mama once more instructs her on something, Ligaya looking up as she speaks to Enrique; Sara scolding her three fat boys, while Mia laughs at me as I, with eyes wide open, realise the camera has caught me unprepared.

Captured for posterity is that look of surprise on my face. "What were you thinking of then?" Marla asks on seeing my expression.

I think for a moment before replying, then I say, "That I had so much . . . I had been given so much." And having spoken those words, I sense their truth.

It was on a spring morning, a Sunday, that the phone rang. Marla took the call in the hall. These days, the phone rang mostly for her. So Jaime and I left her to take the calls.

The toaster had got stuck again. I switched it off from the outlet before fishing out the two pieces of charred bread with a fork. Jaime's breakfast. He glanced up from the travel brochures he'd been reading.

"Don't throw them out . . . I'll just scrape the burnt bits off."

"Oh no, you don't. You'll just make a mess. I'll start again," I said, throwing the two pieces of burnt toast in the bin. Their smoky smell hung in the air.

Jaime had begun to spend most weekends with us. And we'd been toying with the idea of going camping when the weather warmed up. The Kangaroo Valley or Tiona along Lake Wallis, or maybe somewhere in Tasmania if we felt more adventurous. Marla said she'd very likely give it a miss. She had a music composition project to get through. "Besides," she said, "I can't imagine roughing it for a week." But I told Jaime we should still consider it. It's something I'd never done before. He said, "Fine . . . and if we hate it, we can find some place to stay."

Marla came into the kitchen then.

Jaime looked up in surprise. "Through already? That was a quick one."

"It's for Mum," she replied. Then looking at me, she said, "Tia Mia for you and it won't be a quick one." Marla was wrong.

Mia said it was unexpected. That she had seen Mama just three days before. Mama was in good spirits and had insisted Mia stay for lunch. So when the maid, the young one, called her this morning, she could not believe it herself. The maid had gone up to call Mama for breakfast. Mama was an early riser and had breakfast at seven-thirty. Since my last visit home, she had been having her meals downstairs again. So it was the young maid who saw her first.

Mia had gone over with Rey as soon as she heard. On Mama's lap, Mia said, was a photo album, and all around her on the bed were pictures I had sent over the years. And in her hand was the one Mia's son, Iggy, had taken of the family during my last trip home. Mama had been putting them in order at last, the way Papa used to.

She had a smile on her lips, Mia told me; she looked peaceful and happy. And knowing this, the ache in my heart eases, and I think that perhaps in those last moments, Mama felt she had been blessed at last.

ARLENE J. CHAI was born and educated in Manila. She received her Bachelor of Arts degree, with a major in Communication Arts, from Maryknoll College, graduating *cum laude*. Soon after completing her degree, she joined the advertising industry as a copywriter. In 1982, she migrated to Sydney with her parents and sisters and now lives in the Northern Beaches area. After more years in advertising than she cares to mention, she had a year off during which she went for walks, sat in cafes, devoured books, learned Italian, renovated her house, and wrote *The Last Time I Saw Mother*. Today, she is writing ads part-time and has just finished her second novel, *Eating Fire and Drinking Water*.